Old Testame

THE BOOKS OF THE OLD TESTAMENT

TEF Study Guides

This SPCK series was originally sponsored by the Theological Education Fund of the WCC in response to requests from Africa, Asia, the Caribbean, and the Pacific. The books are prepared by and in consultation with theological tutors from all over the world, but have from the outset been as widely used by students and parish groups in the West as by those for whom English may be a second language. More advanced titles in the list are marked (A).

General Editors: Daphne Terry and Nicholas Beddow

1. **A Guide to the Parables**
2. **A Guide to St Mark's Gospel**
3. **A Guide to Genesis**
4. **A Guide to Amos**
5. **Church History 1: The First Advance AD 29–500**
6. **A Guide to Psalms**
7. **Old Testament Introduction 1: History of Israel**
8. **Church History 2: Setback and Recovery AD 500–1500**
9. **Applied Theology 1: 'Go . . . and make disciples'**
10. **Old Testament Introduction 2: The Books of the Old Testament**
11. **A Guide to Romans**
12. **A Guide to Religions**
13. **A Guide to Exodus**
14. **Church History 3: New Movements AD 1500–1800**
15. **Old Testament Theology 3: Theology of the Old Testament**
16. **A Guide to Isaiah 40–66**
17. **A Guide to 1 Corinthians**
18. **A Guide to Philippians**
19. **Applied Theology 2: 'Tend my sheep'**
20. **A Guide to the Revelation**
21. **A Guide to Isaiah 1–39**
22. **Church History 4: Christianity Worldwide AD 1800 Onwards**
23. **A Reader in African Christian Theology (A)**
24. **New Testament Introduction 1: Jesus Christ: His Life and His Church**
25. **A New Teaching, A New Learning: A Guide to Teaching Theology (A)**
26. **New Testament Introduction 2: The Formation of the Christian Scriptures**
27. **A Guide to Acts**
28. **A Guide to Galatians**

IN PREPARATION

A Guide to Deuteronomy
A Guide to Jeremiah
A Guide to Hosea
The Inter-Testamental Period
Readings in Indian Christian Theology (A)

TEF Study Guide 10

Old Testament Introduction 2

THE BOOKS OF THE OLD TESTAMENT

REVISED EDITION

David F. Hinson

SPCK

First published in 1974
SPCK
Holy Trinity Church
Marylebone Road, London NW1 4DU

Reprinted nine times
Revised edition 1992

ACKNOWLEDGEMENTS

Photographs are reproduced by courtesy of the British Library/British Museum (1.1; 1.2; 3.2; 6.1; 7.2; 7.3a & b), Church Missionary Society (4.2), Radio Times Hulton Picture Library (2.3; 8.2; 8.3), Penguin Books Ltd (2.1) and the Mansell Collection.

The map is based on a map in *The Student's Bible Atlas* by H. H. Rowley, by kind permission of the publishers, Lutterworth Press.

ISBN 0-281-04564-X
ISBN 0-281-04565-8 (special edition for Africa, Asia, S. Pacific and Caribbean)

Typeset by J&L Composition Ltd, Filey, North Yorkshire
Printed in Great Britain by
Hollen Street Press Ltd, Slough, Berks.

Contents

Illustrations

Preface to the Revised Edition

When the first edition of this Study Guide was published in 1973 I thanked Dr R. J. Coggins for his detailed and scholarly comments on my manuscript, and three ministers who had had overseas service for their advice and guidance. But above all Daphne Terry, who was then Editor of the series, for giving me the opportunity of writing and for substantial assistance in preparing the book. These still have my gratitude, especially in the light of the value placed by Third World Churches on my three-volume *Introduction to the Old Testament* in the TEF Study Guide Series.

In preparing this second edition I am grateful for the advice of J. H. Eaton of the Birmingham University Department of Theology, and for an opportunity to consult with John Sawyer, Senior Lecturer in Religious Studies at the University of Newcastle upon Tyne. But I am particularly grateful to the present Editor of the TEF Study Guides, Nicholas Beddow, for providing the opportunity to work afresh on this subject, and for challenging me to take serious note of developments in Canonical Criticism.

Some explanation of the outcome of my studies is necessary because this book is substantially different from the first edition. When I wrote the earlier version I took my stand on the belief that every part of the Old Testament needed to be given due consideration, and that not only the original sources, oral and written, but also the subsequent editions of Old Testament books had been prepared by people who had had an experience of God and were writing to share their knowledge of His person, His purposes and His activities with others. The Bible as a whole is a means by which God makes Himself known to subsequent generations, and by which we enter into a living relationship with Him.

The best known writer on Canonical Criticism at the present time is Brevard S. Childs, Professor of Old Testament at Yale University. His main publication which relates to the subject with which I am dealing in this book is *Introduction to the Old Testament as Scripture* (1979). He maintains that the authority of Scripture is that given to it by the Church because the Bible is seen to be a vital source of the knowledge of God. The main thrust of his book is to show that the present format of the various books of the Old Testament arises from editing which is intended to assist in the communication of the faith. You will understand from what I have said that in studying what he says I found myself largely in sympathy with his approach.

However, it seemed right to discover what critical scholars had made of the approach presented by Childs. The main statement of objection to that approach is to be found in a book by James Barr, *Holy Scripture: Canon, Authority, Criticism*. Teachers and tutors who wish to understand the debate on Canonical Criticism ought to study both books. Barr presents some very strong arguments for rejecting the principles of Canonical Criticism. A careful study of the first two chapters of this Guide will give some clues to the difficulties. To name but one, there is no consensus over the content of the Canon. Protestants use the Hebrew Canon, and Childs follows this in his book. But Roman Catholics, and the various types of Orthodox Faith all have their own selections, usefully brought together in the RSV Common Bible.

To place too much emphasis on the Canon is liable to stress the divisions in the Church. Yet Christians of all denominations would agree that the Scriptures they know have been used by God to bring challenge or blessing to them in their devotional lives, and in daily experience. The various Canons were drawn up to indicate where such help could be found. So I believe that we must acknowledge the work of the Spirit of God in bringing the Bible alive for us, and see in this the ultimate authority. The differences which arose among the Churches in determining the Canon reflect the fact that none of the denominations had a full and final knowledge of God. We need each other with our differing insights and understanding if we are to continue our life's pilgrimage in growing knowledge and experience of the Lord.

This preface would be incomplete without an expression of gratitude to the staff of Kingsmead College, Selly Oak for encouraging me to complete my work on the second edition of the book whilst studying there. And gratitude also goes to R. S. Sugirtharajah of the Selly Oak Federation whose lectures on Biblical Interpretation and Third World Theologies have proved an inspiration and encouragement to me in my work.

It is my hope that this Guide will prove to be of real help to students in colleges, and to others studying in groups or alone as they set out to gain a firm knowledge of the contents of the Old Testament, such as will enable them to be effective preachers and pastors as they use their Bibles in their congregations. The words of men of Old Testament times can still be a source of inspiration and blessing as they lead us into the very presence of God Himself. May this Guide lead all who read it to a deeper understanding, and so to a richer experience of all that the Scriptures can mean to us.

Kingsmead College,
Selly Oak, Birmingham

DAVID F. HINSON

Author's Note: Using This Book

In this Study Guide we shall look closely at the books of the Old Testament, and consider how they came to be written, how they found a place in the Bible, and how they reached us in their present form. But before we begin this important study we need to notice a number of things that will help us to appreciate what we read.

BIBLE VERSION

The English translation of the Bible used and quoted in this Guide is the Common Bible edition of the Revised Standard Version (RSV). Other translations are based on the same Hebrew sources in so far as these were available to the translators. Many of the variations between one English text version and another are of the sort that arise whenever two or more people each make a separate translation of something written in one language, into another language. If you use a different English translation, rather than the RSV, you will need to bear this in mind. We shall notice other reasons for differences between the various English versions as we go further with our studies.

ORDER OF STUDY

The books of the Old Testament are dealt with in this edition in the order in which they are printed in the English Bible. We shall not deal with the books of the Apocrypha because a separate Study Guide is planned for these. The order we shall follow is different from that of the first edition of this book, where we followed the Hebrew Canon. The change takes note of the reasons which have been suggested for the order of the Christian Canon (see pp. 5, 6, 12, 14). For the sake of students working in groups who may be using amongst them both editions, the Cross-reference on p. 209 of this volume shows where comparable information is available in each edition. References to Volume 1 also cover both first and revised editions.

HELPS TO BIBLE STUDY

The three basic tools recommended in the previous volume of this course are equally important for use with this Guide, and should be kept ready to hand: i.e. a *Bible Dictionary*, a *Concordance*, and a *Bible Atlas*. In addition, *Commentaries* on the various books of the Bible will be helpful. For a list of these and other useful books see pp. xiv–xvi.

READING THIS STUDY GUIDE

This Study Guide sets out basic ideas about the writers and their books in the Old Testament which are widely accepted among scholars, and which can generally be accepted as a guide to right interpretation. And some alternative views are described and discussed. You should try to assess the value of the different points of view, and accept for yourself what seems the best justified interpretation. In some cases you may disagree with the views put forward here, but if you do, then you should satisfy yourself that there are real grounds for taking the view you wish to hold, and you should try to understand why others may not agree with you.

STUDY SUGGESTIONS

Suggestions for further study and revision appear at the end of each section. They are intended to help readers to study more thoroughly, and to understand clearly what they have read, and also to check the progress made. Topics for research and discussion are also included. These are designed to help you relate your studies to everyday life, and to consider the significance of issues raised by the writers and editors of the Bible for Christian people today.

The best way to use these Study Suggestions is: first read the appropriate section of the Guide carefully, once or twice, looking up all the Bible references as you go along; *then* do the work suggested, in writing or group discussion, without looking back at the Guide except where there is an instruction to do so.

Please note that the Study Suggestions are only *suggestions*. Some readers may not want to use them at all. Some teachers may want to use them selectively, or to substitute questions of their own, especially where they can relate these studies to the circumstances of their own country.

The *Key* (p. 193) will enable readers to check their own work on questions which can be checked in this way. In most cases the Key does not provide the answer to a question; instead it shows where an answer is to be found.

INDEXES

Two indexes are provided. The *Bible Reference Index* (p. 205) shows where the various passages of the Bible are mentioned in this Guide. Most references will be found on the pages where the book in which they occur is studied. But other uses of Bible verses also are listed. The *Subject Index* (p. 199) includes all the people, places, and writings mentioned in the Guide, and shows where they are included in our studies. If you come across a word with which you are unfamiliar, e.g. perhaps Septuagint, Apocrypha, look it up in this Index, and you will be able to refresh your mind about its meaning.

MAP AND CHARTS

The map on p. xvii shows places of importance in the history of the biblical literature. The Summary on p. 188 introduces and explains the time charts of the historical periods to which the various books of the Bible refer, and the periods when books were probably completed. The Comparative Chart on pp. 22–3 lists some modern translations of Deut. 6.4–5 and Psalm 8.4–5.

ABBREVIATIONS

The abbreviations used in this Guide for the titles of the books of the Bible are similar to those listed at the front of the RSV Common Bible, and used in the footnotes of that version.

Further Reading

The books listed below provide further information, some at a rather more advanced level, on the Books of the Old Testament, either taken together or individually. Most theological college libraries have a wide selection of older books on the subject, and tutors and librarians will be able to recommend those that will best suit your needs. For a note on new books, see page 210.

INTRODUCTIONS

Like this TEF Guide, Introductions provide readers starting to study the Old Testament books with a knowledge of their background and textual history. Specially recommended are:

J. H. Hayes and C. H. Holladay, *Biblical Exegesis: A Beginner's Handbook*, Revised. London, SCM Press.
B. S. Childs, *Introduction to the Old Testament as Scripture*. London, SCM Press.
G. Fohrer, *Introduction to the Old Testament*. London, SPCK.
J. H. Hayes, *An Introduction to Old Testament Study*. London, SCM Press.
J. A. Soggin, *Introduction to the Old Testament*, Revised Edition. London, SCM Press.

COMMENTARIES

These offer the best way of getting to understand the Old Testament more fully. Three sorts most useful for students are:

1. *One-volume Commentaries*, containing general articles on subjects relating to the Bible, and concise comments on each book, without extensive interpretation of individual passages. Some have over 1,000 pages, and so are very costly. Recommended are:

G. C. D. Howley, and others, *A Bible Commentary for Today*. Basingstoke UK, Marshall Pickering. A conservative evangelical commentary, with a range of styles of presentation.
W. Neil, *Bible Commentary*. Sevenoaks UK, Hodder & Stoughton.
C. M. Laymon (Editor), *The Interpreter's One Volume Commentary on the Bible*. Nashville US, Abingdon.
R. E. Brown and others (Eds): *The New Jerome Biblical Commentary*. London, Geoffrey Chapman. A Roman Catholic Commentary.
H. H. Rowley and M. Black (Eds), *Peake's Commentary on the Bible*. New Van Nostrand Reinhold. The revised edition published in 1962 of a commentary first produced over forty years earlier.

2. *Background commentaries*, usually giving background information about each Old Testament book or group of books, not verse-by-verse studies. Some are included in series with books on other subjects. Examples are:

Old Testament Guides. Sheffield UK, JSOT Press.
P. R. Ackroyd (OT ed.), *The Oxford Bible Series*. Oxford University Press. (Several books).

H. Mowvley, *Guide to Old Testament Prophecy*. Cambridge UK, Lutterworth Press.

3. *Commentaries on single OT Books*, mostly in series covering the whole OT, with each book giving some background, but mainly detailed studies of the Bible text.

Cambridge Bible Commentaries on the NEB. Cambridge, UK, Cambridge University Press. Clear and concise, explaining the exact meaning of the text and its theological significance for people today.

Daily Study Bible Series. Edinburgh, St Andrew Press. Helps to regular Bible reading, rather than literary and historical studies.

International Theological Commentaries. Edinburgh, Handsel Press. Concerned chiefly with theological significance, not literary or historical questions.

Layman's Bible Commentaries. Atlanta, GA USA, John Knox Press. Expositions by well-known scholars, in everyday English.

New Century Bible. With some literary and historical content, calling for serious study.

Old Testament Library. London, SCM Press. Scholarly books at a more advanced level, requiring a good command of English.

TEF Study Guides. London, SPCK. Language level and presentation similar to this Introduction. For titles available and in preparation, see list opposite title page above.

Tyndale Bible Commentaries. Leicester, UK, Inter-Varsity Press. Brief introductions, with commentary for readers having only basic biblical knowledge

BOOKS ON THE APOCRYPHA

B. Metzger, *Introduction to the Apocrypha*, New York, Oxford University Press.

R. C. Dentan, *The Apocrypha: Bridge of the Testaments*. New York, Seabury Press.

—— *Jewish Literature between the Bible and Misnah*. London, SCM Press.

Cambridge Commentaries on the NEB (see above) include some volumes on the Apocrypha.

BOOKS ON THE DEAD SEA SCROLLS

A. N. Gilkes, *The Impact of the Dead Sea Scrolls*. London, Macmillan.

G. Vermes, *The Dead Sea Scrolls in English*. Harmondsworth, UK, Penguin.

—— *The Dead Sea Scrolls: Qumran in Perspective*. London, SCM Press.

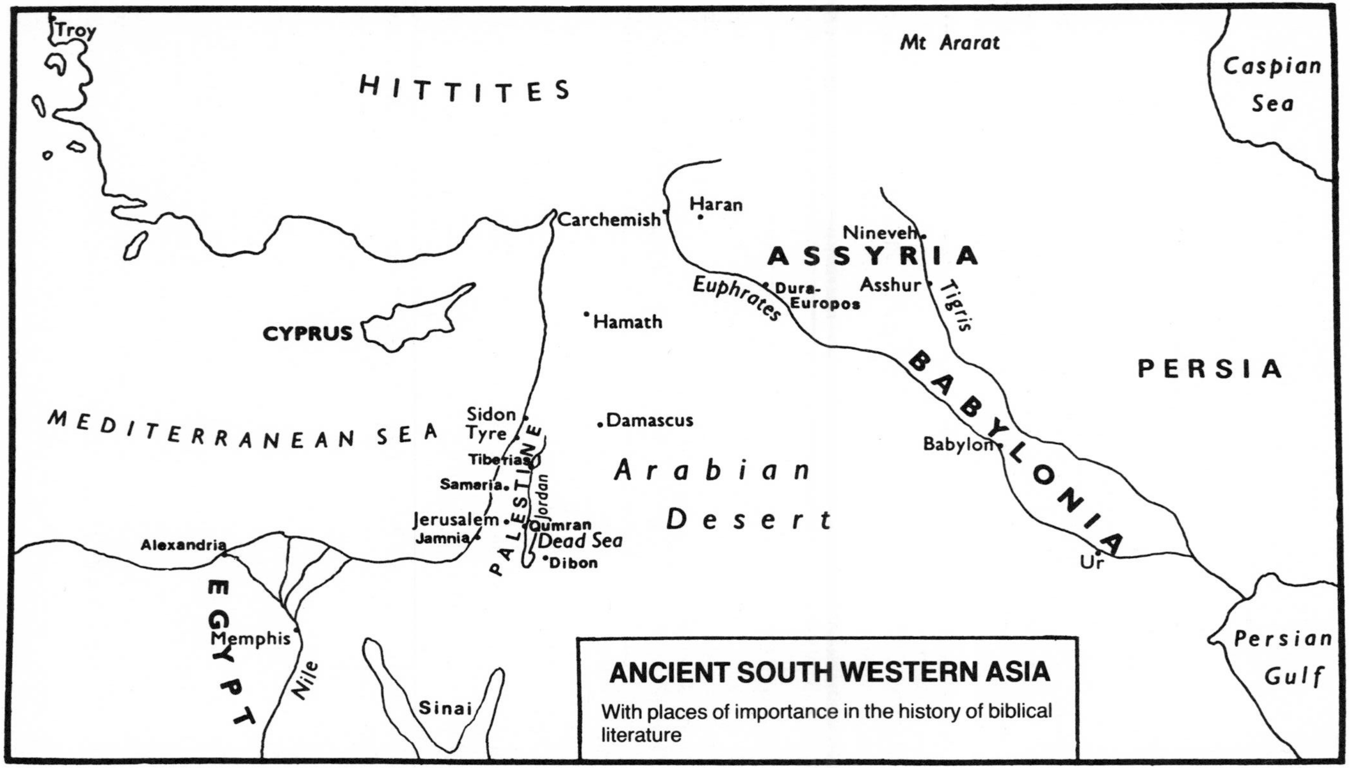

ANCIENT SOUTH WESTERN ASIA

With places of importance in the history of biblical literature

1

Understanding the Old Testament

THREE SEPARATE STUDIES

Some courses on the Old Testament set out to deal with History, Literature and Theology stage by stage. For example they examine the tradition of the Patriarchs, the origin of the book of Genesis which records that tradition, and the religious ideas of that time, all together. But in fact these things cannot be so easily related to each other. As we shall see later, the traditions contained in the book of Genesis did not reach the form in which we know them in that book until the time of the Exile. In the meantime they were passed on by word of mouth, and were written separately into various early documents which we no longer possess. They were only gathered together as we know them now by editors during the Exile, as a way of preserving the traditions of Israel in a time when the Jews could no longer observe many of their traditional customs because they were not living in their own land. A careful study of the book of Genesis shows that over the centuries before Genesis was written various theological points of view were applied to the material, adapting it to meet the needs of people of different generations and centuries.

When we study the history of Israel we need to use the information provided by Genesis to attempt to discover the actual events which underlie the records. In the first volume of this Introduction, on the history of Israel, I made it clear that we are dependent on legend for our understanding of the Patriarchs, and cannot discover an accurate historical account of the events. But we are able to test how far the records are in keeping with the style of life and customs of the period. There is a fair amount of evidence that the picture we receive matches what we know from other sources about the circumstances of the various peoples who lived at the time.

When we study the literature of Genesis we have to try to discover the stages of development which are evident from the way the book is presented today. These traditions cover many centuries. They were preserved during the Exodus, the settlement in the Promised Land, the rule of judges and kings, the end of the Northern Kingdom when it was defeated under the Assyrians and its people exiled, and the destruction of Jerusalem by the Babylonians. We are not of course able to trace every step of the way in which the traditions were passed on from generation to generation; but what we can discover covers a separate study from that of the events which made up the history of the Patriarchs and of Moses.

When we come to the study of the theology of the Old Testament we shall attempt to draw together the things which God revealed to His people down through the centuries and describe them in a systematic way. To do this we have to draw on all the evidence from the whole period of the Old Testament, and we shall not attempt to record developments in understanding stage by stage. This is because there is no one theology which sets out the beliefs of a particular generation. In every age there were people with different points of view, just as there are today. Moses quite clearly understood the LORD in a way which was hidden from Aaron. Moses had a far deeper appreciation of God's intentions for His people than anyone with whom he shared the experiences of the Exodus and Mount Sinai. So it is the overall picture of God's revelation which we need to study, looking for evidence from every age of the ultimate truth which God planned to make known to us through the nation of Israel.

So we see that this 'literary' study, i.e. the study of the literature of the Old Testament, forms a separate study from the history of Israel. We must, however, know the outline of Israelite history in order to understand the importance of the various books which compose the Old Testament. So our study of the literature comes second among the three books of this course. And when we have studied both the *History of Israel* and the *Books of the Old Testament* we shall be ready to study the *Theology of the Old Testament*.

THE BOOKS OF THE OLD TESTAMENT

The list of books which are accepted as having authority for belief and the practice of faith is called the Canon. Its authority comes from the belief that the books listed have been provided by God through His inspiration and revelation to the writers for the guidance and help of those who worship Him. We shall see later in this chapter that there is more than one such list used among Christians, according to their denominations. We shall need to ask, 'What is the significance of this fact?' But first we need to see how the lists accepted by Christians relate to the Canon accepted by Jews.

THE JEWISH CANON

The Jews today accept thirty-nine books as their Scriptures, although some are recorded together on a single scroll. But these are not the only books which were written about the Israelites and about God's dealings with them in Old Testament times. We have already used the Apocrypha, and noticed the existence of the apocalyptic books, in our study of the history of Israel. And the Jews possessed other books besides these towards the end of the Old Testament period.

They came to believe that some of these books were sacred, and must be studied with special care and attention, while others were of less value for the spiritual life of their nation.

The process of selecting which books should be held sacred took several centuries. And some books were formally accepted among the Jews as part of the holy Scriptures long before others were. The main stages in the process are marked by the title given to the Old Testament by the Jews. They call it 'The Law, the Prophets, and the Writings'.

THE LAW

This is the name given to the first five books of the Old Testament: Genesis, Exodus, Leviticus, Numbers, Deuteronomy. These may have been the writings which Ezra brought to Jerusalem in the period after the Exile (Vol. 1, p. 159; rev. ed. p. 172). They were accepted as holy writings by the Samaritans, even though there was a growing conflict between the Jews and the Samaritans from the time of Ezra until the final break between them, when the Samaritans set up their own rival temple on Mount Gerizim. The Jews have always given special respect and attention to the Law among the books of their Scriptures, and to this day they place special emphasis on the revelation of God which they see contained in the Law.

THE PROPHETS

These consist of two groups of books which are placed side by side in the Hebrew Bible. First there are those known as the *Former Prophets:*

Judges,
Joshua,
1 and 2 Samuel,
1 and 2 Kings.

Secondly there are the *Latter Prophets:*

Isaiah,
Jeremiah,
Ezekiel,

together with the Book of the Twelve Prophets, containing:

Hosea,	Nahum,
Joel,	Habakkuk,
Amos,	Zephaniah,
Obadiah,	Haggai,
Jonah,	Zechariah,
Micah,	Malachi

These books came to be regarded as Scriptures in about 200 BC. This was too late for the Samaritans to accept them, but early enough for

1.1 'The Pharisees . . . selected books originally written in Hebrew or Aramaic' (p. 5). This extract from Leviticus is from a Hebrew manuscript of the 10th century AD. The work of the Masoretes (see p. 29) can be seen in the dots for vowel sounds and the marginal notes.

them to be included without major changes in the Greek translation of the Old Testament, called the Septuagint, which was prepared between 250 BC and 100 BC.

THE WRITINGS

These are the remaining books of the Old Testament:

Psalms,	Ecclesiastes,
Proverbs,	Esther,
Job,	Daniel,
Song of Solomon,	Ezra,
Ruth,	Nehemiah,
Lamentations,	1 and 2 Chronicles

These were not finally accepted as being part of Scripture until after the time of Christ. The translators of the Septuagint felt free to include other books, and parts of books, in this section of their Scriptures. At first there was no accepted list of these additional books, and the various editions of the Septuagint differ in the books that they contain.

After the Romans had destroyed Jerusalem, and at a time when Christians were eager to win Jewish converts, the Pharisees held a council at Jamnia (about AD 100) to fix the final contents of the Jewish Scripture. The Septuagint was out of favour with them because it was widely used by the Christians. So they selected books which had originally been written in Hebrew or Aramaic, and which seemed to them to contain sound doctrine, and they rejected the extra books which had been included in the various editions of the Septuagint.

THE CHRISTIAN CANON

The Christians of New Testament times used Greek in their missionary activities outside Palestine, and made use of the Septuagint as their Scripture. They used the books of the Law, the Prophets, and the Writings, together with other books accepted by the Greek-speaking Jews. No formal decision was taken in the early days of the Church about which books were authoritative. In consequence different books were accepted in the various parts of the developing Church.

In AD 382 Pope Damasus, leader of the Roman Church, appointed Jerome to prepare a fresh Latin translation of the Old Testament. Jerome worked from the Hebrew and made use of the Jewish Scriptures. He adopted the Jewish Canon as an indication of the most important books. He treated as inferior the books included in earlier Latin Bibles which had been translations from the Septuagint but did not belong to the Jewish Canon. He made no translation of them. He called them *ecclesiastical books* as distinct from the *canonical books*. He called this 'ecclesiastical' group of writing *the Apocrypha*. The opposite view was expressed by Augustine of Hippo, and in consequence the Latin Vulgate was published later with selected books from among those found only in the Septuagint in the Old Latin translation.

The leaders of the Reformation denied that the books of the Apocrypha were of similar standing for Christians to the books of the Hebrew canon. Luther published a German translation of the Bible in 1534, which contained the Apocrypha between the Old and the New Testaments. He explained that it contained 'books which are not held equal to the sacred Scriptures, and nevertheless are useful and good to read'.

The Thirty-Nine Articles of the Church of England (1571) say of the books of the Apocrypha 'the Church doth read for example of life and instruction of manners; but yet it doth not apply them to establish doctrine'. The English Authorized Version published in 1611 contained the Apocrypha as a separate group of books.

More details of the complicated history of the Canon of the Bible can be found in the Preface to the RSV Common Bible. This is an edition of the English Bible published in 1973, which was based on the earlier Revised Standard Version first published between 1946 and 1957. The RSV Common Bible was produced with the intention that it could gain widespread acceptance and approval in all branches of the Christian Church: Orthodox, Catholic and Protestant. It contains all the books which are included in the various Canons accepted by these Churches. It includes for the Old Testament only the books accepted in the Jewish Canon. But it adds a section with the title, 'The Apocrypha/Deuterocanonical Books' where the extra books and parts of books from the Septuagint are presented.

Most of the TEF Study Guides use the RSV Common Bible as the basis for study of the Scriptures. The three volumes in the series which comprise the 'Old Testament Introduction' do not contain a detailed study of the Apocrypha, although some use is made of it in the *History of Israel* volume, because a separate Study Guide is planned which will deal in detail with the Apocrypha. So this present book deals only with the books of the Old Testament which were included in the Hebrew Canon. This revised edition sets the books out in the order in which they are to be found in the Bible. This is a change from the first edition, which dealt with the books in the order of the Hebrew Canon. (See p. xi.)

We shall not study the Hebrew and Aramaic forms of the Old Testament, because not all students have the opportunity to learn these languages, and there are more advanced textbooks for those who do. But we need to decide which English translation we will use (see ch. 2 below).

STUDY SUGGESTIONS

Before starting work on any of these suggestions please read the section headed 'Study Suggestions' on p. xii.

WORD STUDY

1. What is the purpose of each of the following methods of studying the Old Testament?
   (a) Historical Studies (b) Literary Studies (c) Theological Studies

REVIEW OF CONTENT

2. Why do we need to study the literature of the Old Testament:
   (a) after studying the History of Israel, and
   (b) before studying the Theology of the Old Testament?
3. How did the Samaritans come to accept the first five books of the Old Testament as Scripture, but to reject the other books of the Hebrew Canon?
4. Which of the following are included in the book of the Twelve Prophets?
   (a) Hosea (b) Isaiah (c) Joshua (d) Micah (e) Samuel
5. Daniel is placed among the prophets in English translations. Where does this book find a place in the Hebrew Canon? Why did not the Jews include it among the prophets?

BIBLE STUDY

6. How many of the Latter Prophets are mentioned by name in the New Testament? Using a Concordance, make a list of one reference for each prophet that is named, (e.g. Joel: Acts 2.16).
7. The book of Isaiah shows signs of belonging to more than one period of the history of Israel. Compare Isaiah 7.1–14 with Isaiah 44.21–28. Then answer the following questions, using your knowledge of the history of Israel as well as what you find written in these two passages.
   (a) Who were Rezin, Remaliah and Cyrus?
   Did they all live at the same time? If not, when did each live?
   (b) Which nations were enemies of Judah in each passage?
   (c) What kind of message was there for the people of Judah from God in each passage: judgement or hope?
   (d) Could the same prophet have been at work at both periods of the history?

FURTHER STUDY AND DISCUSSION

8. 'Protestants . . . use the Apocrypha for an understanding of the development of Jewish thought between the writing of the last book of the Old Testament and the time of Christ's ministry on earth.' In what other ways have you seen the books of the Apocrypha used by Protestants?

THE SIGNIFICANCE OF THE CANON

WHICH CANON?

Most denominations of the Christian Church hold the Bible in reverence as an essential source for the knowledge of God, and of His puposes. The Bible is accepted as a guide in discovering how to serve God. Most Christians, before they make a serious study of the Bible, suppose that the edition they use is the one which possesses divine authority and can be used as a secure basis for discussion and understanding of theology and of ethics. Many of them are surprised when they discover that not all Christians accept exactly the same selection of books as the right contents for the Old Testament. Nobody can compel us to accept and use books which we have never before considered to belong to Scripture. We are naturally influenced by the teaching of the denomination under whose influence we become Christians. But we do need to recognize that there are other people who serve the Lord who have a different attitude to some or all of the books contained in the section of the RSV Common Bible headed Apocrypha/Deuterocanonical Books. We ought at least to accept that they have the right to decide, under the guidance of their denomination, what they will read as Scripture. Otherwise we are claiming for ourselves a right which we are denying to others.

The books contained in the Hebrew Canon are accepted by all Christians. Protestants hold these as of supreme importance, but also use the Apocrypha for an understanding of the development of Jewish thought between the writing of the last book of the Old Testament and the time of Christ's ministry on earth. Roman Catholics and people of the Orthodox Faith add additional chapters to some of the books of the Hebrew canon, and also add some additional books to the canon they accept. These additional Scriptures are derived from the Septuagint. Publishers for these denominations place these extra writings in sequence with the books of the Hebrew Canon, and not as a separate third section to the Bible.

There was a time when such differences in accepted Canons were a cause of great controversy between the denominations, because they were used to support distinctive theologies held by different

Churches. But the brief account of the history of the Old Testament Canon which has already been given makes it clear that a fresh approach is necessary, which will cut across these old arguments and help to bring closer understanding between Christians.

WHERE SHOULD WE FIND GOD'S REVELATION?

To answer this we need to go back to the beginning of human knowledge of God. Nobody could ever have known anything about God unless it was the will and purpose of God to make Himself known to us. Many philosophers have attempted to interpret our experiences of life and to provide some meaning and purpose for our existence, but such studies have not provided any secure knowledge of God unless they have accepted the idea of revelation. The whole evidence of the Bible is that God makes Himself known in the hearts and minds of those who seek to know Him.

Revelation did not begin with books and other forms of literature. These came later as an attempt to record what God had revealed. Abraham had no books to guide him on his journeys, nor did he write books or have books written about him during his lifetime. But he knew God, and responded to His rule. Read Genesis 12.1–3. This is the account which has been handed down to us of the beginning of God's plan of salvation through Abraham and his descendants.

Where did this account come from? We have no information about what Abraham told his son, Isaac, about his call to serve the Lord. Nor have we any evidence of what Isaac told Jacob, or Jacob told his ten sons. Some scholars even say that none of these people ever existed, but that they are part of an attempt at later times to explain the origins of God's people. Certainly there was a long period in which the people of Israel were dependent on oral tradition. This was passed by word of mouth from generation to generation and was quite probably adapted and developed over the years. Then there was a time when various accounts were written and later edited, until the book of Genesis was prepared, probably in the time of the Exile in Babylon.

But however the records of Abraham came to be part of the Bible, it is quite clear that from the beginning revelation came as an encounter with God. No clearly defined creed was handed down from generation to generation. No great sculptured image of God was prepared capable of inspiring each generation with a true vision of God's glory. Instead a story was told of Abraham's meeting with God. When a creed was later prepared for the use of God's people in worship it included an account of what Abraham did in response to God's call, and how his descendants came to know God's saving power (Deut. 26.6–10). When poetry was written to provide acts of praise for God's people the story of God's relationship with Abraham was drawn on, and the account of God's continuing relationship with later generations (Ps. 105). These passages of Scripture serve as a witness to God's mercy and love in His dealings with Israel. They pointed each succeeding generation to God's living presence among them, and to the possibility of knowing Him and His activities in their own time.

What matters is that we are offered the possibility of a relationship with God, a personal knowledge of the LORD. The Bible stands as the supreme witness to that glorious possibility. As we read the story of Israel, and as we go on to learn about Jesus Christ and His followers, we discover that central to it all is God's desire for fellowship with His people. He calls us to know Him for ourselves, and this is the purpose and meaning of all revelation (see Jer. 31.33–34). When we witness to other people about God's mercy and love what matters is not simply that they should know what we think, or how we interpret our experiences, but that they should discover for themselves a relationship with the living God.

HOW SHOULD WE UNDERSTAND THE SCRIPTURES?

There are, of course, some questions to be faced at this stage in our studies. How is it that there seem to be so many different ways of speaking about God, and about His purposes? Why do Christians at times disagree about the significance of what they read in the Bible, and especially in the Old Testament? The fact is that each individual discovers some of the truth as a result of his or her relationship with God. Each individual comes to some understanding of the revelation of God contained within the Scriptures. But we do not know God perfectly, and we do not always understand the words which the biblical writers used to express their experience of Him. We have much to learn before we can say that we know God truly, and much to do to discover how to express the truth to others.

But more than this, we make a serious mistake if we suppose that the writers and editors of the Bible somehow escaped human limitations of knowledge and understanding. Each writer used his best skills to prepare some expression of his experience of God, but each was limited in his understanding by the circumstances in which he lived and the way in which people of his time spoke about God, and God's purposes.

How then can we discover a deeper understanding of the Scriptures? For a long time now biblical scholars have been studying the Bible to share with us a fuller knowledge of the significance of what we read in it. Many scholars have felt driven to discover the *original* details of the traditions, history, law, wisdom etc. which are contained in our

Scriptures. They have believed that it is the original revelation which is of supreme importance. There, they seem to say, God Himself speaks. They have tended to treat the editing which they believe underlies the present books of the Old Testament as of secondary importance, needing to be cleared out of the way. But they have been unable to get back fully and clearly to the original revelation in this way, even though their interpretations of the Scriptures have often been helpful. They have mistakenly tended to dismiss the later developments which have in fact contained important evidence of God's revelation. God has in fact been at work down through the generations making Himself known to all involved in the development of the Scriptures.

Let us take a simple example. The prophet Amos preached a message of justice and of judgement to the Northern Kingdom of Israel, and in the event his warnings came to fulfilment. The Assyrians over-ran that country and took the people into captivity, and they were never to be heard of again. Yet in Amos 9.11–15 there is a clear message of hope for the future. What are we to make of this? Most scholars agree that these verses come from a later date, long after the Northern Kingdom had ceased to exist. The editor responsible for adapting the words of Amos applied his preaching to the needs of the people of the Southern Kingdom, which by that time was all that was left of Israel. They needed a warning about obedience to God and compassion for their fellows, but they also needed an assurance that they were not already utterly forsaken by God. A message of hope was not inappropriate. In fact the added words are of significance to all later readers because they do declare the mercy of God. Sinfulness has not been totally removed from God's world. It remains a problem that needs dealing with. But it is still true that God's ultimate purposes are for the salvation of humankind. This interpretation of the book of Amos as a whole, in its accepted form, is a simple example of a new method of studying the Bible which is known as Canonical Criticism.

WHAT IS CANONICAL CRITICISM?

Canonical Criticism is an approach to the study of the Bible which attempts to give full value to every part of it. Nothing is devalued because it is considered to be of a late date, and the work of an unknown editor using an earlier version of the Scripture concerned.

We have already noticed the writings of Brevard S. Childs on Canonical Criticism (see p. ix), in which he sets out his understanding of the significance of the Hebrew Canon for Jewish Faith. He says:

> The shape of the biblical text reflects a history of encounter between God and Israel. The canon serves to describe this peculiar relationship and to define the scope of this history by establishing a beginning and an end of the process. It assigns a special quality to this particular segment of human history which became normative for all successive generations of this community of faith. The significance of the final form of the biblical text is that it alone bears witness to the full history of revelation. (pp. 75–76)

Childs is careful to state that he is describing the development of the Jewish Canon. He sees a specific period of history as the significant time for God's revelation of Himself to that people. He insists that the latest forms of the Jewish Scriptures form the clearest account of that revelation. He recognizes that the work of the editors of the various books which make up the Old Testament was itself part of the process of revelation. He is of course not denying that God was active in Christ, and has been active in the Church through subsequent history, and is available to us today.

Those who use Canonical Criticism as a way of studying the Bible believe that God has been at work at every stage in human history, making Himself known to His people. The study of Scripture is a means to fellowship with God, and all students grow in understanding of God and His purposes as they spend time trying to understand the Bible. Each student needs to look for the guidance and inspiration of God in such studies. Each group of students studying the Bible need to listen to the insights they can offer to each other as they study the record of God's revelation together.

ARE ALL INTERPRETATIONS OF EQUAL SIGNIFICANCE?

There is one question that does need to be faced quite seriously in all this: are those who adopt the approach of Canonical Criticism saying that *any* interpretation of Scripture is to be accepted as revealing the mind of God provided it finds answer in our hearts and minds as evidence of the truth? Throughout the history of the Christian Church there have been people who have put forward ideas which have conflicted with the generally accepted patterns of Christian teaching. They have often done so on the basis of their own understanding of Scripture, sincerely held but not readily approved by other Christians. There are some groups of Christians today who claim to hold the only true interpretation of the Scriptures; and to be commissioned to challenge the teachings of the main-line Churches. Sometimes these groups come into being, at least in part, to emphasize some aspect of the Christian faith which the Churches have neglected. But then these groups tend to over-emphasize the

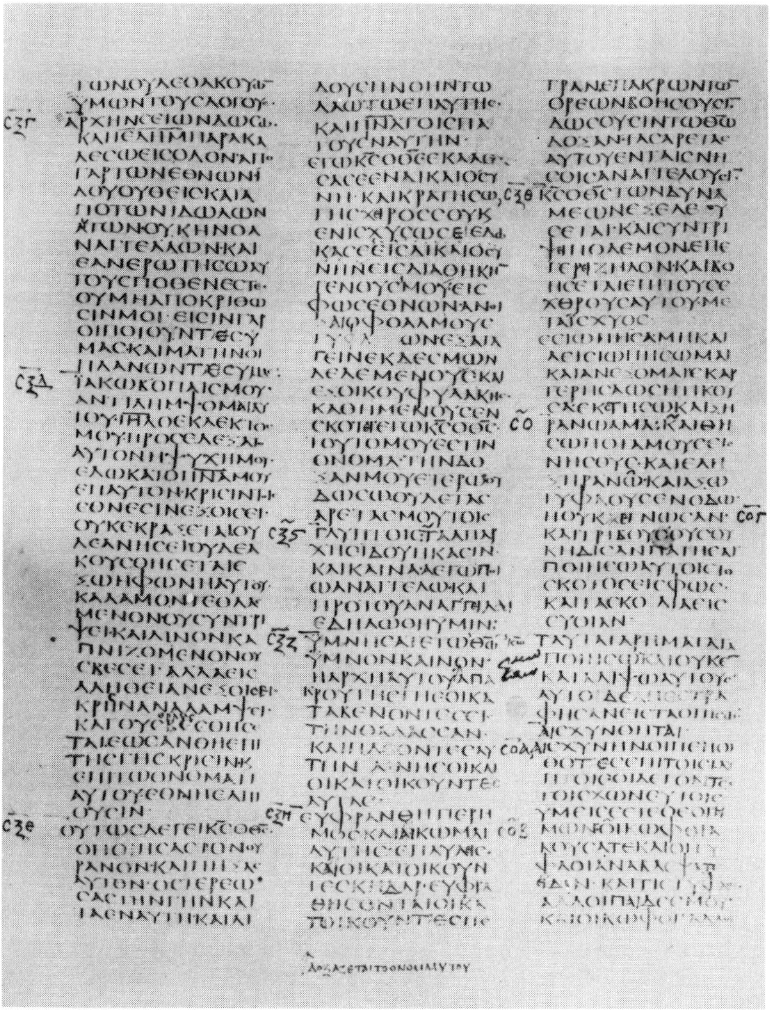

1.2 'The Christians of New Testament times made use of the Greek translation of the Old Testament called the 'Septuagint' (p. 5). This extract from Isaiah 41 and 42 is part of a page from a manuscript of the Septuagint known as the *Codex Sinaiticus* (see pp. 30, 38) probably dating from about AD 350.

things that they teach, themselves forgetting some other important aspects of the truth.

The history of the Canon shows us that those who served the Lord wanted to be able to define the truth which God was revealing by listing the books which clearly presented it. The Jews adopted the Hebrew Canon in reaction to the Christian Church, which they said was heretical! They felt that the Septuagint, and especially the additional writings in it, were being used by Christians to distort the Jewish Faith. The Early Fathers of the Christian Church attempted to limit the spread of heresy by indicating which books should be regarded as authoritative parts of the two Testaments. The leaders of the different denominations defended their own interpretation of Scripture by selecting for use those books which seemed to them to present the truth. Luther, for example, called the Letter of James in the New Testament an 'epistle of straw' because he felt that it disputed the fact that salvation comes by faith, and not by works (see James 2.14–17). His own experience was that nothing he could do could win the approval of God, but that faith in Jesus Christ brought him peace with God. Many Christians today recognize that our new relationship with God through faith brings about changes in our lives and our characters which are evidence that we are living by faith. So we do not find it necessary to reject the teachings of the letter of James.

This example illustrates the fact that, throughout the history of God's People, the real test of any written material which claims to be a revelation from God is: (1) whether or not it brings fresh light and fresh understanding to those who are of the faith, and to those who want to know God; and (2) whether other Christians find the same significance in what is written. The Scriptures carry authority because many Christians over many centuries have found encouragement, guidance and blessing from the study of them.

The lists of books which different denominations accept as authoritative are each an attempt to guide people towards the truth, showing them where they can gain an understanding of the Christian Faith, and knowledge of God. The books of the Hebrew Canon are accepted by all the main-line Churches and are the ones to be dealt with in this Study Guide.

STUDY SUGGESTIONS

WORD STUDY

1. What do the following words mean?
   (a) Canon (b) Septuagint (c) Apocrypha

REVIEW OF CONTENT

2. (a) What was the attitude of the Jews to the Writings and the books of the Apocrypha in the lifetime of Jesus?
(b) Would you expect the writers of the New Testament to make use of the Apocrypha? If so, why? Look through the footnotes of Revelation and make a list of the references you can find to books of the Apocrypha.
(c) What difference did the spread of the Christian Church make to the Jewish attitude to the writings we call the Apocrypha?

BIBLE STUDY

3. Read Jeremiah 29.1–14. What is the significance of this passage for our knowledge of:
(a) the History of Israel?
(b) a possible source for part of the book of Jeremiah?
(c) Jeremiah's understanding of God's nature and purposes?
4. From a copy of the Apocrypha read 1 Maccabees 1.1–10.
(a) Which nation ruled a large part of the world at the time this book was written?
(b) Who was known among the Jews as a 'sinful' ruler. At what date did he become powerful? Find out from a Bible Dictionary what he did to harm the Jews.

FURTHER STUDY AND DISCUSSION

5. 'When we witness to other people about God's mercy and love what matters is not simply (1) that they should know what we think, or (2) how we interpret our experiences. It is (3) that they should discover for themselves a relationship with the living God' (p. 10).
(a) Which of these three things is most important to you yourself?
(b) In what ways are another person's experiences of God important to you?
6. Christians in different denominations, or even within a particular Church, do not always agree about the significance of the Scriptures.
(a) What have you learnt from those who have different beliefs from your own?
(b) What have you been able to help other Christians to understand?
(c) What is your attitude to those whose beliefs continue to conflict with your own understanding of the faith?
(d) Is it right to claim an exclusive knowledge of the truth? Give reasons for your answer.
7. Give an illustration of the way in which the Bible provides a guide to the truth, and say how far your own understanding of the matter in hand depends on the teaching of your own Church.

2

English Translations and the Early Manuscripts

There was a time when most students who used English to study the Bible used the 'Authorized' Version prepared by direction of King James II, and published in 1611. But today many different English versions of the Bible are available. Some students find the range of English Bibles confusing, and are puzzled to know why there are so many versions.

DIFFICULTIES FOR TRANSLATORS

Part of the answer to this problem is the fact that unless we know and use Hebrew and Aramaic, and can read the Old Testament in those languages, we have to use a translation. Students who have attempted to translate a piece of written English into their own language will know how difficult it is to convey the exact sense of the original writing. There can never be an English version of the Bible that is fixed and final, and certain to convey to readers at all times exactly what the original writers intended to say.

1. CHANGES OF MEANING IN ENGLISH

One difficulty for translators is that all living languages change as the years go by. So, for example, many of the English words which were used in 1611 have quite different meanings today. In modern English 'prevent' means to hinder or to stop, e.g. 'Mothers must prevent their children from falling on the fire.' In the Authorized Version we find that verse 13 of Psalm 88 is translated, 'Unto thee have I cried, O Lord; and in the morning shall my prayer *prevent* thee', but it is quite clear from the Hebrew that the Psalmist was not thinking of stopping or hindering God! The translators of the Common Bible have got nearer to the meaning in modern English by saying, 'in the morning my prayer comes before thee'. Other modern versions give a similar translation. Yet the people who prepared the Authorized Version did not make a mistake. In their time the word 'prevent' was taken straight from the Latin *praevenire*, meaning 'come before', and they were right to use it then. But their translation of this verse is confusing for us, because today the word 'prevent' has a different meaning.

If you think carefully about your own language, and discuss it with some of the old people of your language area, you will almost certainly find similar changes there. Such changes are usually more rapid in a language which has little literature, for books help to fix and preserve the meaning of words. In many language areas there has been a need for new Bible translations because the local or regional language has changed so much since the first edition was published. Young people find the earlier translations difficult to understand, whilst older people are happy with them because they remember how words were used in the past.

2. ALTERNATIVE MEANINGS IN HEBREW

Another difficulty for translators is that many words have more than one meaning, and it is not always easy to tell from the Hebrew Text which of several meanings was intended by the writer. *Ruach*, the Hebrew word for 'Spirit' can mean God's Spirit, or a human being's spirit, but it can also mean the wind, and even breath. There are other meanings for the same word. If your library possesses a copy of Young's Analytical Concordance have a look at the section at the end which is headed 'Index-Lexicon to the Old Testament'. Here all the Hebrew words are set out in alphabetical order in the type of lettering we use in writing English. Under *Ruach* you will find twenty different ways in which this one word is translated into English in the King James Version. In making a fresh translation scholars may have different ideas about the best English word to use in any particular verse to convey the meaning of the Hebrew.

3. CONVEYING THE TRUE MEANING OF THE HEBREW

Sometimes English words may convey ideas which really do not suit the sense of the Hebrew. For example the Hebrew word *Shalom* may roughly be translated as 'Peace'. But if you look this word up in an English Dictionary you will find it defined as 'absence of war, freedom from conflict' etc. The Hebrew word is much more positive than this, since it emphasizes harmony, well-being, prosperity etc. So the meaning of a verse where it is used may be quite different from what the English word 'peace' normally conveys. See for example Ps.34.14 where 'Seek peace' might in English convey the idea of avoiding conflict, but should be understood in the sense of the Hebrew word: seeking good relationships, and the consequent harmony.

There is at least one Hebrew word which cannot be expressed adequately by use of a single English equivalent. It is *chesed*, in which the '*ch*' is a hard sound made at the back of the mouth. In the King James Version it is translated 'goodness', 'kindness', 'loving kindness', etc. In the Common Bible the word is normally translated 'steadfast love' when it is used to express the quality of the saving activities of God. Loyalty to His Covenant is an essential part of its meaning. God's faithfulness in His purpose of good for humankind, including His mercy, His patience and His love for sinners are all part of the meaning of this word. The various versions of the English Bible all struggle to make this rich meaning clear. It is useful to compare the way in which each translates *chesed*.

Ideally we need to learn Hebrew and to study the Old Testament in its original language, making our own careful translation in order to help our people. But for most students this is not possible, and the best help available to us is to compare the various translations to see how a verse is translated by different scholars. Otherwise we must choose one version which is reasonably reliable and use that regularly.

4. SELECTING THE BEST HEBREW TEXT

The problem of preparing a translation of the Bible is made even more difficult because we do not possess the original writings of the men who first prepared the books of the Old Testament. What we do have is a fairly large number of handwritten copies dating from various times since the books were first written.

When scholars compare these ancient manuscripts they find that there are differences between them. Words are changed, phrases and sentences are included in some copies and not in others. Whole sections of text are found in one version which are omitted in others, and sometimes the order of the chapters in a book is changed. 'Textual Criticism' is the name which scholars give to the work of comparing manuscripts, and trying to explain the differences between them, in order to come to an understanding of what the original form of the verse or section or book was like.

(a) Many of the changes have resulted from the *difficulties in copying* a passage by hand, or by dictation. Try the following experiment in order to understand the problem. Copy out on to a sheet of paper the words of Psalm 92. Ask a friend to make a copy of what you have written. Give what he writes to another friend to copy. Carry on this process until nine or ten of your friends have each copied what the previous one wrote. Now compare the final copy with what is written in the Bible. There are quite a number of ways in which it is likely to be different. Perhaps somebody missed out a line. Somebody else may have mis-spelt a word. Or somebody may have misunderstood the handwriting that he was copying. In the later stages somebody may have tried to correct an earlier copier's mistakes because he saw that it did not make sense as it stood. Look carefully at the punctuation, and you will probably find that some sentences have been split which really belong together, and others joined which were separate. Mistakes of these sorts frequently occur when copying is done, and it is very difficult to make sure that a copy is true unless we have the original from which it was copied. Similar things have happened over the many centuries in which the Bible was written out by hand.

The Hebrew manuscripts had their own difficulties in addition to all these. For one thing, the Hebrew text was written without signs for most of the vowels. Some modern forms of shorthand give us an idea of what the Hebrew script was like to the Jews. The first verse of Psalm 92 would look like this:

'TSGD TGV THNKS TTHLRD TSNG PRSS TTHNM MST HGH'

Hebrew copyists were used to this sort of 'shorthand' writing, but even so, you will realize how difficult it would be to make an accurate copy. Because the manuscripts were handwritten, the spacing of letters sometimes made it difficult to know where each word began and ended. This too led to differences in the manuscripts.

(b) Some of the differences between the various manuscript copies of the books of the Old Testament were *intentionally introduced* into the text by the people who did the copying. For one reason, or another, they felt that they had a better way of expressing what needed to be said. Perhaps it seemed to them that the original writers had not fully grasped the significance of what God had revealed to them, and that the editors should improve on the text. Or else the changes were made by editors to relate what the text said to the needs of the people of their own generation. Preachers today sometimes do not read all the verses from a passage of Scripture because they feel that some are unsuitable for the guidance of their congregations. For example, look at Psalm 137 verse 9!

(c) Translators need to discover the best text to be the basis of their work. Christian scholars used to consider it necessary to discover the earliest form of the text, setting aside the various later changes, before producing a translation. This was clearly correct where errors had occurred in copying and the text as it stood did not make complete sense. It is unlikely that any of these errors could be considered inspired. But where deliberate changes had been made these could in fact be improvements on the original, and needed to be considered in attempting to produce a translation. Decisions had to be made about the way the text should be reproduced in English, and because they were difficult to make it was important that groups of scholars should work together in preparing a translation. They could discuss carefully the various possibilities for the translation. Even so, sometimes two different forms of the text seemed equally likely to be what the original writer intended, and in some versions of the English Bible another translation is printed as a footnote. Often the existence of alternative versions can only be indicated in a commentary on the book concerned. The writer of a commentary has the opportunity to describe the choices available, and the significance of each for our understanding of the Bible.

People who can study the Old Testament in the Hebrew language need to have a printed version of its text. Various forms have been produced through the centuries which have been an attempt to give as accurate an account as possible of what is written in the early manuscripts. Often the scholar who has produced a Hebrew version of the Old Testament uses the best available manuscript. Thus for example the British and Foreign Bible Society published an edition prepared by Norman Snaith in the years prior to the second world war and printed when that war was over. It contains no footnotes except those which were official to the Masoretic text (see p. 29). For advanced scholars an edition which contains substantial footnotes indicating variations between manuscripts is necessary, for example the *Biblia Hebraica Stuttgartensia* also available from the Bible Society.

You will see from all this what heavy responsibilities rest on those who prepare translations from the Hebrew text. You will perhaps have some idea now of the reasons why the various translations present the material in different ways.

ENGLISH TRANSLATIONS AVAILABLE TODAY

Since so many English translations are now available the different members of any congregation or college class are likely to be using different ones, and you will find it helpful to know something of the origin and presentation of each. The following list includes all the translations of the English Old Testament currently available, which were prepared by groups of scholars appointed to the work. There have been earlier versions that are no longer in print, and you may someday like to read about how the Bible first became available in English. Your library may contain a book on the subject.

The Douai Version This was a Roman Catholic Bible, translated from the Latin. It contains in the Old Testament those books and parts of books which that Church regards as authoritative, but which are often presented in other versions as part of the Apocrypha. The Old Testament was first published in 1609, together with the New Testament which had been issued in 1582. Two major revisions have taken place, beginning in 1749, and the latest published in 1941.

King James Version (AV) This was published in 1611 as an 'Authorized Version'. It was authorized by the British king of the time, who was head of the Anglican Church. Forty-seven scholars worked in six panels and produced a masterpiece of English literature. Italics are used to show where words which are not in the original texts have been inserted in the translation to make sense of what is written in the Hebrew and Greek passages. Chapter headings were provided, which are now printed as headings to each page of the Bible. Each verse begins on a new line, and so a special sign was used to indicate where paragraphs begin. It is like this ¶. Notes were provided in the margins to show related passages from other parts of the Bible, and also possible alternative translations. The Apocrypha was originally included, but is more often issued separately now. A *New King James Bible* (NKJB) was published in 1982 to preserve the literary quality of the original, but remove the difficulties that changes in use of language have created for modern readers.

The Revised Version (RV) In the nineteenth century scholars of various denominations worked together to prepare a revision of the King James Version. They were able to use earlier manuscript copies of the Scriptures than had been available in 1611 as a basis for the revision. They possessed a better knowledge of the biblical languages as a result of research made possible by travel and discovery in the biblical lands. They printed poetry as poetry and dropped the use of chapter headings. The New Testament was produced in 1881, the Old Testament in 1885, and the Apocrypha in 1898. A similar revision was produced in the United States of America under the title *American Standard Version* (ASV) and published in 1901. This has been followed in 1963 by the publication of a *New American Standard Bible* (NASV).

Revised Standard Version (RSV) This version was first published as a whole Bible in 1952, the New Testament having been issued in 1946. The Apocrypha was produced in 1957. Full use was made of all the available texts in the early manuscript versions of the books of the Bible. The style was intended to be simple, direct and modern. The prose is set out in paragraph form, with poetry printed in poetic form. Direct speech is printed with inverted commas, although there is no equivalent punctuation in the original languages. 'Thou' is used only where God is addressed. A Standing Committee continues to supervise the production of new editions, which is able to introduce improvements as study continues. In 1973 the *RSV Common Bible* (RSVCB) was published, based on the Revised Standard Version but presented in a form now officially authorized for use by all major Christian Churches: Protestant, Anglican, Roman Catholic and Eastern Orthodox. This is the version which is used in most of the TEF Study Guides.

The New RSV (NRSV) Prepared like its predecessors under the auspices of the National Council of Churches of Christ in the USA,

Deuteronomy 6.4–5

AV
4 Hear, O Israel: The LORD our God is one LORD:
5 And thou shalt love the LORD thy God with all thine heart, and with all thy soul, and with all thy might.

RSV(CB)
4 "Hear, O Israel: The LORD our God is one LORD; [5]and you shall love the LORD your God with all your heart, and with all your soul, and with all your might."

JB
'Listen, Israel: Yahweh our God is one Yahweh. You shall 4
love Yahweh your God with all your heart, with all your soul, 5
with all your strength.

NEB
Hear, O Israel, the Lord is our God, one LORD, and you must 4 5
love the LORD your God with all your heart and soul and strength.

GNB (TEV)
4 "Israel, remember this! The LORD – and the LORD alone—is our God. [5]Love the Lord your God with all your heart, with all your soul, and with all your strength.

NIV
[4]"Hear, O Israel. The LORD our God, the Lord is one. [5]Love the LORD your God with all your heart and with all your soul and with all your strength.

NJB
'Listen, Israel: Yahweh our God is the one, the only Yahweh. You must love Yahweh your God with all your heart, with all your soul, with all your strength.

REB
[4]Hear, Israel: the LORD is our God, the LORD our one God; [5]and you must love the LORD your God with all your heart and with all your soul and with all your strength.

NRSV
4 Hear, O Israel: The LORD is our God, the LORD alone. [5]You shall love the LORD your God with all your heart, and with all your soul, and with all your might.

Psalm 8.4–5

AV
4 What is man, that thou art mindful of him? and the son of man, that thou visitest him?
5 For thou hast made him a little lower than the angels, and hast crowned him with glory and honour.

Comparative Chart 'You will find it helpful to know something of the origin and presentation of the English translations' (p. 20). Notice the differences between the versions of Deuteronomy 6.4–5 and of Psalm 8.4–5 each compared here.

RSV (CB)
4 what is man that thou art mindful of
him
and the son of man that thou dost
care for him?
5 Yet thou hast made him a little less
than God,
and dost crown him with glory and
honour,

JB
4 ah, what is man that you should spare a thought for him.
the son of man that you should care for him?
5 Yet you have made him little less than a god,
you have crowned him with glory and splendour,

NEB
what is man that thou shouldst remember him, 4
mortal man that thou shouldst care for him?
Yet thou hast made him little less than a god, 5
crowning him with glory and honour.

GNB (TEV)
4 what is man, that you think of him;
mere man, that you care for him?
5 Yet you made him inferior only to
yourself;
you crowned him with glory and
honour.

NIV
4 what is man that you are mindful of
him,
the son of man that you care for
him?
5 You made him a little lower than the
heavenly beings
and crowned him with glory and
honour

NJB
4 what are human beings that you spare a thought for them,
or the child of Adam that you care for him?
5 Yet you have made him little less than a god,
you have crowned him with glory and beauty,

REB
4 what is a frail mortal, that you
should be mindful of him,
a human being, that you should take
notice of him?
5 Yet you have made him little less
than a god,
crowning his head with glory and
honour,

NRSV
4 what are human beings that you
are mindful of them,
mortals that you care for
them?
5 Yet you have made them a little
lower than God,
and crowned them with glory
and honour.

and published in 1990, this is in effect a new work, 'accurately reflecting the most ancient texts available and incorporating the tremendous changes that have taken place in the English language over the last half-century'.

Jerusalem Bible (JB) The Jerusalem Bible is a modern translation prepared for the use of Roman Catholics and published in 1966. In its fullest form it contains introductions to each section, maps and historical charts, and detailed notes about the meaning of the text. Its style and presentation is based on a French version published in Jerusalem in 1956, but it is none the less a direct translation from the original languages.

The *New Jerusalem Bible* (NJB) published in 1988 derives from the 1973 revision of the French version, with introductions and notes based on the results of recent scholarship. It attempts to provide an improved translation, and, like the NRSV, to avoid the use of masculine terms where the meaning includes women as well as men.

New English Bible (NEB) This is a fresh translation prepared for the Protestant Churches. The complete Bible was published in 1970, containing a revised edition of the New Testament which had first been published in 1961. The footnotes indicate where the words used do not fully represent the early texts from which the translation is made: 'Prob.rdg.; Heb . . .'. (See for example the footnote 'c' to Psalm 4.3.) Often the source of the 'probable reading' is given.

The Revised English Bible (REB) has been published in 1989 reviewing 'The New English Bible alongside the ancient texts in Hebrew, Aramaic and Greek, in the light of current English usage in speaking, writing and worshipping'. All major Christian Churches in the British Isles have co-operated in its production, and it was planned from the start to be acceptable to all Christians.

New American Bible (NAV) This is a version prepared by the Roman Catholic Church in America, based on the original languages rather than the Latin Vulgate.

The Good News Bible (Today's English Version) (GNB or TEV) was published in 1976, the New Testament having been published in 1966, and the Apocrypha added in 1979. A Catholic edition has also been published. It uses 'standard, everyday, natural English'. Modern equivalents are given for biblical standards and measurements, e.g. distance in metres. Money is given in dollars in American editions, and pounds in British. Sentences are presented in a simple direct fashion, and sections for paragraphs are shorter than in the Revised Standard Version. Headings are given to each section, and many editions are illustrated with simple but lively line-drawings. There are brief introductions to each book, and footnotes providing information necessary to understand each passage. There is a useful appendix with a brief dictionary, and a selective concordance. Maps on the end papers of some editions are also useful.

New International Version (NIV) This was prepared in the USA with the assistance of scholars from many Protestant denominations, and was published in 1978. It represents a strongly conservative approach to the Bible, accepting 'the authority and infallibility of the Bible as God's word in written form'. It also accepts as the only true understanding of salvation through the death of Christ the theory of the Atonement which teaches that Jesus bore the punishment from God which should have fallen on us because of our sin, and so enabled us to be forgiven. These views affect the way in which the translation is presented. Most other English versions have also been prepared by recognized Old Testament scholars, but who represented various theological traditions, and who all shared in the decisions made about the best way in which to interpret the Scriptures.

The list given above does not include translations which have been prepared by one writer, since this method means that individual style and knowledge will affect them. Translations prepared by a group of scholars are to be preferred to ensure accuracy. Some translations by individuals are paraphrases, and attempt to explain the significance of Scripture by including additions to the original text which are dependent on the scholar's interpretation of the actual wording. Two such versions which are currently available are J. B. Phillips's *New Testament in Modern English*, and K. Taylor's *Living Bible*.

Further new translations will no doubt continue to be prepared individually or by teams of scholars to take account of fresh scholarship and new insights into the meaning of the Hebrew and Greek languages.

STUDY SUGGESTIONS

WORD STUDY

1. The Hebrew word *tub* can be translated into English in various ways. For example it can be expressed as 'the best', 'choice gifts', 'gladness', 'goodness', 'good things', 'prosperity', etc.
   Look at each of the following verses and note the translation used for *tub*. Which, if any, of the other translations can be substituted and make good sense of each of the verses concerned?
   (a) Gen. 24.10 (b) Gen. 45.18 (c) Exod. 33.19
   (d) Deut. 28.47 (e) Job 21.16
2. The English word 'faith' can be used to mean several different things. Use a dictionary to find out as many alternatives as you

can. Then say which of them is the correct meaning for the word 'faith' in the following quotation:
'The righteous shall live by his faith' (Habakkuk 2.4b).

REVIEW OF CONTENT

3. What are the two main difficulties which face scholars who are trying to prepare a fresh translation of the Old Testament?
4. Prepare a chart setting out the information about the various English Versions which are described in this chapter. Use columns to list for each version: its title, its theological background (Catholic, Protestant, Ecumenical, etc.), the dates at which the various parts were published (Old Testament, New Testament, Apocrypha). Use a footnote to indicate the Catholic alternative to publishing the Apocrypha.

FURTHER STUDY AND DISCUSSION

5. Which English Version do you prefer for use in your studies, and for preparation of your sermons? Say why you find it so useful.
6. Compare the contents of the RSV Common Bible with any alternative of your own choosing by setting your answers to the following questions side by side in two columns on a sheet of paper:
   (a) What is the theological background of each? Does each version have a preface explaining this background?
   (b) How has each version been prepared: by an individual or by a group of scholars, and if the latter who was responsible for their selection?
   (c) When was each first published?
   (d) Are there any maps, time-charts or other illustrations?
   (e) Are there footnotes drawing attention to other parts of the Bible where similar or related subjects are dealt with?
   (f) Are there footnotes which explain the sources of the translation, indicating what texts have been used to obtain a clear meaning, and are there alternative translations where this seems necessary?
   (g) Does the English which is used in each translation match the way the language is used in your country today.
   (h) Is there a section at the beginning of each version explaining when it was written, under what circumstances and by whom?
   (i) Is there a commentary provided in each version which explains the significance of each section of the books of the Old Testament in turn?
   (j) Is the Apocrypha included, and if so, where are the various books of the Apocrypha placed in relation to the books of the Old Testament?

7. Which of the items listed in Question 6 are (a) likely to be most helpful in assuring you that the translation in an English Version is accurate and as carefully prepared as possible, and (b) likely to be of most practical value to you in your studies?

USING THE RSV COMMON BIBLE

The RSV Common Bible has been chosen as a basis for Bible study in most of the TEF Study Guides because it is the version most widely used in the colleges and Extension Courses for which the Guides are chiefly intended. Not only is it important because it is accepted by all the main-line Churches; it also contains some useful aids to Bible Study. Many other editions of the RSV contain the same aids. So we need to understand how to use them.

1. *Abbreviations:* At the start of the RSV Common Bible, immediately before the Old Testament title page, you will find a list of the books of the Old Testament, the Apocrypha/Deuterocanonical Books and the New Testament, with the abbreviation for each. For example 'Gen' stands for Genesis, 'Eccles' for Ecclesiastes, etc. These abbreviations are used throughout the RSV Common Bible where reference needs to be made to another book of the Bible, and we are using most of them in the three volumes of this Old Testament course. (In some cases we have enlarged these very short abbreviations to clarify their meaning. Exodus becomes 'Exod' instead of 'Ex', Isaiah becomes 'Isa' instead of 'Is', etc).

2. *Cross References:* Like most versions, the Common Bible contains cross references to other parts of the Bible which deal with similar or related subjects. Look for example at the foot of the first page of Genesis, and you will find the following information: '1.1: Jn 1.1. 1.26–27: Gen 5.1; Mt 19.4; Mk 10.6; Col 3.10; Jas 3.9.' This is a shorthand way of saying that:

(a) When reading Genesis 1 verse 1 you can find a similar statement about the beginning of creation in John's Gospel 1 verse 1. John's Gospel adds the fact that the Word, meaning the Son of God, was with God at the beginning.

(b) When reading Genesis 1 verses 26–27, which is about human beings being made in the image of God, and being made male and female, the same ideas are expressed in Genesis 5 verse 1 and, in fact, verse 2. (You will always find that reading more than the verse quoted, will give you a clearer idea of the meaning of the verse which you have been asked to read.) In Matthew 19.4 Jesus refers to the fact that God made male and female. In Mark 10.6 there is another account of these words of Jesus. In Colossians 3.10 Paul refers to the fact that we are made in the image of God, and in James 3.9 the writer refers to the fact that we are created in the likeness of God. All this reading helps us to understand the importance for faith of the words we are studying in Genesis.

3. *Hebrew Words:* Sometimes the meaning of what is written cannot easily be expressed in another language because the sense is conveyed by the *sound* of the Hebrew word, and not simply by its meaning. Take for example Gen. 4.1. This verse has a small 'g' after the word 'gotten', and the footnote reads 'Heb. *qanah*, get'. This footnote shows how the name Cain has been explained in this verse by relating it to the Hebrew word meaning 'gotten'. The meaning of Genesis 4.1 could not be fully expressed without referring to the actual form of the Hebrew word. But the Hebrew word itself could not be included in the translation of the verse without causing some confusion, so it is placed as a footnote instead.

4. *Information about the ancient versions*: The RSV Common Bible is particularly helpful to students because it contains footnotes which show us some of the difficulties which the translator had to face. We need to understand the footnotes, and what they tell us about the ancient versions of the Old Testament.

Some of the footnotes state that the Hebrew is 'obscure', or 'uncertain'. The translators have to provide some English interpretation even when they are unsure of the meaning of certain unusual Hebrew words. So in the footnote they warn readers that no one today is sure of the meaning of the Hebrew (see Gen. 25.22). Often too, the translators use the abbreviation 'Cn' (see Gen. 16.13), which stands for 'conjecture'; it means that they have done their best to make the passage clear by guessing what was likely to be intended by the original writer.

Some footnotes show where the translators have found support for the way they have expressed a verse. For example, the footnote to Genesis 4.8 says: 'Sam Gk Syr Compare Vg: Heb lacks *Let us go out to the field*.' The list of 'Abbreviations' which is printed below the index to the books of the Old Testament, at the beginning of the RSV Common Bible, shows what this footnote means. In full it becomes 'Samaritan Hebrew text, Septuagint Greek Version, Syriac Version, compare Vulgate Latin Versions: Masoretic Text lacks *Let us go out to the field*.' But to understand this footnote requires a careful study of the way in which the Old Testament has been passed down through the ages to us, and of the forms and versions of the Old Testament which are available to scholars today.

EARLY MANUSCRIPTS

THE MASORETIC TEXT

The need to discover an authoritative version of the text of the Old Testament led to studies which began in the centuries that followed the work of the Council of Jamnia. Once the Pharisees had decided which books were to be counted as Scripture, the detailed study to obtain as accurate a copy as possible could begin. The Jewish scholars who undertook this work were called Masoretes, and the editions which they produced became known as the Masoretic Text. Some worked in Babylon and gradually prepared what is now called the Eastern Text. In the RSVCB footnotes 'Heb' stands for the Eastern Masoretic Text.

When the Muslim armies conquered Palestine and broke the power of Christianity there in AD 638, the Jews were able to start similar studies in Tiberias. They tried to preserve the best evidence of what had been written, and were reluctant to destroy any evidence which might be important. So at times they included two versions of the same sentence, when both looked as if they might be right. They invented a system for expressing vowels in writing by placing signs above or below consonants. This was called 'pointing'. They also introduced a kind of punctuation which marked the main stresses of sentence formation. The result of this work was known as the Western Text. In the RSVCB footnotes 'MT' stands for the Western Masoretic Text.

The work of the two schools of Masoretes was gradualy combined, so that most of the Hebrew manuscripts we now possess contain a mixture of material from the work of both groups.

Unfortunately, the Masoretes were not content to prepare the most accurate manuscripts that they could devise. They deliberately destroyed many of the more ancient copies because they felt it was wrong to preserve those which they believed contained many inaccuracies. So for many centuries, and almost to our own day, there were very few copies of the Hebrew Bible available which came from the time before the Masoretes prepared their editions. Scholars were unable to check the work done by the Masoretes, because they had no earlier manuscripts with which to compare the Masoretic Text. It was difficult to be sure how well the Masoretes had done their work. The main evidence which had been preserved from earlier times was contained in the ancient translations prepared for use in countries where Hebrew was unknown.

THE SEPTUAGINT: GREEK VERSION OF THE OLD TESTAMENT

This translation was prepared for the use of the Jewish community at Alexandria in Egypt during the time of the Ptolemies (see Vol. 1, p. 171; rev. ed. p. 184–5). The Law had been translated into Greek by about 250 BC, and the whole Old Testament together with the Apocrypha was in use in Greek by about 100 BC. In the RSVCB footnotes 'Gk' stands for the Septuagint.

One of the reasons why modern scholars have wanted to be able to check up on the work done by the Masoretes is simply that the Septuagint differs in many places from the Hebrew editions prepared by the Masoretes. We have seen that the early Church regularly used the Septuagint in preaching and worship. The early Church also used it as a basis for translation into other languages, for use in parts of the world where Hebrew and Greek were unfamiliar. By AD 500, translations from the Septuagint had appeared in Latin, Coptic, Gothic, Armenian, and Ethiopic.

TRANSLATIONS FROM THE HEBREW

During the same period other translations had been prepared from Hebrew manuscripts which belong to the period before the Masoretes began their work. These included:

The *Targums*. These were Aramaic translations made necessary by the fact that the people of Palestine had ceased to use Hebrew in normal conversation, and needed the Old Testament in the language actually used; (RSVCB abbreviation: Tg).

Syriac translations; (RSVCB abbreviation: Syr).

The *Vulgate*, produced by the great Christian scholar Jerome, who worked on this new Latin translation at the end of the fourth century, having learned Hebrew at a time when few Christians knew it. He was assisted by Jewish scholars. It has been used by the Roman Catholic Church right up to the present day. (RSVCB abbreviation: Vg).

EARLY EDITIONS OF THE HEBREW

However, early translations are not always a helpful guide to the original form of the Hebrew text. Different translators used different methods. Some tried to find exact equivalents for each of the Hebrew words in the language for which they were preparing the translation. Others tried to give the exact meaning of the Hebrew in their language, but without keeping to a word-for-word substitution. Others again translated freely, adding phrases and sentences which they thought would make the meaning clearer.

Because of these different methods of translation it is not always easy for scholars to know what form of the Hebrew text was used to prepare the translation. And so it becomes difficult to be sure of the value of the evidence provided by comparing the ancient versions with the Masoretic Text. The most valuable evidence must come from very early editions of the Hebrew itself.

The Samaritan Pentateuch is an early form of the Law which has been available to scholars for many years. It contains the Hebrew, but written in a different sort of script from that found in most Hebrew editions. The Samaritan Bible is not always a good guide to the original form of the Hebrew text, because the Samaritan scribes made deliberate alterations and adaptations to the Law in order to support their own ways of worshipping and serving the Lord. Sometimes, too, the Hebrew scribes may have used the same methods to rob the Samaritans of support which may have been there in the earliest editions of the books of the Law. In the RSVCB footnotes 'Sam' stands for the Samaritan Pentateuch.

The Dead Sea Scrolls are manuscripts which provide scholars with excellent evidence of early forms of the Hebrew text. They were discovered in 1947, when a young Arab goatherd was searching for a goat which had strayed from his flock in the Wilderness of Judea, west of the Dead Sea. He noticed a cave on the hillside above him, and sent a stone flying up there from his catapult. When it landed he heard the sound of pottery shattering. This scared him, because he was sure no human lived up there. But eventually he found courage to explore, accompanied by a friend. They found large pots containing ancient scrolls. At first they did not realize the value of what they had found. But before very long they sold part of their discovery to dealers in ancient things, and the scrolls came into the possession of scholars who recognized how important they must be (see p. 33).

This started a widespread search for similar material, because the scholars were willing to pay well. They discovered that these Dead Sea Scrolls are part of the library of the ancient Jewish monastery of Qumran. They were hidden in these caves close to the time when the Romans destroyed Jerusalem in AD 70. Some of the scrolls contain writings which had never been known to modern scholars before. Others are commentaries on the books of the Old Testament. The most important of all for textual criticism were ancient Hebrew editions of the Old Testament, belonging to a time long before the Masoretes began their work. The Common Bible does not adopt any abbreviation to indicate where the Dead Sea Scrolls have been used in preparing the translation.

The results from careful study of manuscripts from eleven caves discovered in the Qumran area over a period of nine years (1947–1956) are significant. Four complete scrolls have been found: two of

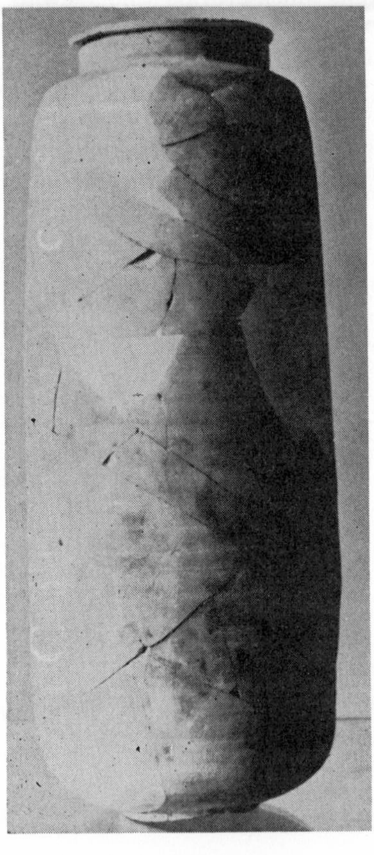

2.1 'He noticed a cave on the hillside . . . a sound of pottery shattering scared him' (p. 31). The largest number of manuscripts found at Qumran came from the cave known as 'No. 4', the larger entrance in the foreground of the picture.

2.2 'They found large pots containing ancient scrolls' (p. 31). The Dead Sea Scrolls have played an important part in Old Testament research in recent times.

Isaiah, one of Psalms with some additional poems, and an Aramaic form of Job. There are shorter passages from every book of the Hebrew Canon except Esther, and some extracts from books of the Apocrypha. The largest number of passages from any one book of the Old Testament are from the Psalms, followed by Deuteronomy and then Genesis and Exodus. There are also a large number of commentaries on Old Testament books. It is clear that members of the community were aware of the Samaritan Pentateuch, the Septuagint and the type of Hebrew text which later was adopted by the Masoretes. No consistent preference is given to any one of these versions. There are instances where they are combined, or, to use the technical term, conflated. The various forms clearly go back to earlier than the time of Qumran, and the community were prepared to accept the existence of a variety of texts.

These discoveries at Qumran have helped to confirm what had been a growing feeling among scholars: that the search for conclusive evidence about the original form of the text of the various Hebrew documents contained in the Old Testament would never prove fruitful. Scholars have had to discard the belief that the Scriptures are best understood by clearing away the effects of later copying and editing and obtaining the pure text of the original revelation, because it is impossible to carry out such a task. They can make some improvement in our understanding of Scripture by carefully comparing existing Hebrew manuscripts and early translations, especially where there is evidence of mistakes in copying. They may be able to discover evidence of editing which has deliberately altered the contents of the books of the Old Testament. But in such cases the original form does not necessarily possess the deepest inspiration.

Canonical Criticism is an approach to the Old Testament which encourages us to take the available evidence of the Old Testament revelation seriously. The scholars who take this approach insist that this is the literature which has been adopted by the Church over many centuries as carrying authority, because it brings us to an awareness of God, and through it we learn His will for us and for others in His world. Because of the varied evidence available from the early manuscripts, we cannot say that a particular form of words carries the final authority of Scripture. But whenever serious and honest study provides us with a deeper understanding of God and His purposes the Bible has done its work. Biblical research will continue, and will be fruitful if through it scholars enable other people to gain a clearer vision of what it is to be servants of God.

Not many people are able to undertake the long hard years of study needed to equip them properly to prepare new translations of the

Bible. Most of us have to rely on the information which such scholars provide in modern commentaries, and in new translations of the Scriptures. But we do also need to know how to use the Old Testament properly, so that all their work may be of real benefit to us. The right way of reading is important, for not all books are to be read in the same way. So the final question we ask in this chapter is: How should we read the Old Testament?

READING THE OLD TESTAMENT

Think about the modern books you have known and used, and the different sorts of books you have seen in libraries and shops. They are not all the same kind of writing, and you would not want to use them all in the same way. A 'story' book presenting a historical or traditional or even a fictional account of events is meant to be read from cover to cover; and the later parts of the story depend on what has been said in the earlier parts. By contrast a dictionary, for example, is meant to provide information when it is needed, telling you the meaning of a particular word, and how it is spelt. A book of this kind is not to be read from cover to cover, although you can discover some interesting things by looking at any page that you choose, without having special interest in one word.

The Bible is a library of different books, and we need to know what sort of book we are handling in it, before we can read the book properly:

(a) There are some very interesting *story* books in the Old Testament, including Genesis, Ruth, and Esther. These need to be read straight through in order to understand them.

(b) Some books such as Exodus, Leviticus, and Deuteronomy contain the *laws* which governed the life of Israel in past ages. We shall understand these best if we try to discover from reading them what laws the Israelites followed, e.g. concerning worship, slavery, the treatment of strangers, and so on.

(c) There are some books which record the *history* of Israel, among them Samuel, Kings, Ezra, and Nehemiah. It is useful to follow the whole account of the experiences of the Israelites, but we can also read separately the parts of the account which are about a particular period of the history of Israel, and so get a detailed knowledge of that time.

(d) Some books contain *poetry*, and the essence of poetry is that it expresses profound ideas briefly and effectively. It is best to read a little at a time, and let it set you thinking about the subject raised by the poet. For example, read one Psalm rather than several at the same time, and one speech from Job rather than several chapters in quick succession.

(e) Many of the books of the Old Testament record the *preachings* of the Prophets. People do not normally listen to several sermons at one time. So try to read a few verses which belong together rather than a whole chapter at a time. You will then take in the meaning and value of those verses, and can read further some other time.

The purpose of this Guide is to introduce you to the books of the Old Testament, so as to show something about their background and history, and what sort of book each one is. This will help you to begin to study each book with a real understanding of what you read. The books are set out in this edition of *The Books of the Old Testament* in the order in which they are found in the English Bible, but do not include the Apocrypha.

STUDY SUGGESTIONS

WORD STUDY

1. 'In the RSV Comon Bible the word '*chesed*' is normally translated 'steadfast love' when it is used to express the quality of the saving activities of God' (see p. 17).
   (a) Compare the translation in the RSVCB with that given in other English versions available to you by examining the following verses:
   Neh. 13.22 Job 10.12 Ps. 33.5 Isa. 54.8 Hos. 2.19.
   Which version do you think gives the most helpful translations, and why?
   (b) The human virtues described in each of the following verses is also expressed in the Hebrew by *chesed*:
   Gen. 20.13 Judges 1.24 2 Chron. 32.32 Prov. 11.17 Hos. 6.4
   Can you suggest why the translators of the RSV Common Bible did not use 'steadfast love' in these verses?
2. The word 'text' is used often in this chapter, and will occur again later in this book. Which of the following definitions expresses our meaning when we use this word in these studies:
   (a) A verse from Scripture used as the basis for a sermon.
   (b) The written words in the language, script, grammar and punctuation of the manuscripts which scholars use in studying the Scriptures.
   (c) The meaning of the things which are written in these manuscripts.

REVIEW OF CONTENT

3. Explain the meaning of each of the following abbreviations used in the footnotes of the RSV Common Bible, and say how each version is related to the original Hebrew text:
   (a) Heb (b) MT (c) Gk (d) Tg (e) Vg
4. (a) What is the significance of the Dead Sea Scrolls for scholars who are preparing a new translation of the Scriptures?
   (b) What difference did their discovery make to the aims and results of textual criticism?

BIBLE STUDY

5. Write out in full the meaning of the RSV Common Bible footnotes to the following verses of the Old Testament.
   (a) Gen. 2.6 (b) Gen. 2.1–3 (c) Gen. 26.20 (d) Gen. 44.4 (e) Isa. 45.9
6. Explain as fully as you can the significance of the footnote to Ezekiel 37.27, which reads as follows:
   '37.27: Ex 25.8; 29.45; Lev 26.12; Jer 31.1; 2 Cor 6.16; Rev 21.3'.
7. Story, History, Law, Poetry, Sermons: these are some of the different sorts of writing to be found in the Bible.
   (i) Which of these sorts is found in each of the following chapters?
   (a) Gen. 3 (b) Exod. 20 (c) Deut. 1 (d) Deut. 27
   (e) Judges 5 (f) Ezra 1 (g) Job 38 (h) Isa. 36
   (i) Jer. 6 (j) John 1
   (ii) Does each book of the Bible contain only one type of writing? Give examples to support your answer.
   (iii) How can you tell from the way the RSV Common Bible is printed whether or not you are reading poetry?

3
The Law

WHICH ORDER TO FOLLOW?

In the first edition of this TEF Guide we studied the books of the Old Testament in the order in which they are presented in modern editions of the Hebrew text. We followed the three main divisions of the Hebrew Canon; the Law, the Prophets and the Writings. The Guide was based on a study of how the Old Testament Scriptures were developed among the Jews, and it made use of the step-by-step adoption of books for the Jewish Canon. This followed the standard practice of Christian scholars in writing books which serve as an introduction to the literature of the Old Testament.

More recently those who adopt the interests of Canonical Criticism ask the very relevant questions: (a) why should we use the Jewish order, and (b) why should we ignore the change of order in Christian Bibles? The Jewish Canon stresses the importance of the Law, and places the Prophets as an interpretation of the Law. It regards the Writings as of least significance. The whole emphasis is on looking back to the time of Moses, who brought salvation to the Jews, and beyond that time, to Abraham. Christians acknowledge the significance of these people in preparing the way for the coming of Christ, but see the New Testament as the climax towards which all else should point.

In order to achieve this emphasis the books of the Old Testament are set out in a quite different order, which can be presented as follows:

1. The Books of the Law:
   Genesis, Exodus, Leviticus, Numbers, Deuteronomy.
2. The Books of the History of the Jews:
   Joshua, Judges, Ruth, 1 and 2 Samuel, 1 and 2 Kings, 1 and 2 Chronicles, Ezra, Nehemiah, Esther.
3. The Books of Poetry and Wisdom:
   Job, Psalms, Proverbs, Ecclesiastes, Song of Solomon.
4. The Books of the Prophets:
   Isaiah, Jeremiah with Lamentations, Ezekiel, Daniel, Hosea, Joel, Amos, Obadiah, Jonah, Micah, Nahum, Habakkuk, Zephaniah, Haggai, Zechariah, Malachi.

It is not clear when this order was first adopted. In the earliest days of the Christian era books existed as separate writings. So long as scrolls were used this was inevitable, because each could only contain a limited amount of literature. The practical difficulties of rolling and unrolling lengths of vellum limited the contents of each scroll. In consequence the question of order for the whole collection of religious writings was not very important. The introduction of codex copies of Scripture helped their readers considerably. The codex copies were produced in the form taken by modern books, with pages sewn together. These could be turned over several at a time, and so made it easier to find particular parts of Scripture. It was at the time when the whole Old Testament was prepared as a single codex that the question of order became crucial. The earliest Christian codex still available for the use of scholars today is probably what is known as *Codex Vaticanus*, or Codex B. It comes from the fourth century AD and includes most books accepted by the Roman Catholic Church, omitting Maccabees. It begins with the books of the Law and the History and ends with the Prophets, placing the major Prophets at the end, finishing with Daniel. The books of poetry and wisdom are presented in a different order from today's Catholic Bibles.

This provides the evidence we need that, from the earliest times in which codices (plural of codex) were used, the Old Testament books were set out in something approaching the same order as is known from modern editions of the Bible, with the books grouped according to what sorts they are. Some of the Christian writers from the fourth century have provided us with lists of books of the Old Testament in approximately the same order.

There are advantages and disadvantages in any order that we may adopt for our studies. The order set out above makes some assumptions that will need to be queried as we work through the individual books. Is 'Law' a good description of the contents of the first five books, and if so why? Why do some of the historical books give a different account of the same period in the life of the Jewish people? Are Ruth and Esther really best described as History, or should we see them as serving another purpose? Do Poetry and Wisdom go hand in hand, or is this group a mixture of different sorts of books? Are the books of Daniel and Jonah each the record of a prophet, and his message? Are the prophetic books set out in a logical order according to the time at which each prophet was at work?

But there is value in the order set out above. The first section sets the scene of creation, the fall of humanity, and the need for God's work of salvation. It records the first steps towards the development of a people who felt called to serve the LORD. The second section sets out the historical background of the Jewish people and their leaders, giving us an account of how their history was interpreted in the light of their developing faith. The third section gathers traditional wisdom showing developments in understanding. It also contains the literature of worship, which cannot easily be dated as belonging to a particular period of Jewish history. The fourth section presents the records of the prophets who taught that God was in control of history, and that He had a purpose for His people which was yet to be fulfilled. The last verse of the Old Testament, Malachi 4.6, points forward to the coming of Elijah to prepare for the Day of the LORD. This is seen by Christians as an introduction to the work of John the Baptist, and the coming of Jesus Christ.

ONE BOOK: FIVE VOLUMES

The first major section of the Hebrew Scriptures is known as 'the Law'. The Hebrew name for it is *Torah*, a word which carries the idea of the Law as the revelation of God's will for His people. The contents of these books is best defined as 'Revelation' rather than 'Law' because the stories of Abraham, Jacob, Joseph and Moses describe how God made Himself known to the earlier generations of the Jews, and how they learnt to serve Him. We shall use the word Torah for this part of the Bible, to avoid confusion with the codes of law contained in it. Another name for this part of the Old Testament is the *Pentateuch*. This name comes from the Greek language and means 'the Five Scrolls'.

The five books of our Bible which belong to the Torah are Genesis, Exodus, Leviticus, Numbers, and Deuteronomy. Their titles have been taken from the Septuagint, the ancient Greek version of the Old Testament. *Genesis* means 'origin, birth, or source', and the title was taken from Genesis 2.4 in the Septuagint. *Exodus* means 'going out, departure' and was taken from Exodus 19.1. *Leviticus* comes from a Greek adjective formed from the name Levi, the priestly tribe of Israel. *Numbers* comes from the Latin translation of the Greek title, which was *Arithmoi*; this refers to the two censuses of Israel which are described in the book (see Num. 1.2–3 and 26.2). *Deuteronomy* comes from the Greek for 'Second Law', and was probably taken from Deuteronomy 17.18, which reads in English 'a copy of this law'.

The titles of the individual books are appropriate, because they tell us something about what is written in each of them. Read a few verses from each of the books in order to get an idea of the sort of writing found in the Torah. The following passages will be helpful: Genesis 1.1–2.4; Exodus 14.5–15; Leviticus 6.8–18; Numbers 3.40–51; Deuteronomy 12.1–11.

The translators of the RSV Common Bible, following earlier translations, gave each of the books a sub-title; 'the First (or Second, or Third) Book of Moses'. A similar title for the Torah is found in some of the later books of the Old Testament (see 2 Chron. 35.12; Ezra 6.18; and Neh. 13.1), and was used by our Lord Himself (Mark 12.26). But note that all these verses refer to 'the book of Moses' in the singular. The five books are to be thought of as one continuous account, which has been divided for convenience into five more or less equal parts. Each section is about the right length to fill a large scroll, but the divisions also mark important breaks in the story. For example, a new scroll is started when the story of Moses and the Exodus is begun.

Together the five books give an account of Israel from the Creation of the world, through God's calling of Abraham and his heirs, to the Exodus from Egypt, the divine revelation at Mount Sinai, and preparations for entering the Promised Land. We can usefully divide up the contents of the five books in the following way:

1. (a) The origin of the world and of nations: Genesis 1—11.
   (b) The Patriarchs: Genesis 12—50:
   Abraham and Isaac: Genesis 12—26,
   Esau and Jacob: Genesis 27—36,
   Joseph: Genesis 37—50.
2. (a) Moses and the Exodus from Egypt: Exodus 1—18.
   (b) The Divine Revelation at Sinai: Exodus 19—40.
3. The Levitical Legislation concerning sacrifices and priests: Leviticus 1—27.
4. (a) The Last Events, and Law-giving at Sinai: Numbers 1.1—10.10.
   (b) The Journey to the Plains of Moab: Numbers 10.11—22.1.
   (c) Events in the Plains of Moab: Numbers 22.2—36.13.
5. The Last Speeches and Death of Moses: Deuteronomy 1—34.

SOURCES

If you stand on the banks of a fast-flowing river you may wonder how it reached such strength and size. To find out, you would need to follow the river back to its source in the hills far away. If you read a book of the Bible, you may wonder how it reached its present form. To find this out, you would need to trace its history back to the beginning, and learn what happened to it over the years. In this volume we shall study the sources of the books of the Bible.

The traditional view of the source of the Torah is that it was composed by Moses, and we have seen that from very early times it was called 'the book of Moses'. But there is very strong evidence in the Torah itself that Moses could not have been responsible for writing it in its present form. In fact we do not know what part Moses

3.1 'In fact we do not know what part Moses played in preserving the memory of the events of the Exodus, and the wanderings of the Israelites' . . . 'The Torah . . . is the book which tells us *about* him' (pp. 40, 42, 43). Carving on a Christian sarcophagus (coffin) of the 4th century AD shows Moses striking water from the rock.

played in preserving the memory of the events of the Exodus, and the wanderings of the Israelites in the wilderness. Those who insist that Moses himself was the author of these five volumes need to find answers to the following questions:

Why did Moses write about himself as though he was someone else, saying '*He* did this . . . *He* said that . . .', instead of saying 'I'? Notice especially Deuteronomy 31.9.

Why did Moses need to make use of earlier written records in order to gain the necessary information to tell the story of events in which he had had a personal part? In Numbers 21.14 the writer used the 'Book of the Wars of the Lord' to provide details of the places where the Israelites camped. In those days people relied more fully on their memories than we do today.

Why didn't Moses know whether he took his wife and children with him into Egypt or not, when he went to confront Pharaoh? According to Exodus 4.20 he took them with him. According to Exodus 18.2–3 he left his wife at her father's house with their children.

Why did Moses think about the events which he recorded as belonging to a time long ago? He wrote about the bedstead of Og as a historic relic (Deut. 3.11). He suggested that there were no longer any Canaanites in Palestine (Gen. 12.6), even though they are often mentioned in the books of Joshua and Judges, which tell what happened after the time of Moses.

Moses never entered the Promised Land, so *why then did he describe things that happened in Moab as happening beyond the Jordan* (Deut. 1.1; compare Deut. 32.52). Why didn't he write of Moab as *this side* of the Jordan?

Why did Moses write about himself with such high praise as is found in Deuteronomy 34.10–12? Can we avoid charging Moses with conceit if he wrote this verse?

How did Moses know the names that were given to places after his own time? Dan (Gen. 14.14—see Josh. 19.47), Hebron (Gen. 13.18—see Josh. 14.15), and Bethlehem (Gen. 35.19) are all later names.

How did Moses manage to write an account of his own death? (See Deut. 34.5–12.)

The most likely answer to all these questions is that Moses did or did not do these things, because in fact he did not write the Torah as we know it today. Most scholars agree that a large number of people had a part in drawing together the stories, laws, poems, and other material that make up the Torah. Some of them wrote at a much later time than the period of Moses and the Exodus. At their own time they quite naturally used the words and phrases which we find difficult to understand *if* we think they came from Moses himself, or from his time.

Some students find difficulty in the fact that Jesus speaks of 'the book of Moses' (Mark 12.26). Was Jesus mistaken like other men of His time? Or ought we to follow His lead by saying that the Torah was written by Moses, despite the difficulties? These are not really the only alternatives. The Torah can be called 'the book of Moses' if we mean by this that it is the book which tells *about* him, rather than the book written *by* him. Also it would be quite natural for Jesus to use the title that everybody used when He wanted to draw people's attention to something in the Torah. He was not passing judgement on the Jewish understanding of the origin of the Torah, nor instructing His disciples what they should believe about it.

STUDY SUGGESTIONS

WORD STUDY

1. What is the difference between a Scroll and a Codex? Which of the two made it necessary to decide the order of the books in the Christian Canon?
2. 'The Book of Moses':
   (a) In what sense is it misleading to refer to the Pentateuch as the Book of Moses, and
   (b) In what sense is it appropriate to give it this title?
3. The word *Torah* means something different from 'code of law'.
   (a) From your knowledge of its books describe the difference between what is written in the Torah and what you would expect to find in a code of law.
   (b) Which two of the following words come nearest to the meaning of *Torah*?
   custom decree instruction revelation rule statute

REVIEW OF CONTENT

4. What is the theological significance of the difference in the order of the books of the Old Testament in the Jewish Canon and in the Christian Canon.
5. Which books of the Bible belong to the Torah?
6. In which of the five volumes of the Torah would you expect to find the following stories:
   (a) The consecration of Aaron and his sons as priests.
   (b) The choice of Joshua as Moses's successor.
   (c) Noah and his Ark.
   (d) The spies in the Promised Land.
   (e) Rebecca chosen as wife.
   (f) The crossing of the Red Sea.

7. Write a sentence about each of the eight questions listed under the heading 'Sources' on p. 42, showing that if somebody else wrote the Torah at a later time than Moses, these difficulties disappear.

FURTHER STUDY AND DISCUSSION

8. What difference does it make to our attitude (a) to the Torah, and (b) to Moses, if we accept that Moses was not the author of the whole of the Pentateuch?

VARIETIES OF WRITING

In chapter 2 (p. 34f) we noted the value which there is for us in understanding what sorts of writings are found in each of the books of the Bible. The first five books of the Bible contain a great mixture of laws, stories and poetry. We shall understand more fully the way in which the Torah was compiled if we distinguish the different sorts of writing, and learn how each was gathered and eventually became part of the five books.

1. LAW CODES

A careful study of the laws in the Torah shows that the same subjects are dealt with more than once, and that there are differences, and even contradictions, in the rulings given in different passages. Compare the answers given in different parts of the Torah to the following questions:

(a) *How many places would God choose for His worship*?
Exodus 20.24 says '*every* place', meaning more than one; but Deuteronomy 12.14 says '*the* place', meaning one only.

(b) *What people might offer sacrifices for Israel*?
Exodus 28.1 says 'Aaron and his sons'; but Deuteronomy 18.6–7 says '*all* Levites'—i.e. not only those of Aaron's family.

(c) *Where might domestic animals be slaughtered*?
Leviticus 17.3–4 says at 'the door of the tent of meeting'; but Deuteronomy 12.15 says 'within any of your towns'.

(d) *What sort of images were forbidden to the Israelites*?
Exodus 20.4–6 (and Deut. 5.8) says 'graven', i.e. 'carved'; but Leviticus 19.4 says 'molten', i.e. 'melted and cast'.

Such changes and variations suggest developments in the law system over a long period of time, made necessary by changing situations in the life of Israel, and by deepening understanding of both justice and compassion. Scholars of the Old Testament have given a great amount of time to examining the laws of the Torah to discover the different codes, i.e. collections of laws, which have been included in these books. These scholars do not entirely agree about the results of their studies. But as a general guide we can distinguish the following groups of laws, and think of them as separate codes drawn up at different times.

(a) THE TEN COMMANDMENTS (Exod. 20.1–17 and Deut. 5.6–21)

It is important to notice where the Ten Commandments are placed in the Torah. They are given first place in two great collections of laws: Exodus and Deuteronomy. The men who edited the Torah clearly believed that they were of supreme importance.

Scholars hold widely different views about the origin of the Ten Commandments. Some say that they are rules suitable for a settled agricultural life, and not suitable for the people of Israel whilst they lived in the wilderness. So they reject the traditional view that these Commandments were received on Mount Sinai. They suggest instead that these Commandments come from a much later time than Moses. But other scholars believe that in their original form these laws do come from the time of Moses. Some basis for the community life of Israel was needed at that time.

Some scholars believe that the Ten Commandments are based on ancient Hittite treaties between kings and their people. But there is no evidence to suggest that Hittite influence reached as far south as the deserts of Sinai. In fact the similarities with such treaties are only those that would be found in all agreements between a great ruler and his subject people.

A careful exposition of the Ten Commandments is given in Vol. 1 of this course (p. 57ff; rev. ed. p. 64ff). It would be helpful to read it through again here; also the more detailed study of the laws of human relationships in Vol. 3, pp. 112ff.

(b) THE BOOK OF THE COVENANT (Exod. 20.22–23.33)

This is another collection of laws which also is studied in Vol. 1 (p. 75f; rev. ed. p. 84f). It shows clear evidence of belonging to the time when the Israelites had settled in Palestine, and were growing crops as well as tending herds. Some of these laws, contained in Exodus 22.29–30 and 23.12, 15–19, are repeated in Exodus 34.10–26 (which some scholars call the Cultic Decalogue, see Vol. 1, p. 62; rev. ed. p. 69f). Compare the following pairs of verses from each of these groups of laws: Exod. 23.12a with Exod. 34.12a; Exod. 23.16 with Exod. 34.22; Exod. 23.17 with Exod. 34.23; Exod. 23.18 with Exod. 34.25; and Exod. 23.19 with Exod. 34.26.

The belief that God wanted all the people of Israel to gather together for worship three times a year is more fully developed in Deut. 16.3–16. Here the Passover (otherwise known as the Feast of Unleavened Bread), the Feast of Weeks (otherwise known as the

Feast of Harvest), and Feast of Booths (or Tabernacles) (otherwise known as the Feast of Ingathering) are all clearly named. The Feast of Weeks was known as Pentecost in New Testament times. Scholars differ about the history of the three copies of these laws; but it is not surprising that laws known early in the history of Israel would be included again at later times when fresh law codes were being prepared.

(c) THE LAW CODE OF DEUTERONOMY (Deut. 12—26)

The book of Deuteronomy is written as though it were a final series of sermons preached by Moses before his death, to encourage the Israelites when they set out to conquer Palestine, and to remind them of the will of God expressed in the law. A careful study of this Law Code of Deuteronomy makes it clear, however, that some of the laws which it contains come from a time much later than the time of Moses.

It was not until the time of Josiah that any attempt was made to limit worship to one central place, and to destroy all other altars. For example, Bethel was a place where God had revealed His purposes (Judges 20.18; 2 Kings 2.2–3). Jeroboam chose it as a suitable centre for worship in the Northern Kingdom (1 Kings 12.29). It became unacceptable later, because pagan forms of worship were used there (Amos 3.14). But it was Josiah who brought an end to worship at Bethel, long after the fall of the Northern Kingdom (2 Kings 23.4, 5). Yet the Code of Deuteronomy makes centralized worship a clear rule for the Israelites, e.g. Deuteronomy 12.13–14, 17–19. Most scholars agree that this code was drawn up close to the time of Josiah, probably in the difficult days of the reign of Manasseh (see Vol. 1, p. 122f; rev. ed. p. 133).

Many of the older laws were set out again as a reminder of what was already known as the will of God, e.g. the Cultic Decalogue in Deut. 16.3–16. But new interpretations of the will of God were included, which were designed to meet the needs of the new time. The centralization of worship was quite possible at the time of Josiah, when the Northern Kingdom had been destroyed. The purpose of this centralization was to prevent the further spread of pagan customs and ideas such as the new inhabitants of northern Palestine were following (2 Kings 17.41). Worship at Jerusalem could be carefully controlled, but in other places it might easily be affected by pagan ideas. So the rule was made that all Israel must worship in Jerusalem.

The centralization of worship involved a radical change in the life of the people of Judah. The Law Code of Deuteronomy provides fresh guidance to meet the changes. Because local centres of worship were no longer to be used there were many Levites out of work. So they became one of the groups of needy to be helped by the community, alongside the widows, orphans and sojourners (refugees) (Deut. 14.28–29; 26.12–13). Sacrifices were no longer to take place at the local shrines and it was not possible to take every animal that was to be slaughtered to Jerusalem, so secular ways of killing them were introduced (Deut. 12.20–25). The great feasts were to be celebrated at Jerusalem, which became a place of pilgrimage three times each year (Deut. 16.16–17). The Passover, which had been celebrated in each home, became a public occasion at the Temple (Deut. 16.2). Personal piety expressed in family life became the study of the Law (Deut. 6.6–9) and the instruction of children about how to serve God (Deut. 6.7, 20–25).

The Law Code of Deuteronomy also shows a new spirit of compassion, which is not so clearly present in the earlier codes. It contains rules about treatment of the poor and slaves (Deut. 15.7–18); strangers, orphans and widows (Deut. 24.17–22); and animals (Deut. 22.1–4, 6–8). And there are laws controlling the appointment and work of Judges (Deut. 16.18–20); and of Kings (Deut. 17.14–20) who were to ensure justice for all, and especially for the needy.

(d) THE HOLINESS CODE (Lev. 17—26)

The whole of this part of the book of Leviticus is given up to a special code of law, which is distinct from the other laws found in Leviticus. It is concerned with holiness, as its modern name suggests, i.e. with ritual purity, especially for the priests, and with the worship in the Temple (see Lev. 19.1–6).

Like Deuteronomy, this Code is written as though it were a sermon of Moses. But again the laws show clear evidence of coming from a much later time in the history of Israel. The prophet Ezekiel shares many of the ideas which make the Holiness Code different from other codes. Compare especially Lev. 17.13 with Ezekiel 24.7; and Lev. 18.10 with Ezekiel 22.11. It is not clear whether Ezekiel influenced the editor who compiled the Holiness Code, or whether Ezekiel was himself influenced by the Code in his own preaching and teaching.

(e) THE PRIESTLY CODE

This law code is scattered in many parts of the Torah. In Exodus chapters 25—31 and 35—40 come from this collection of laws. Leviticus 1—16 also belongs here, and so do the law passages in the book of Numbers. As the modern name suggests, this code is concerned largely with rules for the priests, for sacrifices, and for the ceremonial purity of God's people. Many of these laws belonged to the early times of the history of Israel, but they were gradually adapted and worked out in more detail. The Priestly Code itself probably comes from the time of the Exile in Babylon. It was prepared in time for inclusion in the book of the law which Ezra brought to Jerusalem, probably in 397 BC (Vol. 1, p. 159f; rev. ed. p. 172).

2. TRADITIONS

In addition to the law codes, the Torah consists largely of traditions about the Patriarchs, and about Moses and the Israelites. The remainder consists of poetry. We shall look at both in turn.

Careful study of the traditions has shown that the Torah is composed of several different accounts, which have been combined to provide the present records. The chief evidence for this is that important parts of the history of Israel are told twice in quite different ways. Some of the stories are set down one after the other without any explanation of the differences between them. Others are mixed together phrase by phrase, sentence by sentence. Another method which the ancient editors used was to give one story in full, and then to add to it extra details from another account.

Let us examine two examples where the same event is recorded twice.

1. Take first the Creation: read Genesis 1.1—2.4, and then Genesis 2.4–25. These are two separate and different accounts of the Creation of the world. One starts from oceans (Gen. 1.2), and the other from deserts (Gen. 2.5). One tells how man was made first, and after him plants, animals, and woman. The other explains that God prepared a world with plants and animals before creating men and women together to dwell in it. Clearly the stories are very different, but the editor who worked on the scroll of Genesis included them both. He rightly recognized them both as important myths (see Vol. 1, p. 6) known to the Israelites from ancient times. He felt that both stories taught the same important truths: that this is God's world, that He created it and made humanity the crown of His creation, that human beings are responsible to God for what they do and can have fellowship with their Lord, that marriage and family life are part of God's plan (see Vol. 3, pp. 27, 114).

In recent scholarship attention has been drawn to the fact that the editors of Genesis 1 and 2 have set the stories in a sequence which has theological significance. Chapter 1 deals with the whole of Creation, while Chapter 2 centres its interest in human experience, and prepares the way for the story of the Fall.

2. Secondly, read and compare the following two paragraphs (a) and (b):

(a) When the king of Egypt was told that the people had fled, the mind of Pharaoh and his servants was changed toward the people, and they said, 'What is this we have done, that we have let Israel go from serving us?' So he made ready his chariot and took his army with him, and took six hundred picked chariots and all the other chariots of Egypt with officers over all of them. When Pharaoh drew near, the people of Israel lifted up their eyes, and behold, the Egyptians were marching after them; and they were in great fear, and they said to Moses, 'Is it because there are no graves in Egypt that you have taken us away to die in the wilderness? What have you done to us, in bringing us out of Egypt? Is not this what we said to you in Egypt. "Let us alone and let us serve the Egyptians?" For it would have been better for us to serve the Egyptians than to die in the wilderness.' And Moses said to the people, 'Fear not, stand firm, and see the salvation of the LORD, which he will work for you today; for the Egyptians whom you see today, you shall never see again. The LORD will fight for you, and you have only to be still.' And the pillar of the cloud moved from before them and stood behind them. And there was the cloud and the darkness; and the night passed without one coming near the other all night. And the LORD drove the sea back by a strong east wind all night, and made the sea dry land. And in the morning watch the LORD in the pillar of fire and of cloud looked down upon the host of Egyptians, and discomforted the host of the Egyptians, clogging their chariot wheels so that they drove heavily; and the Egyptians said, 'Let us flee from before Israel; for the LORD fights for them against the Egyptians.' And the sea returned to its wonted flow when the morning appeared; and the Egyptians fled into it, and the LORD routed the Egyptians in the midst of the sea. And Israel saw the great work which the LORD did against the Egyptians, and the people feared the LORD; and they believed in the LORD and in his servant Moses.

(b) Then the LORD said to Moses, 'Tell the people of Israel to turn back and encamp in front of Pihahiroth, between Migdol and the sea, in front of Baalzephon; you shall encamp over against it, by the sea. For Pharaoh will say of the people of Israel, "They are entangled in the land; the wilderness has shut them in." And I will harden Pharaoh's heart and he will pursue them and I will get glory over Pharaoh and all his host; and the Egyptians shall know that I am the LORD.' And they did so. And the LORD hardened the heart of Pharaoh king of Egypt and he pursued the people of Israel as they went forth defiantly. The Egyptians pursued them, all Pharaoh's horses and chariots, and his horsemen and his army, and overtook them encamped at the sea, by Pihahiroth, in front of Baalzephon. The LORD said to Moses, 'Why do you cry to me? Tell the people of Israel to go forward. Lift up your rod, and stretch out your hand over the sea and divide it, that the people of Israel may go on dry ground through the sea. And I will harden the hearts of the Egyptians so that they shall go in after them, and I will get glory over Pharaoh and all his host, his chariots, and his horsemen. And the Egyptians shall know that I am the LORD, when I have gotten glory over Pharaoh, his chariots, and his horsemen.' Then Moses stretched out his hand over the sea, and the waters were divided. And the people of Israel went into the midst of the sea on dry ground, the waters being a wall to them on their right hand and on their left. The Egyptians pursued, and went in after them into the midst of the sea, all Pharaoh's horses, his chariots, and his horsemen. Then the LORD said to Moses, 'Stretch out your hand over the sea, that the water may come back upon the Egyptians, upon their chariots, and upon their horsemen.' So Moses stretched forth his hand over the sea. The waters returned and covered the chariots and the horsemen and all the host of Pharaoh that had followed them into the sea; not so much as one of them remained. But the people of Israel walked on dry ground through the sea, the waters being a wall to them on their right hand and on their left. Thus the LORD saved Israel that day from the hand of the Egyptians; and Israel saw the Egyptians dead upon the seashore.

Each paragraph gives an account of the Israelites' escape from Pharaoh's army. Yet in Exodus 14 they have been combined to make one continuous story. When they are separated as above we notice some important differences which were not clear from the single account in Exodus.

In one account God has to act because His servants are in trouble (Exod. 14.10b); but in the other God lays a plot to punish the Egyptians, directing the Israelites to go where they were likely to be attacked (Exod. 14.1–4).

In one account God saves Israel by His own direct act, by sending the wind (Exod. 14.21); but in the other God uses Moses as His instrument for salvation; it is when Moses stretches out his hand that things happen (Exod. 14.21, 26).

In one account the water was blown back by a strong east wind all night (Exod. 14.21); but in the other the sea was divided instantly so that the waters were a wall to the Israelites 'on their right hand and on their left' (Exod. 14.22).

The disaster that fell on the Egyptians was different too. In one account the Egyptians' chariot wheels were clogged in the mud of the sea-bed (Exod. 14.25), and being unable to fight in their chariots they fled; but in the other account the walls of water collapsed on the Egyptians, drowning them (Exod. 14.28).

If you look closely at the two stories you will notice other differences in detail between them.

We should not be surprised or puzzled by the fact of these different accounts of the same events. In the earliest parts of the Torah we are dealing with myths and legends (see Vol. 1, pp. 6, 7). For various reasons, these are never exact records of what happened. Myths are not based on living memories, but are stories told for the sake of some important lesson contained in them; as in the Creation stories. Legends were preserved for a long time by memory and spoken word alone, and they were adapted and enriched by the imagination of the storytellers.

Even history is often recorded in different ways by different people. Compare the different accounts of a current event in two newspapers of different background, and you will see this happening today. One account will refer to 'the terrorists', while another calls the same people 'nationalists', and immediately the stories look different. It is almost impossible to find an unbiased report, because journalists always need to remember that their readers will be affected in some way by the events, and will want to know what the news means to them. So journalists record what happens by expressing their own interpretation of the events for the sake of their readers. (See Vol. 1, rev. ed. pp. 19–23 for a fuller study of this subject.) Something similar happened in Israel, and through the years the story of the crossing of the Red Sea was interpreted differently and remembered differently by different people. Eventually an editor brought the different traditions together, and rather than choose one and leave out the other, he tried to combine the two accounts.

Scholars have spent much time studying the stories of the Torah, and have come to a fairly general agreement that there are five distinct groups of traditions which have been combined in the first five books of our Bible. They have given each set of traditions an initial letter as a title, to distinguish it from the others.

GROUPS 1 and 2: J^1 and J^2

These two groups are closely linked, and scholars did not at first distinguish them from each other. They were given the title 'J' because in both groups the name Jehovah (*Yahweh*) is used for God, right from the earliest times. Scholars now separate the oldest traditions, and those with the least developed ideas, and give them the title 'J^1'. In these traditions God is described as though He were a man (Gen. 3.8; Exod. 4.24–26). This kind of description of God is called an 'anthropomorphism', from two Greek words which together mean 'in the form of man'. In J^1 immoral attitudes and actions are recorded without comment. It may be that the storyteller was relying on his hearers to recognize the corrupting influences of a developing civilization. (e.g. Gen. 4.24; 9.20–25.) J^1 does not include any laws except the Cultic Decalogue in Exodus 34.10–26.

J^2 is that part of the J traditions which gives a more or less continuous account of the history of Israel from the time of Abraham to the settlement in Palestine. We have already seen in Volume 1 how P. H. Pfeiffer regards J^2 as an account of the way in which God's promises to Abraham have been fulfilled (Gen. 12.2–3, 7) (Vol. 1. pp. 29, 31). Extracts from J^2 are found in Judges, and perhaps also in Samuel, carrying the story through to the death of David. It is generally agreed that this record was first produced in a written form in Judah not later than the time of king Jehoshaphat, and perhaps as early as the reign of Solomon; between 950 and 850 BC. It is not possible to be more exact about the date.

GROUP 3: E

In this group of traditions the name *Elohim* (meaning God) is used for God until the time of Moses, when the new name *Yahweh* (LORD) was revealed (Exod. 3.15; 6.3). So they were given the title 'E'. In them God is described as being more remote than He is in the 'J' traditions. He appears to people in dreams (Gen. 20.3; 28.12), and through angels (Gen. 22.11–12). He is described as appearing directly to Moses only (Exod. 20.19; 32.7–11). There is a clearer awareness of right and wrong shown in these traditions, although actions that we should feel unhappy to copy, in the light of the teachings of Christ, are described by the story-teller as being a response to God's command (e.g. Gen. 22.2). Many scholars believe that these traditions were drawn together into a written document in the northern kingdom of Israel in the reign of Jeroboam II (786–746 BC), at the time when that kingdom was strong and independent, and before Assyria threatened and destroyed it. This written document probably also included the Book of the Covenant.

GROUP 4: D

The book of Deuteronomy begins with eleven chapters written as speeches of Moses. The editors tell us that Moses recalled the experiences of the Israelites from the time when they left Egypt to the time when they were ready to cross into the Promised Land. This material is not set out in a historical order. It begins with the journey from Horeb (Sinai) to the area east of Jordan (Deut. 1—3). Then there are instructions about hearing and obeying the law. Chapters 7 to 10 recall all that God had done for the Israelites, which should make them want to serve Him. All this comes from the 'D' traditions, but the editors who prepared the book of Deuteronomy close to the time of Josiah seem to have taken the details of the wanderings in the wilderness from the 'E' traditions. Deuteronomy 1—11 was written as an introduction to the Law Code of Deuteronomy (see pp. 46, 47).

GROUP 5: P

There are a number of stories which seem closely related to the Priestly Code of Law, to which scholars therefore give the title 'P'. These show a special interest in the way in which Israelite customs began, e.g. the Sabbath (Gen. 2.2); the banning of blood as food (Gen. 9.4); circumcision (Gen. 17.11–14); the Passover (Exod. 12.1–20); the Priesthood of Aaron and his descendants (Exod. 28.1). The writers of these stories seems to have recognized the holiness of God, and the qualities which distinguish Him from human beings. Abraham submits to God, even when his own natural inclination is to think that what God promises is impossible. He discovers the wisdom and authority of God in a difficult situation (Gen. 17. 17–21; 21.1b, 2b–5).

These writers show a great deal of interest in numbers and genealogies. No sacrifices are recorded in these P sections of the Torah as having occurred before the time of Moses, when sacrificial law and priesthood were introduced. Two Covenants are recorded as belonging to the time before Moses came: (1) the Covenant of Noah, which was for all peoples, and (2) the Covenant with Abraham, which was especially for Israel (see Vol. 3, pp. 92, 93).

3. POETRY

It is not always easy for those of us who read only translations of the Bible, whether in English or other languages, to recognize Hebrew poetry. It has a different form and style from anything that we call English Poetry. Yet some of the earliest written material from Israel was poetic in form, and probably was recorded originally on pieces of pottery. Details of the patterns of Hebrew poetry are given in Chapter 6 on pp. 98–100.

For the purposes of this chapter we need only note that in some versions of the English Bible, including the Common Bible, those parts which are poetic in Hebrew are set out differently from the prose. The prose is divided into paragraphs which run straight on, filling the whole width of the page or column. But the poetry is divided into separate lines, with some of them indented in such a way as to show the verse form. If you turn over the pages of the Torah you will find that most pages are filled with prose. But on some pages poetry has been included. Some poetic passages are very brief: only a single verse perhaps; others take up most of a chapter.

It is not known exactly how or when these passages of poetry came to be included. Some are very old indeed, and may have been written

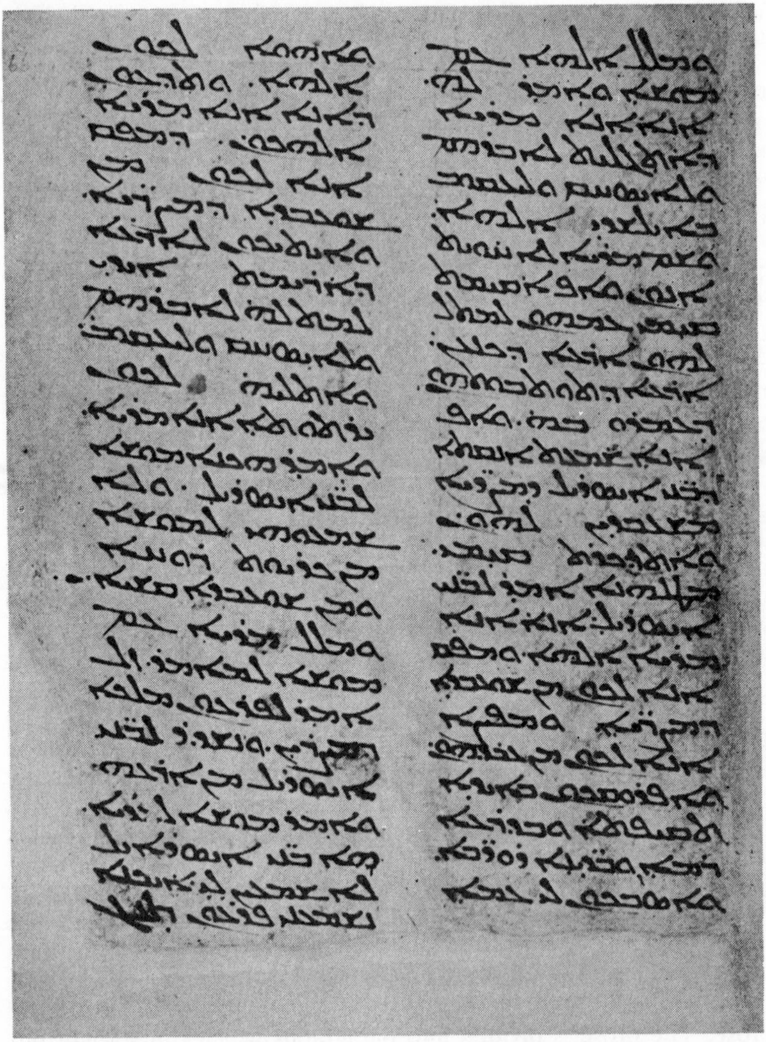

3.2 'The various parts of the Torah'—the five books known as the Pentateuch—'were possibly drawn together between 600 and 400 BC' (p. 55). The oldest *dated* biblical manuscript is a Syriac version of the Pentateuch written in AD 464. This extract from it is Exodus 6.2–12.

down earlier than any of the stories, or most of the laws. Others come from much later times, and may have been added to one or other of the groups of written traditions on which the Torah is based. Scholars with a deep knowledge of the Hebrew language can tell whether the words and grammar used are very ancient or belong to a more recent time. But even they are sometimes confused by the fact that a later writer may deliberately use the language of an earlier time. We have to depend on the writers of commentaries to guide us in understanding the origin of the poetry of the Torah. They tell us that some of the oldest passages of poetry are found in Genesis 4.23–24, Exodus 15.21 and Numbers 21.17–18. These may be the very first of the verses of the Bible that were written down. A long process of writing and editing has followed.

4. THE COMPLETE TORAH

We have seen that the Torah is composed of a number of codes of law, several groups of traditions, and some isolated passages of poetry. These were very gradually collected and set in order over a long period of years until at last the Torah was complete. Scholars disagree about the date when the first written records were produced. Some believe that the codes of law and groups of stories were set down in writing fairly early in their history. Others believe that they were handed down by word of mouth for a very long time before they were put into a written form. It does not greatly affect our own understanding of the Torah, provided we recognize the two chief purposes of those who preserved the material, i.e.

1. To keep the ancient traditions just as they had been handed down, and
2. To complete it by adding other related material from other sources.

The many editors who took part in these processes sometimes added explanatory remarks about the information, and details taken from different sources. Some of these additions increase the confusion of conflicting evidence. But if we are aware of the work which the editors did we shall understand the Torah better.

There are commentaries which show in detail the sources of the various chapters, verses, sentences, and phrases of the Torah. But the following broad account shows clearly enough the steps by which the material in the Torah was put together. The various parts of the Torah which we have already examined were possibly drawn together between 650 and 400 BC.

1. The J-stories were probably linked to the E-stories after the destruction of the Northern Kingdom.

2. Editors influenced by the ideas of Deuteronomy worked over the combined JE material, fitting into it the law code and stories of D. This perhaps took place in the time of the Exile.

3. Towards the end of the Exile, and in the years that followed, the priestly writers of Babylon added the P-stories and the Priestly code.

It may have been the complete Torah which Ezra brought to Jerusalem and read to the people there in 397 BC. And the Torah must have reached its present form not much later than that, for the Samaritans accepted it as their Bible despite the bitter quarrel that developed between them and the Jews at about that time.

Recent scholarship has drawn attention to the significance of the fact that the Torah is traditionally the Book of Moses. Clearly it was not actually written by him, since much of its contents comes from later centuries. Probably the whole Torah was attributed to Moses because by providing the Ten Commandments he had stimulated the belief that the religion of Israel was based on written revelation. After his time the various law codes, traditions and poetry were gradually gathered together as a record of what followed from the initiative of Moses. The Ten Commandments became the basic principles around which other material was collected, and they helped to control the selection of material that was eventually included in the Torah.

THE CANONICAL BOOKS

We have now studied the way in which the Book of Moses was put together from a wide variety of sources, involving both spoken and written traditions, with many different types of material, including law codes, traditions of the beginnings of Israel, and poetry. In this section we are going to look at the Pentateuch, the five books which make up the Torah, and to discover the importance of each of them for our own reading and study. You will find it helpful to begin by re-reading the section headed 'One Book: Five Volumes' on pp. 39 and 40 above.

1. GENESIS

Genesis 1—11: These chapters consist largely of a series of myths which set out for us the eternal nature of God (Gen. 1.1, 2.4), His work in the Creation of the universe (Gen. 1.31), and the central place given to human beings as capable of fellowship with God (Gen. 1.26; 2.7, 18). This is followed by accounts which tell of people's rebellion against God (Gen. 3.1–13), and conflict with each other (Gen. 4.1–16). The account of the Flood is important because it suggests one way in which God could deal with the evil that has entered His world, but reaches its climax in God's rejection of such a plan (Gen. 8.21–22). The narrator seems to be giving an answer to the question, 'Why does not God destroy evil once for all from the face of the earth?' Even Noah, described as a righteous man (Gen. 6.9), is seen to be imperfect in his behaviour (Gen. 9.21–22).

Genesis 12—50: The legends about Abraham, Isaac, Jacob and Esau, and about the twelve sons of Jacob with Joseph the chief among them, all help to present the story of the formation of God's Chosen People the Jews. God's purpose in calling Abraham is that, 'in you all the families of the earth shall be blessed' (Gen. 12.3, see RSVCB footnote). God's intention is to create a community of people committed to His service, who will learn to serve Him in all the changing circumstances of life, and be able to share their knowledge of God with others. The traditions do not attempt to present the patriarchs as perfect men and women, and often recall things they did which were wrong. They frequently failed to distinguish right from wrong, but are shown gradually learning the lessons of loyalty to each other and to God. Joseph stands out as the one who understood the importance of forgiveness, leading to reconciliation and mutual care and support (Gen. 45.3–8; 50.16–21). The circumstances of his life prepare the way for the story of the Exodus, after famine had made it necessary for the Israelites to settle in Egypt.

2. EXODUS

This book sets out to describe the way in which the Israelite slaves in Egypt were set free, given a new awareness of the saving presence of God, and drawn into a new Covenant relationship with Him. At no point is the initiative taken by the Israelites themselves, even Moses is shown as a reluctant servant of the LORD (Exod. 3.6, 11; 4.1, 10; etc.).

Exodus 1—18: The story is told of God's plan to rescue His Chosen People, choosing Moses to be His spokesman, who would overcome the opposition both of the Egyptians, and of the Israelites themselves. God uses Moses to rescue the people at the crossing of the Red Sea, and to provide for them in the desert, eventually leading them to Sinai.

Exodus 19—24: Moses brings the Israelites to the place where he has experienced the presence and glory of the LORD. Two traditions survive side by side:

(a) Moses encourages the people to prepare for a new relationship with God, but they refuse to share his own experience of God. They are prepared to acknowledge God as their Saviour from slavery, and to recognize His right to authority over them, but they expect Moses to interpret God's will to them.

(b) Moses himself assumes authority to speak to the people in God's name and warns them not to attempt to share his special relationship with God.

In both traditions Moses becomes the intermediary between God and the Israelites, and presents the Ten Commandments as a declaration of God's purposes for them. The laws which then follow are to be regarded as an interpretation of the Ten Commandments in the terms of their everyday life and experience, and clearly relate to a time when the Israelites had settled in Palestine.

Exodus 32—34: The traditions on which these chapters are based include the idea that the Ten Commandments were presented to Israel in a written form on two tablets of stone, and are distinct from the traditions of an oral presentation in Exodus Chapter 20. These chapters prepare the way for the many stories that refer to the Ark of the Covenant, which remained a significant witness to God's revelation of His will at Sinai, probably right through to the time when Jerusalem was destroyed by the Babylonians. The account of the destruction of the first stones, following the making of the Golden Calf, underlines the belief that the Israelites were slow to adapt to the rule of the LORD, and frequently fell back into old ideas, customs and behaviour which were inappropriate in the light of God's revelation of Himself and His purpose at Sinai. The prayer of Moses for God's mercy (Gen. 32.11–13), and his willingness to share the people's experience of condemnation (Gen. 32.31–32), show the compassion and concern of a leader committed to the service of God, who has a deep love for His unreliable people. The tension between justice and mercy is a recurring theme in the Old Testament.

Exodus 25—31, 35—40: Here are described both the instructions to build a tabernacle, and the story of how it was done. The purpose was to provide a meeting place between God and humankind, which would serve a similar role to Mount Sinai itself, after the Israelites had left the place where their Covenant with God was first made. Just as Mount Sinai was seen as a place for Moses to meet with God, and to interpret His will to the people, so the tabernacle was set aside for Moses's approach to God. Some scholars believe that the details of the tabernacle are far too elaborate for a movable tent such as could be taken from place to place during the wanderings in the wilderness, and suggest that many of the details come from a much later time when there was a permanent site for the nation to worship God, and the Priests to learn His will. There is no reason to deny that there was some kind of tabernacle in use from the earliest times. Aaron's place as the first High Priest is a very ancient tradition, but the details of his appointment, clothing, duties, etc. belong to the priesthood of a much later time.

3. LEVITICUS

The book of Leviticus is composed of material drawn from many sources and times in the life of the Israelites, but it has been so arranged as to suggest that it belongs to the time of Moses. There are good theological reasons why those who recorded the material in its present form set it out in this way, as we show in the next paragraph. Chapters 1—7 set out the sacrificial system, and chapters 8–10 record its introduction in the life of Israel. Both these sections form a natural sequel to the appointment of Aaron as High Priest as recorded in Exodus. Chapters 11—16 set out rules for acceptable behaviour on a cultic level, and Chapters 17—26 the necessary ethical behaviour for God's people. The final chapter is an appendix giving details of gifts to the sanctuary.

Leviticus has sometimes been thought to present a system of customs and behaviour by which the Israelites could work their own salvation, gaining the approval of God. But in fact it takes place in the Torah as a sequel to God's saving work at the escape from Egypt, and is presented wholly as part of the revelation of God's will at Sinai (Lev. 22.31–33). God has called the Israelites out of the world to be His people, and to serve Him. Their joyful response is to be in accepting and fulfilling His will. Because God is holy, they too must be holy (Lev. 19.2). It is recognized in Leviticus that the Israelites are capable of breaking God's law, and disobeying His will; but God has provided a way for them to return to Him in fresh commitment to His service (Lev. 16.29–31).

4. NUMBERS

This book carries the story of the Israelites from Sinai through the various desert wanderings to the eastern banks of the River Jordan. But it is not simply a historical account of the events involved. The traditions used in preparing the book contain many references to the ritual life of God's people, and the origins of various customs and beliefs. Those who prepared the book in the form in which we have it were clearly more interested in ensuring that their readers were aware of the proper behaviour of the Israelites in their commitment to God, than the precise details of the journeys in the wilderness.

However, the traditions that have been used do suggest the following stages in the experiences of Israel:

Numbers 1.1—10.10: Time spent in the neighbourhood of Sinai, organizing the life of Israel, including a census of the tribes, and the appointment of the Levites as assistants to Aaron the High Priest.

Numbers 10.11—20.14: The early travels of the Israelites, including an unsuccessful attempt to enter Palestine from the south, with many conflicts and difficulties and the presentation of further rules and regulations.

Numbers 20.15—36.13: A fresh attempt to approach the Promised Land, by a route east of Jordan, including encounters with Edom, Moab and Midian. A second census is recorded, and the allocation of land to tribes who were to settle east of the Jordan.

5. DEUTERONOMY

Because the editors of this book have used traditions and a code of law which are quite different from the material used in the preparation of the other books of the Torah, we have already had reason to study its contents. See pp. 46–47, and 52 respectively. We now need to look at the book as a whole, and to understand its significance in the biblical presentation of the tradition of the Exodus and the settlement in Palestine.

The book provides a link between the period of the Israelites' wandering in the desert lands of the Sinai Peninsular and Arabia and that of their crossing of the Jordan under the leadership of Joshua. Moses had lost the right to lead the Israelites into the Promised Land (Num. 14.26–30; Deut. 34.4). So he is pictured as encouraging the new generation who would enter Palestine to serve the Lord.

Deuteronomy 1—11: Moses sets out 'to explain the Law' (Deut. 1.5). These chapters consist of a series of sermons intended to win the commitment of the new generation who were to inherit God's promises, and settle in Palestine. Moses tells afresh the story of the Covenant made at Sinai, and the effects of the Israelites' disobedience. He tells of his own appointment as mediator between God and His chosen people (Deut. 5.28–31). The Ten Commandments are presented as the basic guide for obedience to the will of God (Deut. 5.1–22).

Deuteronomy 12—26: Here the Law is set out in its distinctive form, and Moses is pictured as preparing the way for the new circumstances of life in Palestine. He interprets the will of God for the centralization of worship, the appointment of a king, etc. In this way ideas which come from later times are given the authority of Moses. The intention is that the Israelites should recognize that God's purposes are always to find expression in appropriate ways for the changing times.

Deuteronomy 27—30: In this section of the book Moses is pictured as establishing that the Covenant God had made with the generation who had died in the wilderness was binding on the new generation who would enter the Promised Land (Deut. 29.10–15), and on later generations too (Deut. 29.29). Each new generation needs to renew its Covenant with God.

Deuteronomy 31—34: Moses is pictured as writing down the Law (Deut. 31.9), and arranging for a regular reading of the Torah (Deut. 31.10–13). The will of God is to be kept before the people constantly in this way. Moses's blessing of, and also warning to, later generations follows, and then an account of his death, after seeing the Promised Land.

STUDY SUGGESTIONS

REVIEW OF CONTENT

1. Read again p. 44, and try to discover from which code of law each of the verses quoted there comes. This will help you to understand the reason for the different rulings given on the same subject in different parts of the Torah. Remember that the Ten Commandments have been included at the beginning of both the Book of the Covenant and the Code of Deuteronomy.
2. Explain why scholars have given the titles, 'J', 'E', 'D', and 'P' to various traditions on which the writings of the Torah are based? What do these initials stand for?
3. Read again the five sections of this chapter which describe the groups of stories known to scholars as J, E, D, and P. Can you suggest from which source each of the following stories probably came?
   (a) Flesh for food (Gen. 9.1–7).
   (b) The Tower of Babel (Gen. 11.1–9).
   (c) The driving out of Hagar (Gen. 21.10–21).
   (d) The tables of the Law (Exod. 34.27–28).
   (e) The journey in the wilderness (Deut. 8.14–16).

BIBLE STUDY

4. 'There are differences, and even contradictions, in the rulings given in different passages in the Torah' (p. 44).
   Read the following pairs of passages and say what are the differences between the rulings given in each pair.
   (a) Exodus 20.11 and Deuteronomy 5.15.
   (b) Exodus 23.10, 11 and Leviticus 25.6.
   (c) Exodus 21.2 and 7 and Deuteronomy 15.12.
5. Have a look at what the commentaries in your library have to say about Exodus 15.1–18.
   (a) What sort of writing is this passage?

(b) Does it come from the time of Moses, or are there reasons for thinking that it was written at a much later time?

FURTHER STUDY AND DISCUSSION

6. Give some examples of the way in which the laws of your own country have been adapted over the years to meet changing circumstances. What important laws are being dealt with in the parliament or other legislative body of your country now? Have there been any laws on these subjects before? Why are new laws on these subjects needed?
7. Read the Old Testament parts of the notes in your Bible Dictionary on Law, and on the Ten Commandments. Were Laws in Israel produced by similar legal processes to those in your own country? In what sense were they religious rather than secular? Can Christians do anything to ensure that the laws of their own country are laws approved by God? Give examples.

4

The Historical Books

For our study of the historical books we shall divide them into two groups. The first group covers the history of the people of Israel from their settlement in Palestine up to the Exile of Judah in Babylon. It includes Joshua, Judges, Ruth, 1 and 2 Samuel and 1 and 2 Kings. The second group retells this story and carries it on to the time of the return from Exile, with the rebuilding of the city of Jerusalem and the Temple. It includes 1 and 2 Chronicles, Ezra, Nehemiah and Esther. We shall study the first of these two groups in this chapter and the second in chapter 5.

Both groups are included in the Bible for their value in helping the readers to understand God, and His relationship with Israel. These books are not merely pieces of ancient history, written to set out in order the events of a time long ago. The authors and editors wanted to share with their readers the ideas about God and the world which seemed especially important in their time. These theological insights came from God, and were part of the whole activity by which He reveals Himself to human beings. The Israelites believed that God revealed Himself in the events and experiences of their history, and these were recorded so as to help later generations to understand the ways of God and to do His will.

THE FIRST GROUP

Joshua, Judges, 1 and 2 Samuel and 1 and 2 Kings are together known as the Former Prophets. This title comes from the Hebrew Scriptures where these books are included in the section known as the Prophets. This emphasizes the fact that they were written to pass on to later generations the understanding of God which developed in the time that they record. To these books is added Ruth, because this little book tells a story of a woman who lived in the time of the Judges and became the great grandmother of King David. As we shall see, it was probably written much later in the history of Israel than the other six books.

Most scholars agree that the Former Prophets are based on very much the same insights and understanding as are found in the book of Deuteronomy. But there is evidence too of verses and passages which express similar ideas to those of J in the Torah. Other material may come from sources similar to E.

There is no generally agreed theory about the way in which these books reached their present form. Scholars differ about the

4.1 'The Israelites believed that God revealed Himself in the events of their history, and these were recorded to help later generations understand the ways of God' (p. 63). The stele of king Mesha, found at Dibon and known as the 'Moabite Stone', gives evidence of events in the 9th century BC which relate to the information in 2 Kings.

work done by the editor who introduced the ideas and beliefs of Deuteronomy into the interpretation of the events of this period of history. Either he was able to use earlier written records, including a fairly complete version of J, or he gathered details from many different sources and was himself responsible for the general outline of these books. We have already noticed (p. 52) R. H. Pfeiffer's view that J^2 was an attempt to describe the fulfilment of God's promises to Abraham. This suggests that J may well have covered the period of the settlement in the Promised Land. If so, then the writers of the Former Prophets were able to draw material from J for the periods covered by Joshua, Judges, and perhaps even Samuel.

We shall not attempt to study the sources for the books of the Former Prophets as a group, as we did with the Torah. These books are more distinct from each other than those of the Torah, and the history of the way each was written needs separate study. We shall, however, consider 1 and 2 Samuel as a single book, and 1 and 2 Kings similarly. It is fairly clear that they were first divided when the Greek version of the Old Testament was prepared, and that in older Hebrew editions each pair was a single book.

JOSHUA

THE TITLE

This book is named after the leader of Israel whose story it tells. Joshua was the successor of Moses. He was appointed to lead in the lifetime of Moses (Deut. 31.14–15, 23), and took over leadership when Moses died (Josh. 1.1–9). These verses describe Joshua as a man inspired by the spirit of God. He is also seen as obedient to 'the book of the law of Moses' (Josh. 1.8; 8.31; 23.6). He appears to have added his own interpretation of the purposes of God for His people (Josh. 24.26).

HISTORICAL BACKGROUND

The book tells how Joshua led the Israelites into the Promised Land. Through his leadership the promises of God were fulfilled (e.g. Gen. 13.14–17; 15.7, 18–21. Compare Josh. 21.45 and 23.14).

TYPE OF WRITING

The book consists almost entirely of stories. There are no law codes set down here, and very little poetry. There are details of peoples and villages left unconquered by the Israelites (e.g. Josh. 13.13), and details of the division of the Promised Land between the various tribes (Josh. 20 and 21). And there are speeches of Joshua encouraging the people to serve the Lord, who had done so much for their good (Josh. 23 and 24). But most of the book records the battles in which Joshua led the Israelites against the tribes who occupied the Promised Land. The best known of these stories is about the capture of Jericho, the town which guarded the road into the Promised Land (Josh. 6).

OUTLINE

Joshua 1—5: The Call of Joshua, and the crossing of the River Jordan.
Joshua 6—12: The Conquest of Palestine by the Israelites: Jericho (6); Ai (7–8); Southern Palestine (10); Northern Palestine (11); and a list of Canaanite kings conquered (12).
Joshua 13—22: The division of the Promised Land between the Twelve Tribes, and the selection of cities of refuge, and cities for the Levites who had no territory of their own.
Joshua 23—24: The Last Words of Joshua, leading to the Covenant at Shechem, and then his death.

SOURCES

(a) There is clear evidence in the book of Joshua that the written record did not reach the form we know until long after the Israelites' entry into the Promised Land, and after the time when Joshua actually lived.

The book refers to many things that have continued 'to this day'—the day when the book was written. The writer who used these words thought of these things as having continued for a long time (e.g. Josh. 4.9).

The book mentions another writing, called 'the Book of Jashar' (Josh. 10.13), which also contained the record of David's lament over Saul and Jonathan (2 Sam. 1.17, 18). The Book of Jashar must have been written in, or after, the time of David. So whoever wrote Joshua 10.13 must have done so even later, if he knew that book.

The book refers to the worship at one central shrine, which was established in the time of Josiah, on the basis of the laws contained in Deuteronomy. The writer blames the tribes living in the lands across the Jordan for building another altar (Josh. 22.19), so he must have known the laws contained in Deuteronomy, and he must have believed that these laws were binding on the tribes of Israel in the time of Joshua.

(b) There is also clear evidence that more than one account of the settlement in Palestine has been combined in the book of Joshua. The main outline of the book tells of a swift and successful conquest, after which the land was immediately shared out between the tribes of Israel. But other verses in the book show that many of the major towns were not captured, and that the Israelites only succeeded in capturing rural and hill country (e.g. Josh. 17.11–13). The writer of Joshua must have based his account on earlier records with conflicting evidence. He wrote as best he could, preserving some details which did not fit in with his main idea that success was quickly achieved.

Some scholars believe that the writer used the same sources of information as were used by those who prepared the Torah, namely J^1, J^2, E, D, and P. Each of these earlier sources may have described the settlement in the Promised Land as the climax and completion of the story which began with the Exodus, or even earlier, in the lifetime of Abraham. But if this is so, then each source must have given a different interpretation of the events relating to the settlement in Palestine. For, as we have seen, the book of Joshua contains conflicting ideas of what happened, even though the editor combined the accounts to present a unified picture. See Vol. 1, chapter 3 for a description of the events which lay behind the varying accounts.

Note also that it is certain that the book of Joshua was never part of the Torah, even though some scholars speak of the Hexateuch instead of the Pentateuch (6 Scrolls, instead of 5). The various sources are combined in a different way in Joshua from that in which they are related in the Torah. Also, the Samaritans never accepted the book of Joshua, even though they fully accepted that the Torah was Holy Scripture.

MESSAGE

The book of Joshua records the way in which God fulfilled His promise to give the land of Palestine to the Israelites. Joshua, the leader was chosen by God (Josh. 1.1–9), and worked under God's command (Josh. 5.13–15). The Israelites were certain of victory, except when their sin disrupted the life of the nation (Josh. 7.10–12). The enemy were to be totally destroyed, for fear that they might turn the Israelites away from serving God (e.g. Josh. 8.24–26). However, those who submitted to the Israelites might be saved. This description of the way in which the conquest was carried out is similar to the instructions given in Deuteronomy 20.10–18.

JUDGES

THE TITLE

The 'Judges' of Israel were men who became leaders over groups of the tribes of Israel in times of trouble, before they had any kings, and who rescued the people from their enemies.

HISTORICAL BACKGROUND

The book of Judges tells the story of the settlement of the Israelites in the Promised Land after the time of Joshua (Judges 1.1; 2.8). It describes how the Israelites gradually defeated their enemies between 1200 and 1050 BC. These enemies included the previous inhabitants of Palestine, the Canaanites (Judges 4.2), and also other tribes who either wanted to claim the land for themselves, like Moab and Ammon, or who found it profitable to raid the people who lived there, like the Midianites and Amalekites (see Judges 3.12; 6.3; 11.9). The book also tells of the early conflicts between the Israelites and the Philistines, who were much more dangerous enemies (Judges 3.31; 13.1). (See Vol. 1, chapter 3 for a description of this period.)

TYPE OF WRITING

The book consists almost entirely of prose, with one important story-poem (Judges 5). The accounts are set into a framework of interpretation in which the writer's aim is to explain why the Israelites had to endure the attacks of their enemies, and did not gain complete mastery of Palestine. There is also a preface which sets the scene for the book by describing the Israelites' incomplete conquest of Palestine in Joshua's time.

OUTLINE

Judges 1.1—2.5: Brief details of the incomplete conquest of Palestine by the various tribes. Many of these verses are similar to verses in Joshua.

Judges 2.6—16.31: The Judges:

2.6—3.6. The pattern of Israelite experience: The tribes turn away from God; trouble comes; the people cry to God for help; God sends a leader to help them; the people worship God alone, but later turn away again.

3.7—6.31. Stories of the Judges (Vol. 1, p. 72; rev. ed. p. 81): Othniel against Edom (3.7–11); Ehud against the Moabites (3.12–30); Shamgar against the Philistines (3.31); Deborah and Barak against the Canaanites (4.1—5.31); Gideon against the Midianites and Amalekites (6.1—8.35); Abimelech (internal strife) (9); Tola (10.1–2); Jair (10.3–5); Jephthah against the Ammonites (10.6—12.7); Ibzan (12.8–10); Elon (12.11–12); Abdon (12.13–15); Samson against the Philistines (13.1—16.31).

Judges 17.1—21.25: Stories which are not about the Judges at all:

17.1—18.31. The tribe of Dan seeks new territory, and steals Micah's graven image.

19.1—21.25. The tribe of Benjamin does a great wrong and is severely punished, but enabled to survive.

SOURCES

The book is made up from a number of legends which were known among the tribes of Israel. They were probably first recorded in two separate groups, which some scholars call J and E. Later these were combined, and set into the background of interpretation already described. The ideas emphasized in the final version of the book are closely similar to those of the source D, and this suggests that it was edited by someone who was influenced by the thoughts and beliefs expressed in Deuteronomy.

MESSAGE

The writer believed that God is able to keep His promise of giving the land of Palestine to the Israelites. He tried to explain why the land did not come quickly into their full and firm control. It was because the Israelites were disobedient, and God had sent their enemies against them to punish them (e.g. Judges 3.7–9, 12–15). When the Israelites repented, God sent Judges to deliver them. They then had a time of peace (Josh. 3.11, 30). In the closing section of the book this idea is developed. The Israelites were so rebellious that they could only be united under the leadership of a human king. Until one was appointed they would continue to do 'what was right in their own eyes' (Judges 17.6; 21.25).

RUTH

TITLE

The book has as its title the name of a Moabite woman whose story it tells. A family of Israelites visited Moab in the days of the Judges in order to escape a famine in their own land. The father died. The two sons married Moabite women, and then they too died, leaving their mother Naomi and her two Moabite daughters-in-law, Orpah and Ruth. Naomi set out to return home to Israel, and Ruth decided to accompany her. When they reached the family's home village, Bethlehem, they found the barley harvest in progress. Ruth gleaned in the field of a man called Boaz, who turned out to be a close relative. He decided to help Naomi and Ruth, and to do so bought the land which had belonged to their family, and married Ruth. Their son later became grandfather to king David. So David was descended from a Moabite woman, Ruth.

HISTORICAL BACKGROUND

The book of Ruth gives a picture of life in the time of the Judges which is too peaceful and settled to be a true account of life in those times. It suggests that Israel was at peace with Moab, which was not true in the time of the Judges (Judges 3.12–30). David had peaceful relations with them at a later time, so that he was able to leave his parents with the king of Moab for safety (1 Sam. 22.3–4). But this may have been because he was descended from Ruth, and was out of favour with the king of Israel.

The writer of the book of Ruth looks back on the customs of the time, and explains them to his readers (e.g. Ruth 4.7). This shows that he was writing at a time when the old customs were forgotten, e.g. when the sandal was used in a different way among the Israelites (Deut. 25.5–10).

The title of the book gives emphasis to the part played by the Moabite woman, rather than by her mother-in-law who was an Israelite. Ruth 4.17–22 serves as the climax of the book in its present form, and shows that the writer wanted to emphasize that David was descended from a Moabite woman. Probably he recorded this story as a defence of the foreign wives of some men of Israel. This became an important subject in the time of Nehemiah, when the Jews thought that foreign wives were a danger to their community life in Jerusalem, and drove them out (Neh. 13.1–3, 23–27). This was probably the time at which the book of Ruth was published, based on a traditional story. This would explain why the book is included among the Writings in the Hebrew scriptures, and not among the Former Prophets.

OUTLINE

Ruth 1: Ruth becomes daughter-in-law of Naomi, and accompanies her home to Bethlehem.
Ruth 2: Ruth gleans grain in the field of her kinsman Boaz.
Ruth 3: Ruth wins the love of Boaz at the harvest celebrations.
Ruth 4: Ruth becomes the wife of Boaz and bears him a son.

SOURCES

Some scholars disagree with the idea that the book was written as a protest against the enforced divorce of foreign wives, and suggest that an older story has been adapted for this purpose. They believe that the references to Ruth as an ancestor of David have been added in order to make the book into a suitable defence for foreign wives. They compare the naming of Obed, Ruth's son, with similar verses about the way names were given to other people, and suggest that the child's name was not Obed at all, but Bennoam, 'son of Naomi'. (See Ruth 4.17.)

However, it is difficult to see how this could be true. If the book was suddenly introduced, based on a traditional story but with an entirely new ending, it is very unlikely that people would have accepted it as having any value. Those who believed that foreign women were a danger to Israel, and who could support their belief by quoting the law, would soon have exposed the book as a fraud (Deut. 23.3). Yet it survived and was included among the Scriptures. It must have been regarded as soundly based on traditions from ancient Israel, or else it would have been rejected. We may note that the writer of Matthew's Gospel includes Ruth among the ancestors of 'Joseph the husband of Mary, of whom Jesus was born' (Matt. 1.5, 16).

MESSAGE

The book of Ruth tells how a Moabite woman became fully committed to the life and faith of the Jews (Ruth 1.16–17). It tells how the LORD provided for the needs of the two women when they returned to Bethlehem, how Boaz felt it natural that the LORD should bless Ruth; and how the LORD used her in His purposes (Ruth 2.11–12, 20; 3.10; 4.13). The message of the book seems to be that the Jews must be careful that they were not less charitable and appreciative than Boaz, for the women who married into Jewish families were capable of true faith, and the LORD would honour their sincerity.

The book of Ruth is one of the Five Scrolls which are used in the Synagogues as readings in the celebration of the various Jewish Festivals. It is used at Pentecost, which was originally the Feast of Harvest, and now celebrates the giving of the Law at Sinai. The other books among the Five Scrolls are the Song of Solomon, Lamentations, Ecclesiastes, and Esther: each related to a different religious ceremony (see the chapters which describe these books).

STUDY SUGGESTIONS

WORD STUDY

1. What are the differences in meaning between (a) information, (b) knowledge, and (c) understanding?

REVIEW OF CONTENT

2. 'The first group . . . are together known as the Former Prophets'. Where and why is this title used, and which books are included?
3. The writers of the books of Joshua and Judges express the belief that God is able to achieve what He sets out to do. They also record that the conquest of Palestine was incomplete. This made it difficult for people to understand the ways of God. Compare the way in which each writer treats this difficulty.
4. Why did Joshua make a covenant with all the tribes of Israel at

Shechem? What was the significance of the covenant, and what was the significance of the place where the covenant was made?

5. (a) Why is the book of Ruth placed between Judges and Samuel in the English versions of the Bible?
   (b) In what way is it connected with each of these books?

BIBLE STUDY

6. Read Judges 4 and answer the following questions. Then read Judges 5 and answer the same questions from the information given there.
   (a) Who were the leaders in Israel at the time of this story?
   (b) What part did the tribes of Benjamin and Ephraim play in this story?
   (c) Who was Jabin, and what part did he play?
   (d) Where did the battle take place?
   (e) What was Sisera doing when Jael struck him?
   There is enough in these two chapters to show that they are accounts of the same event. How would you explain the differences in detail between the two accounts, especially in the answer to (e).

FURTHER STUDY AND DISCUSSION

7. (a) What difficulties are likely to arise when a man marries a woman from a different tribe or race?
   (b) In what circumstances is such a marriage likely to be a success, judging by the experiences of Boaz?
   (c) How would you advise a young person who planned to enter into a mixed marriage?
   (d) Do you think similar problems can arise if Christians of different denominations marry? If so, how would you counsel young people who were planning such a marriage?

1 AND 2 SAMUEL

THE TITLE

Samuel was the last of the great Judges. He was an important leader among the Israelites, and helped them to face the problems created by the power of the Philistines, and by the need to find a leader able to inite the Twelve Tribes in their fight for freedom. Samuel did not write the books which bear his name, for he was only alive and involved in the history of Israel during the period covered by the first twenty-four chapters (see 1 Sam. 25.1).

The two books of Samuel were originally written as one book in the ancient Hebrew scrolls. It was first divided into two books when the

Greek translation was prepared. The Septuagint needed two scrolls because the Greek contained vowel letters, and was one and three-quarter times as long as the Hebrew. The division was retained when Jerome prepared the Vulgate, even though he was working from Hebrew manuscripts. Much later the Hebrew was presented in versions that make the division.

HISTORICAL BACKGROUND

The books of Samuel tell how Israel suffered at the hands of the Philistines, and how Samuel helped the people to choose a king. The books tell how the first king, Saul, failed to fulfil his responsibilities and was eventually replaced by David. They also tell how David conquered his enemies and made Israel a powerful nation. (See Vol. 1, chapter 4 for fuller details.)

TYPE OF WRITING

The greater part of these two books consists of accounts concerning Samuel, Saul, and David. There are some short items of poetry which probably come from the time of the events to which they are related. These include Samuel's rebuke of Saul for disobedience (1 Sam. 15.22–23); the women's song in praise of David (1 Sam. 18.7); and David's lament over Saul and Jonathan, and over Abner (2 Sam. 1.19–27; 3.33–34). The longer poetic passages in 1 Samuel 2.1–10 and 2 Samuel 22.2–23.7 are probably later compositions, written to suit the occasion to which they relate. Some scholars see each of these two passages as theological comments on the history recorded in these two books.

OUTLINE

1 Samuel 1—7: The early life of Samuel, and the Philistine victories.
1 Samuel 8—31: The kingdom of Saul:
1 Samuel 8—15. Samuel and Saul.
1 Samuel 16—31. Saul and David.
2 Samuel 1—24: The kingdom of David:
2 Samuel 1—4. David, king of Judah.
2 Samuel 5—8. David, king of Israel.
2 Samuel 9—20. The reign of David.
2 Samuel 21—24. Miscellaneous additions.

SOURCES

The books of Samuel were not written by a single eye-witness of the events they describe. They were composed later from more than one source of information. The result is that they contain contradictory evidence about what happened at a number of important points in the story, e.g.:

(a) In the time of Samuel *the Philistines were finally conquered*, and driven out of Israel (1 Sam. 7.13). Yet very soon *the Lord appointed a king to save the Israelites* from the Philistine power (1 Sam. 9.16).

(b) The appointment of *the king was part of God's plan* to save Israel (1 Sam. 9.16); *but God was quite able to save His people without a king*, and only appointed one because the people demanded it (1 Sam. 10.18–19, 24).

(c) *Saul was rejected by God* for making unlawful sacrifice (1 Sam. 13.8–15), and again later for not destroying all the enemy (1 Sam. 15.10–26). *Yet he remained king* until he died (2 Sam. 1.6–10).

(d) *David came to the king's court at Saul's command* to play soothing music for him, and was made Saul's armour-bearer (1 Sam. 16.14–23). But later David came to the battlefield to carry a message for his father, and conquered Goliath. At that time *he was quite unknown to Saul* (1 Sam. 17.55–58).

These contradictory details in the story can best be explained by supposing that there was more than one source of information available to the writer of the books of Samuel. Each of these accounts developed separately, at a time when the memory was passed on by word of mouth. It was only later, when written records of the traditions were prepared and then compared, that the differences between them were recognized. By that time it was impossible to discover the exact details of what had happened. So writers and editors set down the different accounts side by side, with little attempt to show how they were related to each other.

Many scholars believe that the traditions in the book of Samuel can be separated into two distinct but continuous accounts of the events described. They say that the details are consistent within each account, and that the differences arise only between the two accounts. And some scholars think that these two accounts came from the same J and E sources as the book of Judges (see p. 69), and perhaps even from J and E in the Torah.

There is very little evidence of the ideas of the writer of Deuteronomy in the books of Samuel. It is reasonable to suppose that the books of Samuel were first written down before the time of Josiah, and then altered a little by later editors.

MESSAGE

The two books give an account of God's dealings with the leaders whom He appointed to rule over Israel. Each leader in turn served God, but also at some point failed Him. For example:

Eli pronounced God's blessing on Hannah, which had a far-reaching effect (1 Sam. 2.20–21), but he failed to rebuke his own sons (1 Sam. 3.10–14).

Saul defeated the Ammonites in the power of God's spirit (1 Sam. 11.6–11), but was unwilling to obey God's commands (1 Sam. 15.18–19).

The glory of it all is that God's purposes for the world are achieved even though His own servants sin, and fail Him. For a time God used the reign of David to establish a fine and just kingdom, and He was quite capable of maintaining that kingdom (2 Sam. 7.15–16). The Messianic hopes of the Old Testament spring from this promise. The subsequent troubled history recorded in 1 and 2 Kings and the prophetic books nonetheless shows us that God was still active among His people, and that the Messiah had a central place in His plans for salvation.

There is a great deal of evidence in these books that the writers believed in a personal relationship between the prophets and God. Samuel heard God's voice so clearly that he thought Eli was calling him (1 Sam. 3.6–8). Saul and David received the command of God through the words and actions of Samuel. Later Nathan fulfilled a similar role. The kings all recognized the right of the prophets to speak in God's name.

1 AND 2 KINGS

THE TITLE

These books record the reigns of the kings of Judah and the kings of Israel. At first there was only one book of Kings, but like the book of Samuel it was divided into two parts when the ancient Greek version was prepared. In the Septuagint the parts are called 3 and 4 Kingdoms, as the books of Samuel are called 1 and 2 Kingdoms. Some scholars believe that at one time all four books were written as one continuous record, describing events from the appointment of the first king till the time when the Babylonians captured Jerusalem.

HISTORICAL BACKGROUND

The books of Kings tell the story of the kingdoms of Israel from the reign of Solomon, through the time of the divided kingdom (Judah and Israel) to the destruction of Israel, and the exile of the people of Judah. (See Vol. 1, chapters 5 to 7, for fuller details.)

TYPE OF WRITING

The two books contain interwoven accounts of the kings of Judah and the kings of Israel. The writer describes each reign by relating it to the reign of the king of the other kingdom. The length of each reign is given, and a judgement is passed on the way in which each king ruled. For the kings of Judah the age of the king when he came to the throne is given, and the name of his mother. The death of each king is mentioned and the name of his successor is given. The information about each king is limited to matters which the writer thought to be important, and readers are told where they can find more details if they want them.

Some quite important facts are not given, and careful study shows that the writer chose to include those events which would illustrate that success or failure depend upon the king's attitude to centralized worship. Those who allowed worship anywhere other than Jerusalem are condemned. The kings of Israel are especially accused of approving of Jeroboam's sinful action in setting up rival places of worship in Bethel and Dan, and placing golden bulls there for worship (1 Kings 12.26–33). The books of Kings only give eight verses to the account of the reign of Omri (1 Kings 16.21–28). Apart from condemning him for following 'the way of Jeroboam', the only information provided about his reign is that he established Samaria as capital of the Northern Kingdom. The writer of Kings fails to draw attention to the importance of Samaria as a city easily defended, and well placed to strengthen the unity of the Northern Kingdom. He also fails to record that Omri was successful in regaining rule over Moab, which had been part of David's kingdom.

The writer of the books of Kings interprets history according to the ideas of Deuteronomy. He draws his authority for this approach from the discovery of 'the book of the law' which he records in 1 Kings 22. In addition, the books of Kings contain a more detailed account of the life of Solomon; a diary recording the main events in the history of the first Temple; and collections of stories about Elijah (1 Kings 17–21; 2 Kings 1.1–2.18), and Elisha (2 Kings 2–9; 13.14–21).

There is very little poetry in these books. 1 Kings 8.12–13 probably came from the Book of Jashar, as suggested in the Septuagint; and so can be accepted as an authentic work of Solomon. 1 Kings 12.16 is typical of early fragments of poetry in praise of great deeds, and was probably handed down from the time of the actual event to which it is related. 2 Kings 19.21–28 is part of a passage which is also found in the book of Isaiah (see Isaiah 37.22–29). Many of Isaiah's utterances were poetic in form, and this seems clearly to belong to the time which the writer of 2 Kings used it to describe.

4.2 'The two books carry forward the idea that God chose men . . . to speak to the kings in His name' (p. 79). Since then God has continued to send prophets to speak to national leaders in His name—people like Archbishop Janani Luwum of Uganda, seen here with President Amin, whose violent and oppressive rule he condemned, and as a result was arrested and killed.

OUTLINE

1 Kings 1—11: The reign of Solomon.
1 Kings 12—2 Kings 17: The Divided Kingdom, and the destruction of Israel by Assyria.
2 Kings 18—25: The survival of Judah, followed by the exile of her people to Babylon.

SOURCES

We have already noticed the different sorts of writing which were included in the two books of Kings. The editor who prepared the parallel accounts of the kings of Judah and Israel certainly got his information from the books to which he refers his readers for further details. The Book of the Chronicles of the Kings of Judah (1 Kings 14.29, etc.), and the Book of the Chronicles of the Kings of Israel (1 Kings 14.19, etc.) were records of the main events in the lives of each king. They had been prepared separately in the two kingdoms. The editor used both to compile the books of Kings now in the Bible, and he did so at a time when Israel was already destroyed and Judah remained as the source of hope for the future of the Israelites. These source books are not to be confused with 1 and 2 Chronicles, but consist of records no longer available to us except from their use in 1 and 2 Kings.

Most scholars agree that the first version of the book of Kings ended at 2 Kings 24.7. Up to that point each king is introduced in the same sort of way, but this pattern is not found in the remaining verses of the book. This suggests a change of writer. But more important than this is the fact that the first editor clearly believed that David's kingdom would survive against all attack, and that Jerusalem would remain independent (1 Kings 11.36; 2 Kings 8.19). He wrote that the Temple was still standing as it was originally built (1 Kings 8.8).

2 Kings 24.8—25.30, however, describes how Jerusalem and the Temple were captured and destroyed. So this passage must have been added to the book by a later writer. This second editor seems to have adapted some of the earlier parts of the book, in order to prepare the reader for the bad news at the end. See 2 Kings 22.20, and 23, 26–27, where God is shown to plan the punishment of Judah. Probably the stories of Elijah and Elisha also were added at a later time, and did not belong to the first edition of the book of Kings.

The final paragraph of 2 Kings points to a sign of hope for the future. King Jehoiachin of Judah gains favour in the eyes of a new king in Babylon, Evilmerodach.

MESSAGE

The first edition of the books of Kings was written in the years that followed the discovery of Deuteronomy, in the reign of Josiah. The writer wanted to prove that the laws in Deuteronomy can be used to interpret the history of the Israelite kingdoms. When kings obeyed God, and led their people in worship in Jerusalem, they found blessing. When they allowed men to worship in other sanctuaries, with all the dangers of idolatry and the service of other gods, they lived under God's condemnation. Obedience led to success, while disobedience brought trouble. Hezekiah was the outstanding example of obedience (2 Kings 18.3–8). Manasseh was the outstanding example of disobedience (2 Kings 21.2–18). Some kings who did good works failed in the matter of worship, and so enjoyed only limited success, and received limited praise (e.g. Asa: 1 Kings 15.9–24).

The writer also gave special emphasis to the Temple. He gave an account of it through many changes of history from the time of Solomon until the reform of religion under the leadership of Josiah. The writer of the first edition of the book of Kings clearly assumed that Jerusalem and the Temple had a special place in God's plans. Even when it became necessary to add an epilogue about the destruction of Jerusalem and the Temple, the book served to remind Jews that it was their disobedience and idolatry which had led to this trouble. It thus prepared the way for the prophets who proclaimed that a purified Israel would return to Jerusalem, and would rebuild the Temple.

The two books carry forward the idea found in Samuel that God chose men, and sent them in the power of His Spirit to speak to the kings in His name. Their messages were often of a deeply political kind, and are evidence of God's concern about the whole life of His people.

Among these prophets were:

Ahijah, who warned of the coming division of the kingdom, but also condemned Jeroboam (1 Kings 11.28–39; 14.6–16);

Shemaiah, who prophesied at the same time as Ahijah, warning Rehoboam not to fight the people of Israel (1 Kings 12.21–24);

Jehu, who rebuked Baasha of Israel (1 Kings 16.1–10);

Elijah, who led the conflict with Jezebel and the priests of the fertility gods, the Baalim (1 Kings 17–21; 2 Kings 1.1—2.18);

Elisha, who was deeply involved in the conflicts between the small nations, especially involving Syria (2 Kings 2—9; 13.14–21).

STUDY SUGGESTIONS

REVIEW OF CONTENT

1. When were the books of Samuel and of Kings each first divided into two, and why?
2. (a) What sort of writing do we chiefly find in the books of Samuel and Kings?
   (b) What sorts of writing do we *not* find much of in the books of Samuel and Kings?
3. Where did the writer of the book of Kings get his information?

BIBLE STUDY

4. 'The books of Samuel contain contradictory evidence about what happened at important points in the story' (pp. 73–74).
   Read the following groups of passages and say what were the contradictions in the story within each group.
   Group (a): 1 Sam. 9.16; 1 Sam. 10.20–24; 1 Sam. 11.11–15.
   Group (b): Sam. 19.17; 1 Sam. 20.25–29.
5. 'Each leader in turn served God, but also at some point failed Him' (p. 74).
   (a) Read the following two groups of passages, and for each group say (i) who was serving God, (ii) in what way he served God, and (iii) in what way he failed God.
   1 Sam. 3.19 and 1 Sam. 8.1–3;
   1 Sam. 16.12, 13 and 2 Sam. 12.7–12.
   (b) What evidence, if any, is there in these stories of a growing understanding of God's willingness to forgive?
6. The books of Kings contain 'a diary recording the main events in the history of the first Temple'. Make a list of the stories about the Temple which they contain, and give the chapter and verses where each may be found. (Do not attempt to retell each story.)
7. Read the chapters which tell the story of Elijah, and summarize the main events of his life. How did he know what to say and do in God's name? Use a concordance to find the passages you need.

FURTHER STUDY AND DISCUSSION

8. Who, if anyone, today is generally regarded as having 'the right to speak in God's name'? Do you yourself think that they have that right? Give reasons for your answer.
9. 'God's purposes for the world are achieved even though His own servants sin and fail Him' (p. 75). Do you agree? Give examples from your own experience to support your answer.

5

The Historical Books (continued)

THE SECOND GROUP

1 and 2 Chronicles, Ezra and Nehemiah together make up a second record of the history of God's People. They tell us what happened from the time of Adam until the resettlement of Israel in Jerusalem after the Exile. To these are added the book of Esther, which tells the story of a Jewish heroine in the time of the Persian empire. In the Hebrew Scriptures all these books are among the Writings, the latest group to be included in the Canon.

We shall first study the four books which tell the story of Israel. The general style of the writing, the material selected, and the interpretation of events all suggest that the same editor prepared all four books. Originally they were one complete account of the History of Israel.

In the Hebrew Bible the order of the books is reversed, so that 1 and 2 Chronicles come after Ezra and Nehemiah. Probably Ezra and Nehemiah were accepted as part of the Scriptures before 1 and 2 Chronicles, because the former two books record a period of history not dealt with in other parts of the Scriptures. 1 and 2 Chronicles repeat, adapt, and add to information found in the books of the Law, and in Joshua, Samuel, and Kings. They were not accepted as a necessary part of the Scriptures until a later time, and then they were placed at the end of the Writings, i.e. after Ezra and Nehemiah.

In the English versions the books are set in their natural order, following the custom established by the Septuagint. We shall study them in that order, taking 1 and 2 Chronicles first, and Ezra and Nehemiah after them.

1 AND 2 CHRONICLES

TITLE

The Hebrew title for these books means 'Events of the Days', suggesting that the books describe what happened at each stage of the history of Israel. The Greek title means 'things omitted', suggesting that the books record details about the history that were left out of earlier accounts. The Vulgate follows the Greek title, but Jerome suggested that these books should be called 'A Chronicle of the whole of Sacred History'. The English title follows this suggestion. A chronicle is a record of events in the order in which they happened. Chronicles was divided into two books fairly late in the passing on of the Scriptures, and they are still counted as one book in the Jewish scrolls used in Synagogues today.

HISTORICAL BACKGROUND

As the outline shows, these two books tell the story of Israel from the time of 'Adam' through to the fall of Jerusalem, and the Exile. They end with Cyrus's proclamation that the Jews could return to Jerusalem, and should rebuild the Temple.

The editor selected material from the earlier historical books, and added information from other sources. In doing this he showed an interest in special aspects of the story which help us to understand why he thought a new account of the history was necessary. They also show the probable time at which he wrote.

He only mentioned Saul briefly. He ignored the sins and troubles of David. He did not say much about the revolt that split the kingdom after the death of Solomon. And he said very little about the Northern Kingdom, and then only when this was necessary in order to explain events in Judah.

Instead, he emphasized the building of the Temple in Judah. He described how David made most of the preparations: how he drew up the plans, gathered the materials, and appointed officers who could lead the worship. The editor also showed great interest in the part which the Levites played in history, and in the use of music in worship.

All this was an introduction to the story of the rebuilding of the Temple in Jerusalem after the Exile, and the re-establishment of the worshipping community there under Ezra and Nehemiah. But it also provided a background to the conflict between the Jews and the Samaritans, which reached its climax in about 400 BC, when the Samaritans built a rival temple on Mount Gerizim. The editor minimized the importance of the Northern Kingdom, and emphasized that the true servants of the LORD were the people of Judah.

For reasons connected with the Ezra-Nehemiah part of this history book, it seems likely that the date of the whole record was rather later than 400 BC, perhaps about 350 BC.

OUTLINE

1 Chronicles 1—9: History of the tribes between the time of Adam and the time of David. Most of the information provided is in the form of genealogies, that is, lists of ancestors and their descendants.
1 Chronicles 10—29: David's reign, and the preparation for the building of the Temple.
2 Chronicles 1—9: Solomon's reign, and the building and dedication of the Temple.

2 Chronicles 10.1—36.21: The history of Judah until the Exile.
2 Chronicles 36.22–23: The Proclamation of Cyrus.

SOURCES

The editor of Chronicles used a great deal of information which he obtained from other books of the Old Testament, i.e. from the books of the Law and from the Former Prophets. Several times he records where he gained his knowledge. He refers to the book of Kings (e.g. 2 Chron. 16.11), and also mentions books compiled by the prophets (e.g. 1 Chron. 29.29; 2 Chron. 9.29; 13.22).

Some scholars believe that the latter verses simply record other ways of naming the books of Samuel and Kings, because all the prophets whom the editor mentioned are in fact named in these books (e.g. Samuel in 1 Sam. 7.6; Nathan in 2 Sam. 7.2; Gad in 2 Sam. 24.11; Ahijah in 1 Kings 11.29; Iddo in 1 Kings 4.14; Shemaiah in 1 Kings 12.22; etc.).

In two verses the editor said that the information preserved by the prophets had reached him through the books of Kings (2 Chron. 20.34 and 32.32). But he also included important details that were not available to him through the book of Kings, and must have come from another source, or sources. He mentions a 'Commentary on the Book of Kings' (2 Chron. 24.27), which may have been written to include additional information, and to fill out the details contained in the book itself.

The editor shows a knowledge of the ritual laws included in the Priestly Code (see pp. 47, 48), as well as those of the earlier codes. He presents the history of Israel in such a way as to suggest that these rules always applied to worship among the Israelites, as though there had been no development or change of customs over the centuries (see p. 44). He must have worked at a time when the five books of Law were known, after Ezra's return from the Exile. He also introduced further information about the Temple cult, which was not included in the books of the Law, and showed that there were developments even after Ezra's time.

In recent times some scholars have suggested that the writer of Chronicles was deeply influenced by the fact that the earlier records were already taken as authoritative in the life of Israel. He is thought to have attempted to draw them together in a harmonized account of God's people. He corrects the information from his earlier sources to dispose of conflicting information. Two examples will be sufficient to make the point.

In 1 Samuel 17.31–47 it is recorded that David killed the Philistine giant Goliath, but in 2 Samuel 21.19 Elhanan the son of Jaareoregim

5.1 'The editor' of Chronicles 'emphasized the rebuilding of the Temple . . . as an introduction to the rebuilding after the Exile, and the re-establishment of the worshipping community under Ezra and Nehemiah' (p. 82). This wall-painting, believed to be of Ezra reading the Law to the people, was found when archaeologists uncovered a synagogue of the 2nd or 3rd century AD at Dura-Europos.

slew Goliath. The writer of Chronicles records that Elhanan 'slew Lahmi the brother of Goliath' (1 Chron. 20.5).

In 2 Samuel 6.12–16 the story is told of David and all the house of Israel bringing the Ark to Jerusalem. In Deuteronomy 10.8 the work of carrying the Ark is given to the Levites as a regular duty. The writer of Chronicles retells the story of the bringing of the Ark to Jerusalem to include reference to the Levites while still mentioning the involvement of all Israel (1 Chron. 15.1–3).

For many years scholars were very doubtful about the accuracy of the stories recorded in the book of Chronicles. They believed that the writer had adapted the information to suit his own expectations of what happened in the light of his understanding of how God works. But his emphasis on sources suggests that he was able to draw on fresh evidence that was not available to the writers of Samuel and Kings. Scholars are now more cautious about rejecting the evidence provided by Chronicles. The writers of both the records of the History of Israel, Samuel-Kings and Chronicles, had their own way of interpreting the facts. As I have already suggested, all history-writing involves selection of what the author considers significant information. What is written is always an interpretation of what happened. We cannot be certain, for example, that the Levites did not carry the Ark into Jerusalem. It may have been unimportant to the writer of Samuel, but was significant to the writer of the Chronicles. Scholars warn us not to be dogmatic about what we believe to be the actual facts.

MESSAGE

The editor seems to have written these historical books in order to show that only the people of Judah were the Chosen Race, and to reject the Samaritans' claim to be God's People. Perhaps he was so deeply convinced of the fact that God was at work in and through the history of Judah, that he could not see the Northern Kingdom of Israel as significant except in its impact on Judah. The Samaritans were of mixed racial origin and he did not recognize them as part of the People of God.

This editor was convinced that every human action is followed immediately by punishment or reward from the LORD. He took considerable trouble to show in the book that the success or failure of the various kings of Judah depended directly on their response to God. If they were faithful, then God rewarded them with success. If they were sinful, He brought them to experience failure.

The editor was unhappy with some of the information given in the book of Kings, and found it necessary to adapt it in order to support his own conclusions. For example:

1. He found it difficult to believe that God had 'incited' David to do evil by carrying out a census and had then punished him for doing so (2 Sam. 24.1, 10–14). So in 1 Chronicles 21.1 he records that it was Satan who incited David, and God who punished him. This is in line with later thinking about the nature of temptation (see Matt. 4.1).

2. The writer of Kings gives no explanation for the fact that King Manasseh reigned for forty-five years, even though he was a very bad man (2 Kings 21.1–18). That writer shared the view that God's blessing followed obedience, but he simply describes the bad things Manasseh did. The writer of Chronicles says that in fact Manasseh was deported for a time to Babylon, and that he experienced conversion while he was there and was allowed to return to Jerusalem (2 Chron. 33.10–13). Assyrian records exist which tell of the fact that early in his reign Manasseh was summoned by Esarhaddon. This is ignored in the book of Kings. So it is possible that the writer of Chronicles had some fresh information to present. The strongest evidence scholars have presented against Manasseh's conversion is their belief that at least a first edition of Deuteronomy was produced secretly in his reign in the hope of a reformation once he was gone.

3. King Josiah, who had done much to encourage his people in the service of God, died young at the hands of Pharaoh Necho of Egypt. The writer of Kings does not give a clear explanation of what happened to lead to the death of Josiah at the meeting described in 2 Kings 23.29–30. He seems to have believed that Josiah suffered because of the evil done by Manasseh (2 Kings 23.26–27). The writer of Chronicles says that Josiah met his death because Pharaoh Necho was not coming to attack Judah, and had the blessing of God in what he was doing, but yet Josiah opposed him (2 Chron. 35.20–24). He thus finds reason for Josiah to be suffering for his own sins in line with the teaching of Ezekiel 18.20, 26–27, and the beliefs of Job's friends (Job 4.7–9, etc.).

The editor was very certain that God rules over human affairs. He even went so far as to suggest that the people of Judah did not need to defend themselves against their enemies, because God delivered them by His own personal action on the battlefield (e.g. 2 Chron. 13.15; 14.12; 20.17). The idea matches the belief that God rewards or punishes people immediately, within their own lifetime, for their service or rebellion against Him.

STUDY SUGGESTIONS

WORDS

1. What are the meanings of the three distinct titles given to Chronicles in Hebrew, in Greek and by Jerome?

Which of them seems to you the most appropriate title for these books and why?

REVIEW OF CONTENTS

2. What attitude did the editor of Chronicles have towards death, for example, the death of kings?
3. The writer of Chronicles 'was unhappy with some of the information given in the Book of Kings, and found that he had to adapt it in order to support his own conclusions' (p. 85). In which passages of Chronicles, if any, did he make use of the details:
   (a) in 1 Kings 12.1–20, of the division of the two kingdoms in the time of Rehoboam?
   (b) in 1 Kings 12.25–33, of the golden calves set up by Jeroboam in Bethel and Dan?
   (c) in 1 Kings 16.29–34, of the founding of a temple of Baal in Samaria?
   What reasons can you suggest for his decisions about using or not using these details?

BIBLE STUDY

4. Read 2 Samuel 6.12–20 and 1 Chronicles 15.25–29, and answer the following questions:
   (a) Who were the people who carried the Ark up to Jerusalem? Which version of the story gives this detail?
   (b) Who carried out the sacrifice on the way to Jerusalem?
   (c) What made Michal despise David?
   Which version of the story gives this detail?
   (d) Which account describes the musical instruments used on this occasion?
   (e) How would you explain the differences between the two accounts of this event? Which do you think is likely to be the most accurate account?
   (f) Which is more important: (i) the fact that David brought the Ark up to Jerusalem, or (ii) the details of the ceremony by which it was brought?

FURTHER STUDY AND DISCUSSION

5. What is the real nature of God's personal action in the world? And how does He help those who are facing trouble or danger? Give examples to support your answer.

EZRA AND NEHEMIAH

TITLES

These two books are known by the names of the two great Jewish leaders of the period of history which they describe. The history of Ezra is shared between the two books, and the record of Nehemiah's work is contained in the book which bears his name. In addition the book of Ezra begins with a description of events from the time of the Jews' first return from exile in 538 BC until the rebuilding of the Temple in Jerusalem which was completed in 516 BC.

We have already noticed that these two books belong together with 1 and 2 Chronicles as part of a second account of the History of Israel. At first in the Canon Ezra-Nehemiah was one book, which was divided later to make the two books we know in the English Bible.

Jerome's Latin translation of the Bible, the Vulgate, contains four books of Esdras, of which Ezra and Nehemiah are two. The others were another version of the events described in Ezra-Nehemiah, and an account of the visions of Ezra. The latter two books are included in the Apocrypha as 1 and 2 Esdras.

HISTORICAL BACKGROUND

Ezra and Nehemiah contain an account of the experience of the Jews during the Persian Empire. It covers the release from Exile, to the rebuilding of the Temple and the city of Jerusalem, the establishment of a sub-province with a Jewish governor, and the introduction of the book of the Law, which probably contained the first five books of the Old Testament. (See Vol. 1, chapter 8, for a full account of this period.)

The books of Ezra and Nehemiah are the source of most of our information for this period of history. Haggai, Zechariah, Isaiah 56–66, and Malachi record the work of prophets who belong to this period, but they do not give very much information about the political and social life of the time.

Because there are no written records of this period it is difficult to discover how accurate an account the books of Ezra and Nehemiah provide. As a result, scholars differ widely in their interpretation of the history of this period.

Many scholars believe that the editor of Ezra-Nehemiah was seriously mistaken when he supposed that Ezra came to Jerusalem before Nehemiah, and that this caused him to make other mistakes in presenting his account of the period. We shall understand the view of these scholars and the reason for the editor's mistake if first we see how he put his book together.

OUTLINE

Ezra 1—6: From the return from Exile, to the rebuilding of the Temple:
Ezra 1.1—4.6: An account of the early part of this period: including work on the house of God.
Ezra 4.7—6.18: A record, addressed to Artaxerxes in Aramaic, of the hindrance to the rebuilding of the walls created by the governors of the 'Province beyond the river'.
Ezra 6.19–22: A Passover to celebrate Artaxerxes's permission to continue rebuilding the Temple.
Ezra 7—10: Nehemiah 1—13: The stories of Ezra and Nehemiah:
Ezra 7—8: The return of exiles led by Ezra, by authority of Artaxerxes (see Ezra 7.12–26).
Ezra 9—10: Ezra deals with those who had married foreign wives.
Nehemiah 1—7: Nehemiah leads the people in rebuilding the walls of Jerusalem.
Nehemiah 8.1—12.26: Ezra presents the book of the Law.
Nehemiah 12.27–47: The dedication of the walls of Jerusalem.
Nehemiah 13: Nehemiah's second visit to Jerusalem, and his enforcement of laws concerning the Sabbath and foreign wives.

SOURCES

The editor of these two books used earlier records in order to prepare his account of the period. These include:

(a) *Ezra's own account*: directly copied in Ezra 7.27–28 and 8.1–34; and summarized in Ezra 7.1–10 and 9.1—10.44, and in Nehemiah 7.73—8.18 and 9.1–38.

(b) *Nehemiah's own account*: directly copied in Nehemiah 1.1—7.73; 11.1–2 and 13.4–31, and summarized in Nehemiah 12.27–47; 13.1–3.

(c) *Official documents in Aramaic*: Ezra 4.8—6.18 and 7.12–26. Aramaic was a language widely known among the peoples of Western Asia from Persia to Egypt, and beyond. The Jews regularly used it in making contact with their foreign rulers at least from the time of Hezekiah, because it was related to Hebrew and so was easy to use in communicating with others whose language was also related to it (see 2 Kings 18.26). It was the mother tongue of Jesus and His disciples, by which time classical Hebrew was not so widely known.

(d) *Lists of names from official records*: Ezra 2.1–70; Nehemiah 11.3–36 and 12.1–26, and similar lists probably included first in the personal records of Ezra and Nehemiah: Ezra 8.1–14 and 10.18–44, and Nehemiah 7.6–72.

(e) *Nehemiah 10 as it stands in our Bibles* is a record of a covenant which the people and their representatives made in response to

5.2 'Ezra and Nehemiah describe the experiences of the Jews during the Persian Empire' (see p. 88). Cyrus's own account of his conquest of Babylon, and his policy of allowing captives to go back to their own country, is recorded on the 'Cyrus Cylinder'.

Ezra's presentation of the Law. But Nehemiah's name heads the list of those who took part, while Ezra is not included. The promises made are closely related to the problems which Nehemiah raised in his time as governor, and there is no mention of a new law book such as Ezra introduced. So probably this chapter belongs with the story of Nehemiah rather than that of Ezra.

(f) *There may have been an earlier record* of the return from Exile and the rebuilding of the Temple, on which the editor based Ezra 1—6. But some scholars believe that the editor himself composed these chapters, with the help of the official records and documents which we have already noticed. It is significant that Ezra 4.7—6.18 refers to the rebuilding of the walls, while the rest of this section is only concerned with the rebuilding of the Temple. The editor has used an Aramaic source which does not belong to the time about which he is writing in this section.

WHO CAME FIRST: EZRA OR NEHEMIAH?

The editor of these two books clearly believed that Ezra came first, that Nehemiah followed, and that for a time they worked together. The sources of his information deal with the two men separately, but he has woven them together to create the single account of their work given in these books.

He mentions several dates as he presents the story, but most of these do not name the year, only the month and day. Those which do name the year use the reign of 'Artaxerxes the king' as a basis for their counting. According to Ezra 7.7–9, Ezra returned from exile in the seventh year of Artaxerxes's reign. Nehemiah 1.1 and 2.1 mention the twentieth year as the date when Nehemiah first heard of the hardships of the Jews in Jerusalem and arranged to visit them. Nehemiah 13.6 gives the thirty-second year as the date of Nehemiah's second visit to Jerusalem.

If all these dates refer to the same king's reign, then Ezra reached Jerusalem before Nehemiah, as the editor believed. But there were three kings of Persia called Artaxerxes, and the editor does not say which one he meant in each case. If Nehemiah worked in the reign of Artaxerxes I, and Ezra in the reign of Artaxerxes II, then Nehemiah reached Jersualem before Ezra. Scholars differ on this matter. Some take the editor's view, and others believe that the dates which the editor took from the records he used to compile Ezra–Nehemiah referred to the reigns of different kings.

The only way in which we can decide which view is most likely to be correct, is to see what evidence, if any, there is in the two books, to confirm the idea that Nehemiah came to Jerusalem before Ezra, and that they were not there together. The following facts seem to give support to this idea:

(a) The records which Nehemiah and Ezra themselves prepared provide important evidence, because neither one mentions the other. It is unlikely that Nehemiah would have written critically of the 'former governors' without clearing the name of Ezra if he was one of them (see Neh. 5.15). Only the editor himself mentions them both together (Neh. 8.9). We know that editorial work has been done on this verse because the verb 'said' is in the singular, but it is given several subjects, 'Nehemiah . . . Ezra . . . the Levites'. These would require a plural form of the verb if they were in the original document used at this point in the book. The editor inserts the extra people, Ezra being the original subject. Verse 10 confirms that only 'he' was speaking.

(b) Both men were given authority by the king of Persia. It is difficult to see how they could both have exercised this authority at the same time, as their responsibilities overlapped (Ezra 7.25–26 and Neh. 2.5; 13.6–9).

(c) The work of Nehemiah was to lead the Jews in rebuilding the walls of Jerusalem. Ezra expresses joy that there is a wall 'in Judea and Jerusalem' (Ezra 9.9: see footnote). The Hebrew word translated in the text of the RSV Common Bible as 'protection' is a normal word for 'wall'. It comes from the same root as the word for 'mason' (e.g. in 2 Kings 12.12).

(d) The laws known and enforced by Nehemiah were those of the Law Code of Deuteronomy. Compare Nehemiah 13.5 with Deuteronomy 18.1–8; Nehemiah 13.15–18 with Deuteronomy 5.14; and Nehemiah 13.23–25 with Deuteronomy 23.3–4. There is no evidence that Nehemiah knew any other book of law such as the one introduced by Ezra; for example, the Day of Atonement is not mentioned.

(e) Ezra was given special authority to teach the laws of God (Ezra 7.25). Yet according to the book of Ezra, when he reached Jerusalem the only question he had to deal with was that of mixed marriages. He did not present the book of the Law until several years later, when Nehemiah had already organized the rebuilding of the wall of Jerusalem. If the book of the Law was of supreme importance to Ezra it is difficult to explain the delay. If, however, we remove the stories of Nehemiah, there is nothing to suggest that there was such a delay. Ezra's action over mixed marriages may even have followed the reading of the law.

All this seems to provide strong evidence that Nehemiah was in Jerusalem well before the time of Ezra. We ought to accept that the editor was confused by the use of the name Artaxerxes in the sources from which he drew his information, and that he constructed his account of this period on the basis of his mistaken ideas about the dates. Probably Nehemiah worked in the reign of Artaxerxes I, and Ezra in the reign of Artaxerxes II. Using the dates of these kings of Persia we may suppose that Nehemiah reached Jerusalem in 444 BC, and Ezra in 397 BC. Since the editor was unaware of the real sequence of events, he must have been at work some time after the days of Nehemiah and Ezra. An interval of two generations would be sufficient to account for his confusion; perhaps he compiled Ezra–Nehemiah in about 350 BC.

MESSAGE

The editor presents the story with similar emphasis to that found in the book of Chronicles. The rebuilding of the Temple and the establishment of worship there are matters of supreme importance. God's people find favour with foreign nations and are triumphant over their enemies. 'The people of the Land', the Samaritans, have no right to be counted among the servants of the LORD (Ezra 4.1–3). The Jews must accept and obey the written law of the LORD, and order their whole lives by it. The goal of Israelite history is reached with the establishment of a worshipping and obedient community in Jerusalem.

ESTHER

TITLE

This book has as its title the name of the leading character in the story that it tells. According to the story Esther was a Jewish woman living in Persia, who married the king of that country and was able to save her people from a cruelly planned massacre.

HISTORICAL BACKGROUND

The events of the story take place at Susa, the capital city of the Persian Empire, in the reign of a king named Ahasuerus. This almost certainly means Xerxes I, who reigned between 486 and 465 BC. Very little is known about the reign of this king, but we do know that there was an important Jewish settlement at Susa at that time. It is quite possible that the Jews faced a serious threat of persecution there in the reign of Xerxes I.

OUTLINE

Esther 1—2: Esther becomes Queen of Persia:
Esther 1: Vashti, the former queen, angers her husband and is dismissed.

Esther 2.1–18: The king chooses Esther as his new queen, from among the beautiful women in his harem.
Esther 2.19–23: Mordecai, Esther's guardian, warns the king of a plot to kill him.
Esther 3—7: Haman plots a massacre of the Jews:
Esther 3: Haman, honoured by the king, persuades him to punish 'a certain people' for disloyalty. His real reason is hatred of Mordecai.
Esther 4: Mordecai persuades Esther to plead for their protection.
Esther 5.1–8: Esther prepares two feasts for the king and Haman, and holds the first one.
Esther 5.9–14: Haman prepares gallows for Mordecai.
Esther 6: The king orders Haman to give Mordecai public honour for saving the king's life (see 2.19–23).
Esther 7: At the second feast Esther denounces Haman, and he is executed on the gallows which he built.
Esther 8—10: Victory for the Jews:
Esther 8: Mordecai is given Haman's place of honour. The decree ordering a Jewish massacre cannot be withdrawn, so the Jews are given authority to kill anyone who tries to carry it out against them.
Esther 9.1–19: The Jews take their revenge.
Esther 9.20–32: The Feast of Purim is officially appointed among the Jews.
Esther 10: The king honours Mordecai.
Notice that in the Common Bible Esther appears twice, the second time as part of the Apocrypha. In other versions the book appears once, with additional material in the Apocrypha entitled 'The rest of the chapters of the book of Esther'. These passages were included in the Septuagint version of this book, and not simply as an appendix. As you can see in the RSV Common Bible, the additions belong at various places in the book, and not only at the end. These extra chapters contain further details for the story, showing that Mordecai was warned in a dream what would happen. They contain prayers to God for help, and copies of the king's written commands. Probably these sections were added to the original version in order to give the book a deeper religious significance. In the Hebrew version there is no mention of God at all, except in a veiled way in Esther 4.14.

SOURCES

Scholars vary greatly in their attitude to this book.

(a) Some believe that it is firmly based in the actual experience of Jews living in Persia.

(b) Some believe that it is based on a pagan tradition and cult, perhaps originally celebrating a victory of the Babylonians over the Elamites. It has been suggested that the leading characters in the story are really the gods of these two people, and that their names provide evidence of this. Mordecai and Esther are supposed to be Marduk and Ishtar of the Babylonians, and Vashti and Haman are supposed to be Mashti and Humman of the Elamites.

(c) Other scholars believe that the story of Esther was composed as a piece of fiction to support the introduction of a new festival among the Jews: the feast of Purim (see below).

Neither the book, nor the feast of Purim are mentioned anywhere else in the Old Testament, or in the New Testament. In the Apocrypha the only other reference is in 2 Maccabees 15.36, where the date of the defeat of a Greek general is given by reference to 'the day of Mordecai'. Probably the feast was at first only celebrated among the Jews in Susa. Probably, too, the book was written for their use, as a reminder to them of the purpose of the festival. If so, it was probably written towards the end of the Persian Empire, a hundred years or more after the events which it describes.

Later, the custom was taken up by the Jews in other places, including Palestine. Perhaps it became popular in Palestine in the time of the Maccabees, who survived the persecution under Antiochus Epiphanes, and helped the people to regain their freedom.

Among the Jews this book is counted as one of the Five Scrolls which are read each at a different festival.

MESSAGE

The book is extremely nationalistic in outlook. The Hebrew version makes no mention of God, but the whole story is about the survival and victory of His people the Jews in the face of persecution. The feast of Purim has become a time of secular festivity, but probably it began as an occasion to celebrate God's care of His Chosen People.

There is much in the book which makes it unsuitable for use in Christian worship, especially the details of the way in which the new queen was chosen, which Esther seems to have approved. The joy of the Jews as they celebrated the killing of 75,000 'of those who hated them' (Esther 9.16–19) does not give us any insight into the ways of God with humankind. It expresses the hatred and contempt which is only too common between people of different races and nationalities.

STUDY SUGGESTIONS

WORD STUDY

1. Read the footnote in the Common Bible to Ezra 9.9. If the Hebrew means 'a wall', give two reasons why the translators insert the word 'protection' in the main text of this passage.

REVIEW OF CONTENT

2. What is Aramaic? Who used it, and in what period of history? Would the Jews who lived after the time of Nehemiah have been able to understand what was written in Ezra 4.8—6.18 and 7.12–26?
3. 'The laws known and enforced by Nehemiah were those of the Law Code of Deuteronomy' (p. 92). What aspects of that law code were used by Nehemiah in guiding the life of the community in Jerusalem? What problem does his ignorance of the Priestly Code of Law create for us in understanding the books of Ezra and Nehemiah?
4. What is unusual about the Hebrew version of the book of Esther compared with the other biblical books, and how did the writers of the Septuagint attempt to correct it?

BIBLE STUDY

5. Use the information in the section headed 'Sources' on pp. 89, 91 to set out the chapters and verses of Ezra and Nehemiah in the order in which they are presented in the Bible, indicating the source of each part. Your answer should continue the following list:
   Ezra 1.1 to 6.21: An earlier record of the return from exile and the rebuilding of the Temple, including a list of names from official records and an official document in Aramaic.
   Ezra 7.1–10: A summary from Ezra's own account
   Ezra 7.12–26: An official document in Aramaic.
6. Read Ezra 6.13–15, and answer the following questions:
   (a) What was the 'Province beyond the river' which was ruled by Tattenai and his friends?
   (b) What did Darius order these men to do? Was there any change from their previous attitude involved?
   (c) Who was Zechariah the son of Iddo?
   (d) What was 'their building' which the elders of the Jews finished?
   (e) If the building was completed in the reign of Darius, why does Ezra 6.14 refer to a decree of Artaxerxes who ruled later?

FURTHER STUDY AND DISCUSSION

7. Why were Ezra and Nehemiah so disturbed about marriages with foreign women? What differences do you think there would have been in the later history of Israel if they had taken a different attitude?
8. What is the place of each of the following in building a stable national community?
   (a) good government (b) personal morality (c) shared worship of God

6

Poetry and Wisdom

We can easily understand why those who prepared the Christian Canon placed the Law and the historical books first. The Christian faith is based on the story of God's saving action in making Himself known to human beings. This revelation began in the time of Abraham and his descendants, and continued with the experiences of Moses and the tribes of Israel. It led to the reign of David, and the record of the adventures of God's people in the times of the Philistines, and the Assyrian and Babylonian empires. All this needed setting out as clearly as possible in the books which stand at the beginning of the Christian Old Testament.

We can also readily recognize why those who prepared the Christian Canon placed the books of the Prophets at the end. These books record the preaching of men who believed that God had plans for His people and for the world. The books look forward to new things that God would do for the salvation of humanity, and for the establishment of His Kingdom. So they prepare the way for the Gospels which record the life and activities of Jesus Christ, the Son of the Living God. They introduce the records of people's response to the coming of Jesus as they are set out in the book of Acts and the Epistles of the New Testament.

Between these two major groups of books come five books which could be described as miscellaneous: Job, Psalms, Proverbs, Ecclesiastes and the Song of Solomon. Each is different in style and content from the others of the group. They all belong to the Writings in the Jewish Canon, and were only adopted formally as authoritative Scripture after the lifetime of Jesus. Like other Old Testament books, they each had a long history of development. Two of them, Proverbs and Psalms, are anthologies; that is, they were collections of material from different sources. All of them contain some poetry, ranging from human love-songs to hymns in praise of God. Three of them, Job, Proverbs and Ecclesiastes, are concerned with wisdom, that is, the results of human efforts to understand life and the problems raised for people of faith by their experiences of suffering.

We must begin our study of this group of books by looking more closely at the two major sorts of literature which they contain: Hebrew Poetry and Hebrew Wisdom.

TYPES OF LITERATURE

1. HEBREW POETRY

In chapter 3 we noted the practical difficulties in distinguishing poetry when we read the Old Testament in English. Not all versions of the Bible indicate where the Hebrew text consists of poetry. Those versions which do indicate where poetry is used do not always agree with each other about which passages of Scripture are poetical in the Hebrew. For example compare Proverbs 1—7 in the RSV Common Bible with the same chapters in the Good News Bible. This is partly because Hebrew manuscripts do not normally set out poetry in the style we are used to in English, but fill every line with writing whether or not the breaks in the poetry fall at the end of the line. It is time now that we should look at the way in which poetry is presented in Hebrew.

STRESSED SYLLABLES

The basic form of Hebrew poetry is a single line composed of a set number of stressed syllables. Stressed syllables are those which would correctly be spoken with more emphasis when making sense of a sentence. Stress is important in all speaking. Notice the difference it makes to the meaning of the sentence 'John went to visit Peter' according to the stress. If we stress 'John' then we are saying it was John rather than James or Andrew. If we stress 'went' we are saying that although John had said he was doubtful whether he would go, he did in fact do so. If we stress 'visit' we are saying that the purpose of his journey was to spend time with Peter, not to buy some food or deliver a letter, etc. If we stress 'Peter' we are saying that his visit was not for the sake of Peter's wife, or perhaps we are saying that after a long time of quarrelling John was at last prepared to make friends with Peter. Hebrew poetry makes use of the stressed words in what is written or said.

Between each stressed syllable at least one unstressed syllable is used. The number of stresses in each line is either two, three or four. Usually each single line of poetry is twinned with another, and sometimes a triplet is used. The number of stressed syllables can vary from line to line. Combinations in couplets are usually 3 + 3, but can be 4 + 3, 3 + 2 etc.

Clearly a detailed knowledge of the Hebrew text and how it should be spoken is needed to discover what patterns have been used. Another reason why scholars differ about which verses are poetry is that they have different ideas about the original form of the text. Those of us who have to study in English can recognize poetry both from the way it is presented in English, and from other qualities which come from the Hebrew forms of poetry.

COUPLETS AND TRIPLETS

The most significant evidence available to us is the fact that Hebrew Poetry usually consists of couplets and triplets. These normally compare and contrast ideas from line to line, often with a stronger expression of an idea in the second line. This is known as 'parallelism'. For example, look at Psalm 8 v.3:

'When I look at thy heavens, the work of thy fingers,
the moon and the stars which thou hast established;'

Both lines talk about what the Psalmist sees: 'thy heavens' and 'the moon and the stars'. These are different ways of talking about the same sight. Both lines also tell what the Psalmist believes about what he sees. They are 'the work of thy fingers' and things 'which thou hast established'. So two ways are used to say the same thing. There is perhaps a little development in the thinking between the first line which talks about the whole sky, and the second line which tells us about the things it contains at night.

In verse 4 of the same Psalm there is a definite development of thought in both parts of the two lines:

'What is man that thou art mindful of him,
and the son of man that thou dost care for him?'

The poet asks God a question: what is special about 'man' and about the 'son of man'? Both 'man' and 'son of man' are Hebrew terms meaning 'all human beings'. Probably a development is intended, in that God might be thought to be concerned chiefly about adults, but in fact is also interested in their offspring. Each line also tells us of the remarkable fact that despite the glories of the heavens God is 'mindful of' and 'cares for' human beings. The two terms used about what God does develop from one line to the next. In the first He remembers people, and in the second He does what is necessary to look after them.

In verse 5 there are two related ideas which both indicate the importance of human beings, but from opposite sides of their relationships:

'Yet thou hast made him little less than God,
and dost crown him with glory and honour.'

The upper limits of human status are set in the first line, in that we cannot claim equality with God. The second line indicates that humans do have a special status in creation that brings them respect from all other created things. (The Hebrew word *Elohim*, used in this couplet and translated in the Common Bible as 'God', is sometimes used in the Hebrew Scriptures to mean angels, and sometimes other gods. So scholars differ about how it should be translated here, and this affects the translation in the various English versions: see AV for 'angels', and NEB for 'a god'; and see pp. 22–23 above.)

This then is the chief feature of Hebrew poetry: two, or maybe three, lines which set similar ideas side by side, but in which there is usually a development of thought from one line to the next.

OTHER MARKS OF HEBREW POETRY

There are other features which often appear in this poetry:

(a) There is a widespread use of *metaphors*, that is, of picture-language used to express important ideas about God and about life. Psalm 23 gives a detailed comment on why we should think about God as a shepherd. The qualities of a shepherd helped the people of Israel to understand God.

(b) There can be a *refrain*, or *chorus*, which is repeated throughout a poem. Psalm 107 uses 'Let them thank God for his steadfast love' in verses 8, 15, 21 and 31.

(c) Some poems are *acrostics*. Each line, or each couplet, begins with a different letter of the alphabet in its normal order. Psalm 119 has eight lines of poetry for each letter of the alphabet. That is the reason for the wider spaces between lines 8 and 9, 16 and 17, etc.

(d) *Unusual words*, or words no longer used in ordinary conversation, are sometimes included in poetry. Psalm 74.14 refers to 'Leviathan', a many-headed sea monster mentioned in Canaanite literature, which was a symbol of chaos or evil.

2. HEBREW WISDOM

The twentieth century could be described as a time of great knowledge. Modern man has discovered many new facts about the world. These facts have led to many new inventions for our comfort and convenience. But often knowledge has taken the place of wisdom. We have known many things but we have not always lived wisely. Wisdom can be described as the understanding of human life and of our relationship with the universe and with each other. It can lead to personal well-being, and communal harmony.

Many tribes and nations possess traditional wisdom in the form of proverbs, or of stories which can help to explain our experiences in life and so encourage us to behave in ways which will lead to our welfare and that of our communities. Many of the peoples of ancient South Western Asia possessed similar wisdom. The book of Proverbs illustrates the traditions of Israel and, as we shall see, draws on the wisdom of other nations.

There is evidence in the books we have already studied that wisdom was highly valued among the people of Israel.

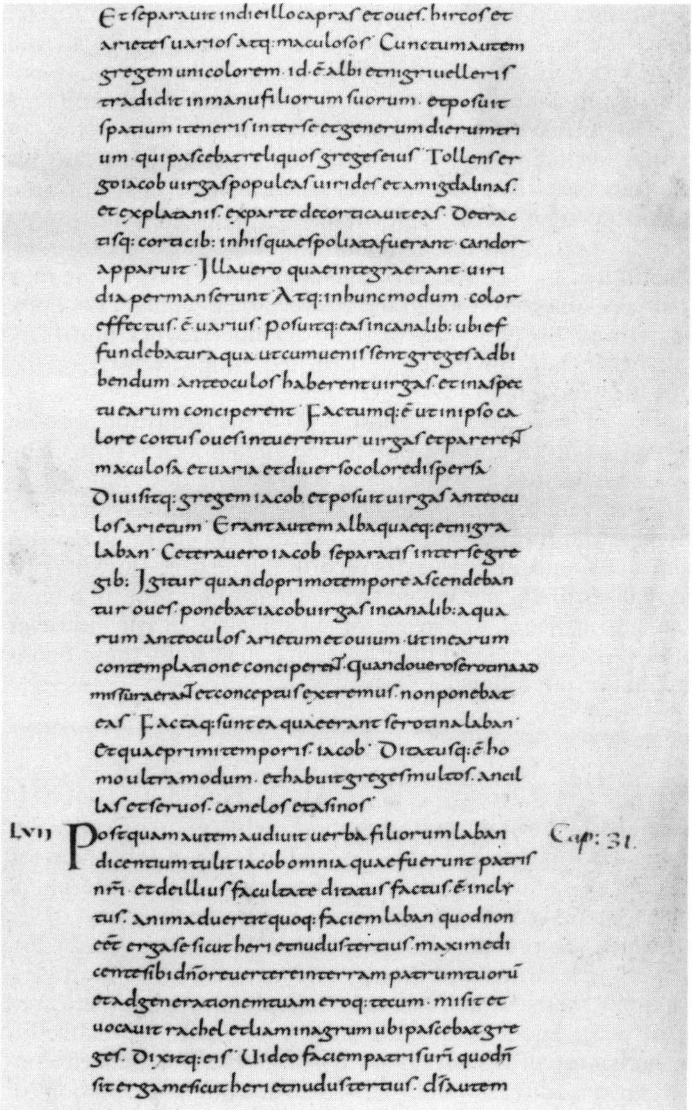
Et separauit in die illo capras et oues. hircos et
arietes uarios atq; maculosos. Cunctum autem
gregem unicolorem id ē albi et nigri uelleris
tradidit in manu filiorum suorum. et posuit
spatium itineris inter se et generum dierum tri
um qui pascebat reliquos greges eius. Tollens er
go iacob uirgas populeas uirides et amigdalinas.
et explatanis. ex parte decorticauit eas. Detrac
tisq; corticib; in his quae spoliata fuerant candor
apparuit. Illa uero quae integra erant uiri
dia permanserunt. Atq; in hunc modum color
effectus ē uarius. posuitq; eas in canalib; ubi ef
fundebatur aqua ut cum uenissent greges ad bi
bendum ante oculos haberent uirgas. et in aspec
tu earum conciperent. Factumq; ē ut in ipso ca
lore coitus oues intuerentur uirgas et parerent
maculosa et uaria et diuerso colore dispersa.
Diuisitq; gregem iacob et posuit uirgas ante ocu
los arietum. Erant autem alba quaeq; et nigra
laban. Cetera uero iacob separatis inter se gre
gib; Igitur quando primo tempore ascendeban
tur oues. ponebat iacob uirgas in canalib; aqua
rum ante oculos arietum et ouium ut in earum
contemplatione conciperent. Quando uero serotina ad
missura erat et conceptus extremus. non ponebat
eas. Factaq; sunt ea quae erant serotina laban.
Et quae primi temporis. iacob. Ditatusq; ē ho
mo ultra modum. et habuit greges multos. ancil
las et seruos. camelos et asinos.
LVII Postquam autem audiuit uerba filiorum laban Cap: 31.
dicentium tulit iacob omnia quae fuerunt patris
nr̄i et de illius facultate ditatus factus ē incly
tus. animaduertit quoq; faciem laban quod non
eēt erga se sicut heri et nudiustertius. maxime di
cente sibi dn̄o reuertere in terram patrum tuorū
et ad generationem tuam eroq; tecum. misit et
uocauit rachel et liam in agrum ubi pascebat gre
ges. Dixitq; eis. Uideo faciem patris uri quod n̄
sit erga me sicut heri et nudiustertius. ds autem

6.1 When the great Christian scholar Jerome prepared the new Latin version of the Bible known as the Vulgate, he began his revision of the Old Testament with the Psalms, before embarking on the Torah and other Jewish Scriptures. The page of it shown here is Genesis 30.5—31.35, about the birth of Joseph.

(a) They preserved the story of the Pharaoh who looked to Joseph for wisdom. The wise men of Egypt had failed him (Gen. 41.8), and the king was deeply impressed by the response of Joseph (Gen. 41.37–40). Joseph not only had a deep insight into the problem faced by Egypt, but provided a practical solution which was to benefit many people, including his own family. We should notice also his compassion and his ability to forgive, which helped to restore the unity of God's people (Gen. 50.15–21).

(b) They also recorded that Solomon was famous for his wisdom, and was consulted by the Queen of Sheba (1 Kings 10.1–6). He may have personally collected some of the wisdom to be found in the book of Proverbs. Sadly, Solomon's wisdom did not prevent him from making many enemies in Israel, and so preparing the way for the division of the kingdom.

The books of Job and Ecclesiastes take the study of wisdom further. Their writers are well aware that in human society wise living does not always lead to blessings, and wrongdoing does not always receive its just punishment. The book of Job tells the story of a righteous man who suffered many troubles, and discussed the reasons with his former friends. Ecclesiastes records the puzzled thinking of a man who realizes that according to the teaching of his time all human beings end up in Sheol, the place of meaningless death, however wisely or well they have lived their lives. We shall study these books in more detail in the following pages.

JOB

TITLE

The people of Israel treasured stories about righteous people. One of these was called Job (Ezek. 14.14, 20). In the book of Job, the story of Job is used as a starting point for a discussion of the suffering of righteous people. According to the book, Job lived in the land of Uz (Job 1.1), which was probably Edom (Lam. 4.21, compare Jer. 25.20). He was a very rich farmer with herds and lands of his own (Job 1.3). He was happily married, and had a large family for whom he cared deeply (Job 1.5). Suddenly he faced the loss of all his wealth, his children, and most of his servants (Job 1.13–19). He himself contracted a serious disease (Job 2.7–8). The whole discussion of suffering is presented as a debate between Job and his friends, and towards the end of the book, as a debate between Job and God.

OUTLINE

Some slight rearrangement of the chapters and verses of the book is necessary if we are to see clearly the steps of development which the editor of Job may have intended to follow. Most scholars think that the present text is out of order, but not all are agreed on what the outline should be.

Job 1—2: The Introduction
Job 1: Job suffers personal loss.
Job 2: Job suffers personal sickness.
Job 3—31: Job's debate with Three Friends:
Job 3.1–26: Job's lament.
Job 4.1—14.22: The first round of debate: Eliphaz (4.1—5.27)—Job (6.1—7.21); Bildad (8.1–22)—Job (9.1—10.22); Zophar (11.1–20)—Job (12.1—14.22).
Job 15.1—21.34: The second round of debate: Eliphaz (15.1–35)—Job (16.1—17.16); Bildad (18.1–21)—Job (19.1–29); Zophar (20.1–29)—Job (21.1–34).
Job 22.1—27.33: The third round of debate: Eliphaz (22.1–30)—Job (23.1—24.17); Bildad (25.1–6; 26.5–14)—Job (26.1–4; 27.1–12); Zophar (27.13–23)—Job (24.18–24).
Job 28.1–28: A hymn of wisdom.
Job 29.1—31.40: Job's oath of innocence.
Job 32—37: The speeches of Elihu.
Job 38.1—42.6: The speeches of the LORD:
Job 38.1—40.2: The LORD's first speech.
Job 40.3–5: Job submits.
Job 40.6—41.34: The LORD's second speech, including poems about Behemoth and Leviathan.
Job 42.1–6: Job submits again.
Job 42.7–17: The Conclusion: Job is restored.

SOURCES

Most scholars would agree that the book of Job was not written by a single author. Some of the sections listed above do not fully fit in with what is said in other places in the book. The main substance of the book can perhaps be taken as Job's debate with his friends (Job 3.1—27.23), his oath of innocence (Job 29.1—31.40), and the speeches of the LORD (Job 38.1—42.6 but perhaps omitting the poems about Behemoth and Leviathan). Most scholars would perhaps agree that the following parts of the book involve independent thought not fully in accord with the rest of Job.

(a) *The introduction: Job 1.1—2.13.* This section is in prose, but the rest of the book is in poetry. References to the heavenly court and to the Satan are not to be found in the rest of the book. The explanation of Job's suffering given here is not taken up again later.

(b) *A hymn of wisdom: Job 28.1–28.* This section makes no mention of the suffering of the innocent, but sets out the general belief of the wisdom literature that 'the fear of the LORD, that is wisdom' (28.28). Some scholars believe that it robs the speeches of the LORD of their significance by setting down already as words of Job himself the things which God finds it necessary to say to him at their meeting.

(c) *The speeches of Elihu: Job 32.1—37.24.* These verses are clearly an interruption, because Job 38.1 begins God's answer to Job's oath of innocence which ends at Job 31.40. Job never gives answer to Elihu; Elihu is not mentioned anywhere else in the book, and his answer to Job's problem is not mentioned either.

(d) *The poems of Behemoth and Leviathan: Job 40.15—41.34.* Scholars are divided in their interpretation of this passage. The footnotes to Job 40.15 and 41.1 in the RSV Common Bible show that some scholars believe these are poems about the Hippopotamus and the Crocodile, but the translators of the Common Bible leave the Hebrew names in the main text. This is because they believe that 'Behemoth' and 'Leviathan' are two mythical creatures which are described as submitting to God but which will not submit to humans.

(e) *The conclusion: Job 42.7–17.* This is a second passage of prose in the book of poetry. We might think that it belongs with the introduction, but it makes no mention of the heavenly court or the Satan. It gives a different answer to the problem of the suffering of the righteous from that set out in Job 1.1—2.13. It does mention the three friends of Job for whom he must pray because they 'have not spoken of me what is right, as my servant Job has.' (Job 42.8b.)

MESSAGE

The book of Job is concerned with the problem of the suffering of righteous people, which is part of what we today should call the 'problem of evil'. But it does not provide any answer which fully explains the reasons for suffering. The writer merely reviews the various answers which were given among the Jews, and concludes that although it is impossible for human beings to know the reasons for such suffering, they can submit to God without fearing that their trust and obedience will be betrayed.

The different sections of the book contain various attempts to answer the problem of suffering:

(a) In the introduction suffering is presented as a test of human righteousness. Truly righteous people do not live righteously for the sake of rewards of wealth, family happiness, or health. They do so because of their relationship with God, which continues in adversity as well as in prosperity (Job 1.21; 2.10).

Notice the place which is given to the Satan in this section of the book. He is an angel of God, whose function is to test people's hearts to see whether they are 'blameless and upright' (Job 1.8; 2.3). Later biblical teaching seems to be a development from this into a belief that Satan is openly rebellious against God. The Jews were taught to reject any view of the powers of evil which suggests that they have independent existence, and are not created by God, and so are capable of eternal opposition to the LORD. But God was not to be blamed for creating evil beings. Satan had been an angel with a rightful place in the service of God, but had rebelled, and had fallen into sin, just as human beings had done (see Vol. 3, pp. 49–52).

(b) In Job's debate with the three friends they argue that suffering results from sin, and that although Job appears righteous the fact of his suffering shows that he must be guilty of some serious fault (Job 4.7–9). Job admits that if he had sinned his suffering would be deserved. But he is confident that he has lived a righteous life yet God overwhelms him (Job 9.13–24). The friends are unable to comfort him, and continue to accuse him of sin (Job 22.6–10).

(c) In the hymn of Wisdom human security is in the fear of the Lord, and 'to depart from evil is understanding'. The traditional view in Israel is expressed, that people's well-being is to be found in obedience to God. Job has not found peace in the fullness of the Hebrew meaning of that word. He is suffering in spite of his innocence. The only contribution the poem makes to the debate on suffering is that wisdom is hard to find, and needs our full attention.

(d) In Job's oath of innocence we see how fully he has understood the nature of righteousness. He has done everything required of him, and can boldly say that he would fully accept his punishment if he had been deceitful, unfaithful to his wife, uncaring for his servants or lacking in compassion for the needy. He even recognizes that he must care what happens to his enemy (Job 31.5–29).

(e) In the speeches of Elihu this young man tells Job that the only hope of salvation is in the mercy of God, and that thanksgiving should be his song (Job 33.26–28). Job should be humble enough to look to God for further guidance in righteousness, rather than suppose that his righteousness gives him a claim on God (Job 34.31–32, 35.7).

(f) The climax of the book comes in the speeches of the LORD, who reminds Job that there are many things in creation which he does not understand and cannot control. His life is not dependent on such knowledge, it is sufficient for him to know that God is in control. So too with suffering, Job must leave all things to God's control and be content to know that God cares for all His creation. Job's personal experience of God is the final answer to his need:

I had heard of thee by the hearing of the ear
but now my eye sees thee:

therefore I despise myself,
and repent in dust and ashes. (Job 42.5)

He knows that God is not a distant being unable to hear or understand human troubles. God's care is shown in the fact that He has revealed Himself to Job. That is all that matters.

(g) The conclusion describes how all Job's fortunes were restored, 'twice as much as he had before' (Job 42.10). This expresses a view of suffering and prosperity often found in the Psalms. The prosperity of the wicked, and the suffering of the righteous are both temporary experiences, and both will quickly pass away, leading to times of just punishment and reward. This section of Job assumes this to be true in this world, and does not suggest that justice is complete only in the life to come.

According to the book of Job, suffering is a purely personal thing. There is no suggestion that because people live in a sinful community they have to share in the sufferings caused by their fellows. Job and his friends all expect that righteousness will be rewarded by blessing, and that suffering should only be the result of personal sin. This view of suffering is closely related to the teaching of Ezekiel: 'the soul that sins shall die' (Ezek. 18 and 33.10–20).

The writer of Job does not seem to have known the teaching of Deutero-Isaiah about the suffering of the 'Servant'. It is not suggested in the poetic part of the book that the sufferings of the righteous may help to redeem a nation, nor that it makes forgiveness possible for sinners, and restores their relationship with God, and their fellow human beings. There is a hint of this idea in the Conclusion, where the friends are instructed to ask Job to pray for them, because he is righteous and they are not. But the idea is not fully developed, and the writer probably mentioned it without having been influenced by the teaching of Deutero-Isaiah.

If the book of Job was written under the influence of the ideas of Ezekiel, but without any influence from the ideas of Deutero-Isaiah, then it was probably written during the Exile. But there is not enough evidence to decide for certain the date by which the book reached its present form, with the various additions which we have noted.

STUDY SUGGESTIONS

WORD STUDY

1. Explain the meaning of each of the following words which are used in the study of Hebrew Poetry:
   (a) stress (b) couplet (c) metaphor (d) refrain (e) acrostic
   Give an example to illustrate each word.

2. What are the differences in meaning between the following words:
   (a) knowledge (b) wisdom (c) understanding
   When you have answered this question, compare your answer with the answers you gave to question 1 on p. 71. What do you notice?

REVIEW OF CONTENT

3. (a) What are (i) the *basic form* and (ii) the *chief feature* of Hebrew poetry?
   (b) List *three* other features which often appear in Hebrew poetry.
4. What losses did Job suffer that led to his distress about his sufferings?

BIBLE STUDY

5. In which of the five major sections of Job would you expect to find the following verses, or parts of verses?
   (a) The LORD said to Satan, 'Whence have you come?'
   (b) Do you know when the mountain goats bring forth?
   Do you observe the calving of the hinds?
   (c) Think now, who that was innocent ever perished?
   Or where were the upright cut off?
   (d) My servant Job shall pray for you, for I will accept his prayer.
   (e) If you are righteous, what do you give to him;
   or what does he receive from your hand?
6. Use a concordance to discover: (a) how often the name 'Satan' is found in the Old Testament; (b) which books use the name; (c) from what period in the history of Israel these books come; (d) in what ways the writers of these books describe the relationship between Satan and God.

FURTHER STUDY AND DISCUSSION

7. How would you comfort a man whose wife had died of cancer, leaving him with several small children to care for? How would you respond to his complaints against God?

THE PSALMS

TITLES

The Hebrew title for this book is *Tehillim*, which means 'Hymns of Praise'. The Greek title *Psalmoi* (Luke 20.42; Acts 1.20) was a translation of a different Hebrew word, *Mizmor*. It means 'Songs to be sung to stringed instruments', and it is used in the heading of fifty-seven of the Psalms. Neither of these titles provides a description which fits all the Psalms, for there are several quite distinct sorts of religious poetry included in this book, and we know that wind and percussion instruments, as well as strings, were used in the Temple.

HISTORICAL BACKGROUND

The book of Psalms is like a present-day hymnbook in that it contains poems written at many different times. Scholars differ in their ideas about the dates when the various Psalms were written. Some believe that many of them come from before the Exile, others believe that almost all were written after the Exile.

Almost half of the Psalms are headed 'A Psalm of David', but though David may have composed some of them, there are many which he could not have written. Some of them, for example, mention the Temple, which had not been built in David's time (e.g. Pss. 5.7; 68.29).

The Psalms which refer to an Israelite king as a living person ruling over a free kingdom must have been written before the Exile (e.g. Pss. 2.6; 45.1). Psalm 137 clearly comes from the time of the Exile itself, and Psalm 126 belongs to the period after the Exile.

Whatever the date of the individual Psalms, the collecting together of Psalms to form one book was a long process which largely took place after the Exile, and was probably not completed until about 100 BC.

OUTLINE

The book of Psalms in the Bible is divided into five sections, themselves called 'Books', each with a numbered heading, starting at Psalms 1, 42, 73, 90, and 107 respectively. But careful study shows that 'Books' II and III belong together, and that 'Books' IV and V do also. Thus there were three main collections which were later put together to form the book we know:

(a) **'Book' I. Psalms 1—41:** The earliest collection, said to be Psalms of David, perhaps put together between 1000 and 900 BC.

(b) **'Books' II and III. Psalms 42—89:** including:
Psalms of the Sons of Korah, i.e. Psalms 42—49, 84, 85, 87, 88;
Further Psalms of David, i.e. Psalms 51—72, and 86;
Psalms of Asaph, i.e. Psalms 50, 73—83.
An editor corrected these Psalms by using the name *Elohim* (God) for God in place of the name *Yahweh* (LORD). These psalms were perhaps put together in one collection about 700 BC to 600 BC.

(c) **'Books' IV and V. Psalms 90—150:** including:
The Songs of Ascent, i.e. Psalms 120—134; sung going up to Jerusalem;
Further Psalms of David, i.e. Psalms 108—110, 138—145;

Miscellaneous Psalms, i.e. Psalms 90—104.
Between the groups are:
The Hallelujah or Hallel Psalms, i.e. Psalms 105—107, 111—118, 135, 136, 146—150.

Most of these Psalms begin or end with the Hebrew word 'Hallelujah', translated as 'Praise the LORD'.

Books IV and V were perhaps collected after the Exile, about 450 BC.

Notice that some of the Psalms are repeated in different sections of the book of Psalms. Psalm 14 is the same as Psalm 53; Psalm 40.13–17 is the same as Psalm 70; Psalm 108 is Psalm 57.7–11 plus Psalm 60.5–12.

Notice also that some Psalms were divided in half when the book of Psalms was produced, and that they need to be treated as belonging together: Psalm 9 plus Psalm 10; Psalm 42 plus Psalm 43.

SOURCES

We have already noticed that about half of the Psalms are said to be 'of David', but that many of these could not have been written by him. Later editors have added these notes in an attempt to explain the origin of the Psalms, but their guesses are not always reliable evidence. They too easily assumed that Psalms were written by David. Probably they were also wrong to suggest that Moses wrote Psalm 90, and that Solomon wrote Psalm 72 and Psalm 127.

When these editors mention the names of people who were not famous for any other reason than that they wrote Psalms, we can be more confident that the information they give is correct. Two groups of Psalms are headed with names of this kind: those of the Sons of Korah (Pss. 42—49, 84, 85, 87, and 88), and those of Asaph (Pss. 50, 73–83).

Asaph was the first man, other than David, to be remembered for composing Psalms (see 2 Chron. 29.30). His descendants are listed among the Levites working in the second Temple after the Exile (Neh. 7.44; 11.22). The Psalms said to be 'of Asaph' probably do not all come from the same time, so Asaph's descendants must have been responsible for collecting or composing some of them.

Korah is mentioned in Numbers 16, where he is described as a layman who opposed the exclusive authority of the priests. The sons of Korah claimed a right to lead the worship in the Temple, and found the opportunity to do this in Psalm singing. Heman seems to have been one of the sons of Korah (see Ps. 88). He seems to have founded his own family of singers (see 1 Chron. 25.1, 6; 2 Chron 5.12). Jeduthun, who is also mentioned in these verses, seems to have had something to do with Psalms 39, 62 and 77. But two of these are called Psalms of David, and the third is a Psalm of Asaph, so it is not clear how Jeduthun was involved; perhaps he provided some special musical setting for the Psalm. Jeduthun seems to have had an alternative name: Ethan (see 1 Chron. 15.19), and this name is given as the composer of Psalm 89.

MESSAGE

The Psalms cover a wide range of religious thought and experience, and they cannot be summarized in any simple statement of faith. But we shall find it helpful to know which Psalms are concerned with the same kind of experience. So we classify them below according to subject, using the suggestions made by Georg Fohrer. Under several of the headings the Psalms can be divided into two groups: (1) those expressing the experiences of the nation, described here as *community* Psalms, and (2) those expressing the experiences of one particular person, described here as *individual* Psalms.

Hymns, expressing praise to God.
General: 8; 19.1–6; 29; 33; 77.16–20; 89.1–18; 95; 100; 103; 104; 113; 114; 117; 134; 135; 145; 146; 147; 148; 149; 150.
Monotheistic, expressing the belief that God rules over all creation: 47; 93; 96; 97; 98; 99.
Zion Songs, expressing the belief that Jerusalem has an important place in God's plans for the world: 46; 48; 76; 84; 87; 122.
Pilgrimage Songs, expressing the joy of Jews visiting Jerusalem for one of the feasts: 15; 24; 121.

Laments, expressing distress in face of trouble.
Community Laments: 12; 60; 74; 79; 80; 83; 85; 90; 94.1–11; 123; 126; 137.
Individual Laments: 3; 4; 5; 6; 7; 13; 14 (= 53); 17; 25; 26; 27.7–14; 28; 35; 38; 39; 40.13–17 (= 70); 42—43; 51; 52; 53 (= 14); 54; 55; 57; 59; 61; 64; 69; 70 (= 40.13–17); 71; 77.1–15; 86; 88; 102; 109; 120; 130; 139; 140; 141; 142; 143.

Confidence, expressing faith in God, and in His power to save.
Community Songs: 125; 129.
Individual Songs: 11; 16; 23; 27.1–6; 62; 131.

Thanksgiving, expressing praise for God's care for His people.
Community Thanksgiving: 65; 66; 67; 107; 118; 124.
Individual Thanksgiving: 18.1–30; 30; 32; 40.1–11; 41; 63; 94.12–23; 111; 116; 136; 138.

Royal Psalms, expressing belief in God's rule, exercised through Israel's anointed kings: 2; 18.31–50; 20; 21; 44; 45; 72; 89.19–52; 101; 110; 132; 144.

Wisdom and Teaching Psalms, expressing the belief that upright living is pleasing to God, and brings blessing: 1; 19.7–14; 34; 37; 49; 73; 78; 91; 105; 106; 112; 119; 127; 128; 133.

Judgement Liturgies, expressing God's condemnation of the unrighteous: 50; 81; 82.

Mixed Psalms, expressing more than one theme.
Individual Lament and Thanksgiving: 9; 10; 22; 31; 56.
Other Mixtures: 36; 68; 75; 92; 108; 115.

MUSICAL DIRECTIONS IN THE PSALMS

Some technical words are included in the headings to the Psalms. Some of these describe the sort of Psalm that follows: e.g. *Psalm* means a song for use with a musical instrument; and *Maskil* probably means a song that gives meaning to the experiences of life (Pss. 32; 42 and 43; 44; etc.). *Miktam* (Pss. 16; 56; etc.) and *Shiggaion* (Ps. 7) were probably other sorts, but the meaning of these Hebrew words is no longer known.

Other technical words give instructions to the singer. The commonest of these is *Selah*, which frequently occurs between the sections of a Psalm (e.g. Ps. 66.4, 7 and 15) and probably means that the stringed instruments are to be played alone for a time before the next words are sung. *Higgaion* (Ps. 9.16) also may refer to the music of stringed instruments. *Sheminith* (see the headings to Pss. 6; 12) seems to mean 'on the octave', but some scholars doubt whether Hebrew music used the octaves, on which most Western music is based.

The names of popular tunes are given at the beginning of some of the Psalms to indicate the music to be used in singing the Psalm. *Gittith* (Pss. 81; 84) probably means 'the wine-press song'. 'Do not destroy' (Pss. 57; 58; 59, and 75) is the title of a song of the grape harvest, which is also mentioned in Isaiah 65.8. 'Lilies' (Pss. 45, 69, and 80), 'The Dove on far-off Terebinths' (Ps. 56), and 'The Hind of the Dawn' (Ps. 22) are all titles of songs which were popular at the time. Unfortunately no written music exists to preserve any of the tunes that were used to sing these songs.

PROVERBS

TITLE

The Hebrew title for this book is the word '*Mashal*', which can be translated in several different ways: taunt song (Mic. 2.4), byword (Ps. 44.14), discourse (Num. 23.7), allegory (Ezek. 17.2), as well as proverbs (Ps. 49.4). The English title has been copied from the Vulgate, Jerome's Latin Bible, where the word *Proverbia* is used.

6.2 '*Psalm* means a song "to be sung to stringed instruments" . . . wind and percussion instruments . . . were also used in the Temple' (pp. 107, 108). One stringed instrument of that time was the zither, as shown in this carving from Caanan.

6.3 These synagogue musicians (from the Joel ben Simeon commentary), belong to the 15th century AD, and both Jews and Christians still sing the Psalms to music today.

The book contains a wide selection of wisdom literature, more than can be covered by the word Proverbs.

HISTORICAL BACKGROUND

The first verse of the book provides a title: 'The Proverbs of Solomon, son of David, king of Israel'. Unlike the first verse of many of the prophetic books, this title is not intended to describe the whole book. Other titles are given in Proverbs 10.1; 22.17; 24.23; 25.1; 30.1; and 31.1.

Two of these other titles repeat the idea that the Proverbs belong to Solomon (Prov. 10.1 and 25.1), but the remainder mention different sources. Two teachers from Massa in the northern part of the lands across the Jordan are named (Prov. 30.1 and 31.1). Their 'words' come from a foreign source. As we shall see there is evidence that other parts of the book of Proverbs have been adapted from Egyptian and Assyrian sources.

The book of Proverbs is in fact a collection of what is known as Wisdom Literature. This sort of writing was used to pass on, from one generation to the next, information about the best way to live happily and peacefully with one's neighbours. Similar writings were found among the Egyptians, and in Mesopotamia and Palestine, from very early times. We do not know exactly when the collection in the Bible was put together, and it contains material from widely different times and sources. It could not have reached its present form earlier than 400 BC, and may not have done so before 150 BC (see p. 114).

OUTLINE

Proverbs 1—9: The Proverbs of Solomon: fairly long poems in which a father speaks to his son, or in which 'Wisdom' is made to speak to all people.
Proverbs 10.1—22.16: The Proverbs of Solomon: about 375 separate sayings with very little evidence of order.
Proverbs 22.17—24.22: The words of the wise: 30 sayings (Prov. 22.20) partly based on an Egyptian source.
Proverbs 24.23–34: Sayings of the wise.
Proverbs 25—29: Proverbs of Solomon, which 'the men of Hezekiah king of Judah copied'.
Proverbs 30: The words of Agur son of Jakeh in two parts: Proverbs 30.1–10 and 30.11–33.
Proverbs 31.1–9: The words of Lemuel, king of Massa.
Proverbs 31.10–31: A good wife: A poem in which each line begins with a different letter of the Hebrew alphabet in turn.

In the Septuagint, the first Greek translation, some of these sections are in a different order, which helps us to recognize where each section ends.

SOURCES

Proverbs 10.1—22.16 and 25—29 contain the sort of sayings that were likely to be known and used around the time of Solomon, and some of them may have been composed by the king himself. But some of the sayings about kings seem to be too boastful to have been written by him, and probably come from other sources (e.g. Prov. 16.10, 14; 20.2, 8, 28; 25.2, 6). It is quite probable that the servants of king Hezekiah did collect and preserve the sayings in Proverbs 25—29.

Proverbs 22.17—24.22 contains material borrowed from foreign sources. Proverbs 22.17—23.12 is clearly adapted from an Egyptian book of wisdom, called 'The Instructions of Amen-em-Ope', which was probably written around 1000 BC. The verses in the book of Proverbs are not a word-for-word copy of the Egyptian book, but like that book they are divided into thirty sections, and many of the ideas are the same. Proverbs 23.13–14 is probably adapted from 'The Instructions to Ahikar', which describes life in Assyria in its time of power.

The short section 24.23–34 is too brief to give us any idea of its origin.

Proverbs 30 and 31.1–9 come from the writings of men belonging to a northern Arabian tribe, who lived in Massa. Agur and Lemuel are not known to us apart from the information in the book of Proverbs, and no date can be given for their work. The poem in 31.10–31 cannot be easily dated either.

Proverbs 1–9 is probably the most recent part of the whole book. Its long well-constructed sentences are similar to those found in other literature from after the Exile. The ideas about Wisdom given here are similar in some ways to ideas found in Greek literature.

The book as a whole had not reached its final form in Hebrew at the time when it was translated into Greek in the second century BC. The writers of the Septuagint felt free to arrange the various sections in a different order from the order we know in the Hebrew version. The writer of Sirach, in the Apocrypha, knew the Proverbs of Solomon when he wrote his book around 180 BC (Sirach 47.17), but not necessarily in their final order and form. The book may only have reached its final form by about 150 BC.

MESSAGE

The book of Proverbs is typical of Wisdom Literature. Its writers were concerned to share with their readers an understanding of how to live well in the world that God has created. Just as there is a physical order that can be recognized and used for the benefit of human beings, so there is a moral order which needs study and understanding (Prov. 25.23; 26.20; 27.17). Children need to be taught wisdom, even if this demands stern discipline (Prov. 13.24; 22.15; 29.15, 17). For adults two chief dangers may hinder wise living. The first is laziness (Prov. 6.6; 13.4; 20.4; 24.33–34); the second is drunkenness (Prov. 20.1; 21.17; 23.29–30). It is important to choose the right companions because the wrong ones will turn us away from wisdom (Prov. 13.20; 24.1–2; 28.7). Faithfulness to a good wife brings blessings (Prov. 5.18–19; 18.22; 19.14). What we think and what we say will show the measure of our wisdom (Prov. 11.12–13; 16.23; 21.23).

Other qualities encouraged in this book are obedience (Prov. 10.1); humility (Prov. 11.2; 15.33); self-control (Prov. 14.17; 18.13; 25.28); truthfulness (Prov. 10.10; 12.22); kindness (Prov. 11.17); generosity (Prov. 11.25); cheerfulness (Prov. 15.13); justice (Prov. 21.15); and faithfulness (Prov. 25.13).

The first section of the book is later in origin than the others, and contains poems about the importance of wisdom. Much of this section is similar in its message to the rest of the book, but a few passages stand out because in them Wisdom herself is heard to speak. These passages are 1.20–33; 8.1–31; 9.1–6. One section among these is so remarkable that it needs special attention.

Proverbs 8.22–31 is a passage of poetry in which the writer attempts to express difficult ideas in a way that will stimulate his readers to think deep thoughts. Every reader is likely to present a different interpretation of the significance of these verses. Here are the thoughts it rouses in my mind:

(a) Only living, active, thinking beings can possess wisdom, because its very nature is to understand life and its relationships. Some animals develop wisdom to meet their experiences of life, but human beings are capable of a deeper and more widely related wisdom. No human can claim to possess all wisdom. We recognize that we need to learn from wisdom. But where does that wisdom find full expression? Who can teach us day by day? We could say that God possesses wisdom, and that it is part of His nature, and part of what He reveals.

(b) But the writer of this passage seems to want to explore that idea further. As humans we can learn from wisdom. Does God then, like ourselves, look to wisdom as a greater authority than Himself which can guide His activities? If He did that He would cease to be God. Yet it is quite clear that God used wisdom in creating the universe. The world is designed with true knowledge and understanding. Where did God's wisdom come from? The writer of this passage sees wisdom as coming from 'the first of his acts of old'. He says on behalf of wisdom, 'The LORD created me at the beginning of his work ... I was beside him, like a master workman; and I was daily his delight'.

(c) What is the nature of the relationship between God and Wisdom in this passage? The Hebrew word for '*created*' in verse 22 is used in Gen. 14.19 and 22 where it is translated as 'maker' in the phrase 'maker of heaven and earth'. But it is used elsewhere in the book of Proverbs simply to mean 'get' in the phrase 'get wisdom' (Prov. 4.5; 16.16; 19.8). Either could be the meaning here, but several modern translations share with the Common Bible in using the word 'created'. The Hebrew word for '*set up*' in verse 23 is also used in Ps. 2.6 where God says 'I have set my king on Zion'. The same word occurs in Is. 29.10 where the prophet says, 'For the LORD has poured out upon you a spirit of deep sleep'. In all three cases the emphasis is on the fact that God is in control, and able to achieve His purposes. The Hebrew word for '*brought forth*' in verses 24 and 25 is regularly used of a woman giving birth, as in Ps. 51.5, but it is also used of the first human being created, as in Job 15.7, which is a close parallel to the use in the passage we are studying. No clearer language can be found to describe what happened, since we are dealing with the unique mystery of God's creative powers.

(d) This passage has been taken up by Christians as being comparable with what is said about 'the Word' in John 1.1–3. It probably assisted the early Christian Church in thinking about the relationship between Jesus and His father.

ECCLESIASTES (or THE PREACHER)

TITLE

The Hebrew title for this book is *Koheleth*, which is translated as 'Preacher' in Ecclesiastes 1.1, 12; 7.27; and 12.8–10. It is an unusual word in Hebrew, but it seems to mean 'One who speaks to an assembly'. The English title comes from the Septuagint, where it stands for the leader of an *ekklesia*, the Greek word later used for 'Church', meaning assembly, congregation, community.

HISTORICAL BACKGROUND

In Ecclesiastes 1.1 the Preacher is said to be 'the son of David, king of Jerusalem'. This suggests that the writer was Solomon. But the book contains evidence that the writer was not Solomon. The Preacher speaks of 'all who were over Jerusalem before me' (Eccles. 1.16; 2.9). Solomon was only the second king in Jerusalem and would not have used the word 'all' to describe one king, David. The Preacher also speaks as though he had once been king, and was no longer ruling (Eccles. 1.12). Solomon was king until he died, and never gave up his throne, so he could not have written these words.

The Preacher is also described as a teacher of wisdom (Eccles. 12.9). This could be a description of Solomon, who was believed to have collected and taught many of the wise sayings of his time. But since, as we have seen, the writer is unlikely to have been Solomon himself, the later teacher of wisdom probably thought of himself as a disciple of Solomon, inheriting his wisdom and using it in his own work. We shall see later what part the writer of Ecclesiastes played in the development of Jewish ideas about God, and human life.

OUTLINE

Ecclesiastes 1.1—6.12: Human life is filled with meaningless effort:
Ecclesiastes 1.1—3.15: Strivings for the satisfaction of desires, for knowledge, for pleasure, and for wisdom are all useless,
Ecclesiastes 3.16—5.20: Justice and fair rewards are not to be found in this life,
Ecclesiastes 6.1–12: All hopes and ambitions remain unfulfilled.
Ecclesiastes 7.1—12.7: How to live out human life:
Advice to those who know the uselessness of human striving: be moderate in all things.
Ecclesiastes 12.8–14: The Preacher and his Message described.

SOURCES

The language of the book is a very late form of Hebrew, with many Aramaic words and constructions. Some scholars have even suggested that it was first written in Aramaic and then translated into Hebrew, but there is not really enough evidence for this. It was probably written some time between 250 and 200 BC, when Aramaic had become widely known and widely used among the Jews. Copies of the book in Hebrew have been found among the Dead Sea Scrolls, and these appear to have been prepared between 200 and 150 BC.

The general pattern of the teaching contained in the book suggests that it belongs to a late stage in the development of Hebrew wisdom literature. The writer expresses the traditional belief that obedience to God is the source of wisdom, but sets against this the idea that even wisdom cannot provide a meaning for life (e.g. Eccles. 2.21, 26). The idea of fate, as a pattern of life that is fixed beforehand and cannot be changed, is also found in this book (Eccles. 2.14; 3.19; 9.2–3).

Scholars have suggested that foreign ideas may have influenced the style and contents of this book. And they have tried to show a connection between the teachings of the Preacher and the ideas of the various schools of Greek Philosophy. There is no doubt that Greek ideas were known in a general way among the Jews when this book was written, but Egyptian writings may have influenced the thought of the Preacher even more. The earlier Jewish writers passed on a whole range of ideas to the Preacher, who seems especially to have known the book of Job; e.g. compare Ecclesiastes 5.15 with Job 1.21.

MESSAGE

The book presents a number of conflicting ideas about life. For example we are told that Wisdom brings no reward and is a vanity, and yet it is a gift from God (Eccles. 2.15, 16, 26). Feasting is the best way of life but so is mourning (Eccles. 2.24; 7.2). It is better to be dead, but it is also better to be alive (Eccles. 4.2; 9.4).

Scholars vary considerably in their explanation of these opposing ideas. Some think of a single writer whose ideas changed according to his mood at the time he wrote. Others think that he quoted traditional ideas in order to oppose them. Yet others believe that the verses which present the more usual Jewish view of things were added by a later editor to make the book more acceptable. It has even been suggested that the whole book is a discussion between two people, even though it is impossible for us now to divide the book into two separate parts to form a dialogue.

Probably the first of these ideas is correct. The writer was deeply troubled by his failure to understand his experiences of life. As soon as he put forward one interpretation he found equal reason to support an opposite point of view. Nothing made sense to him any more. Every idea seemed a foolish vanity.

But he did not lose his faith in God, who created all things and controls all things (Eccles. 3.11, 14; 9.1; 12.1). He believed that it was God's intention that people should enjoy life (Eccles. 2.24; 3.13). He also believed that God is the judge of all human beings (Eccles 3.17; 8.12–13; 11.9). Yet he had discovered that there is no justice in this life (Eccles. 8.4; 9.15; 10.5–6). Whatever sort of life we live, we all come to the same end, we all die (Eccles. 2.15–16; 3.19–20).

The writer accepted the traditional Jewish view of death. He believed that after death all human beings enter a place called *Sheol*. There they live an empty, meaningless sort of life, with 'no work, or thought, or knowledge' (Eccles. 9.10). Everything that a person has lived for and valued comes to an end (Eccles. 9.5–6). What then is the purpose of life? What can be achieved that is worthwhile? Does it really matter whether a person tries to live a good upright life, or chooses lust, greed, and violence? The writer concluded that life is meaningless because death is so empty and useless.

At one point in the book the writer thought briefly about the possibility that human death leads to something better than Sheol.

But he had no confidence in the idea, and quickly dismissed it from his mind (Eccles. 3.21–22). This explains the attitude of despair which we find so frequently expressed in the book.

Earlier wisdom literature had simply expressed ideas that would provide a guide for life in this world. Ecclesiastes shows that worldly wisdom, even when it is based on the fear of God, does not provide a wholly adequate interpretation of life. Death throws everything else out of gear, making all effort and all wisdom pointless, mere vanities.

THE SONG OF SOLOMON

TITLE

Scholars use several different titles for this book. These titles all come in one way or another from the first verse of the book: 'The Song of Songs, which is Solomon's'. In the AV and Common Bible the title is 'the Song of Solomon'. In the RV and NEB the book is called 'the Song of Songs'. This title is also used in Hebrew Bibles. It is based on a Hebrew idiom which should perhaps be translated 'the best of songs'. This would be similar to the translation of a Hebrew phrase as 'the most holy', which would in a more literal translation read 'the holy of holies' (e.g. 1 Kings 8.6). Notice also that in Ecclesiastes 'Vanity of vanities', means 'the most vain', that is, 'completely worthless' (e.g. Eccles. 1.2).

Solomon had a reputation for writing songs, so the title could mean that this was the best of them all (1 Kings 4.32). Roman Catholics prefer to call the book 'Canticles'. This title comes from Jerome's Latin translation, the Vulgate, and means 'Hymns'.

HISTORICAL BACKGROUND

Song 1.1 suggests that the book belongs to Solomon. This king is mentioned in Song 1.5; 3.7, 9, 11; 8.11, 12, usually to make a comparison with his glory. But there is very little evidence to support the idea that the poems in this book were written by Solomon, or that they describe his experiences of love.

Tirzah is mentioned in Song 6.4 as a city comparable with Jerusalem. It was the capital of the Northern Kingdom after the time of Solomon and before Samaria became the capital in the reign of Omri (e.g. 1 Kings 15.21, 33). So this verse at its earliest must belong to a time after the division of the kingdom, and thus later than Solomon.

The book contains many Aramaic language forms which belong to the period after the Exile, when this language was in common use among the Jews. The word translated 'orchard' in Song 4.13 has been borrowed from the Persian language, and the word translated 'palanquin' in Song 3.9 is Greek in origin. These words also must have been included after the Exile.

Apart from this evidence there is no other way of discovering the historical background to this book. Probably it was compiled from poems from many different times in the history of Israel, but was put into its final form between 300–250 BC.

OUTLINE

There is no clear outline, and little evidence of order in the book. Scholars have given widely different interpretations of the Song of Solomon, and have divided the book into sections which suit their idea of its purpose and contents. All we can say for certain is that the different parts of the book are addressed to different people, and from this fact we can discover natural divisions in the text, as follows:

Song 1.2–4, 15–17; 7.10–12: A girl addresses her lover, and
Song 1.12–14; 2.8–17; 6.11–12; 8.1–3, 10: A girl thinks about her lover.
Song 1.9–11; 4.1—5.1; 6.4–10; 7.1–9: A man addresses his beloved, and
Song 6.13; 8.5: A man thinks about his beloved.
Song 1.7–8; 2.1–3; 8.13–14: Dialogue between the girl and the man.
Song 1.5–6; 2.4–7; 3.1–11; 5.2—6.3; 8.4: The girl speaks to her woman friends (with their replies in **5.9** and **6.1**).

MESSAGE

The book has been interpreted in several different ways, apart from the most obvious idea that it is a book of love poetry. Scholars have tried to find hidden meaning in the book, because they have not felt satisfied that ordinary human love poetry would have been preserved in Israel and included among the sacred writings, as this book has been. The following interpretations have been suggested:

1. Perhaps the subject of the book is God's relationship with Israel, or Christ's relationship with the Church, or else the relationship of God or Christ with a human soul. This sort of interpretation explains why the book is read at the festival of Passover, to celebrate God's work as Saviour of Israel. Some of those who favour this interpretation believe there is a hidden meaning for each part of the human body mentioned in the book, e.g. they take the woman's navel (Song 7.2) as a symbol standing for the Communion cup. Such an idea is foolish, and illustrates the danger in getting away from the natural meaning of the words.

2. Perhaps the book was originally written in connection with pagan fertility rites, and was later altered and adapted for use in Israelite worship at the New Year Festival. However, the Jews were

unlikely to adopt a thoroughly pagan book and use it in their own religious ceremonies. And there is no clear evidence that the Jews observed a New Year Festival in biblical times.

3. Perhaps the book records a romantic drama concerning Solomon's relationship with a country girl. According to one view his love was accepted, but according to another the girl rejected Solomon and returned to the shepherd whom she loved. Some scholars have connected this interpretation with 1 Kings 2.13–25, which they say tells the story of Solomon's failure to take Abishag the Shunammite as his wife. They note the fact that the 'beloved' in the Song of Solomon was a Shulammite (Song 6.13). However, the fact that there are two different ideas of the form of the story shows that the book cannot easily be set out in a dramatic form as this theory suggests. And the tribal origins of Abishag and the beloved are not the same.

4. Perhaps the book consists of the ritual songs for a marriage feast, and in its original form was prepared for Solomon's marriage to Pharaoh's daughter. It is true that such ritual songs were known in the ancient Near East, but not all the poems in this book are concerned with marriage. Some scholars try to show that the book records the progress from attraction to courtship, and finally to marriage and the bliss of love's fulfilment, but there is no real evidence of order and development in the book.

So we are left with the idea that the book is a collection of love poetry. The only religious interpretation that can rightly be given to it is that it sets the seal of God's approval on sex, love, and marriage. This is a subject wholly worthy of inclusion in the sacred writings of Israel.

STUDY SUGGESTIONS

WORD STUDY

1. What sorts of literature can be described by the Hebrew word *Mashal?* Give an example of each.

REVIEW OF CONTENT

2. What evidence is there in the following Psalms regarding the date at which they were written?
   (a) Ps. 18.50 (b) Ps. 27.4 (c) Ps. 126
3. Proverbs 22.17–23.12 is related to an Egyptian book of wisdom
   (a) What is the title of the Egyptian book?
   (b) Was it right or wrong for a servant of the LORD to make use of ideas that come from pagan writings?
   (c) What evidence can you find in the biblical passage that it has been adapted to serve faithful Israelites?

BIBLE STUDY

4. Explain the headings to each of the following Psalms:
   8 42 75 113 125
5. The book of Proverbs is largely concerned with Wisdom. The 'wise man' is contrasted with the fool. Use a concordance to help you list at least six things which a fool will do, which a wise person will avoid.
6. (a) What is the meaning of *vanity* in the book of Ecclesiastes?
   (b) Use a concordance to make as complete a list as you can of all the things that the Preacher called 'vanity', giving the relevant verse reference for each.
   (c) What belief did the Preacher lack that caused him to feel that life was meaningless?
7. (a) Examine the following Psalms and say whether they express (i) Individual Laments, (ii) Individual Songs of Confidence, or (iii) Individual Thanksgiving:
   3 23 32 64 116 131
   (b) Do you think these Psalms can properly be used for public worship? Give reasons for your answer.

FURTHER STUDY AND DISCUSSION

8. It has been said about the composers of the Psalms that 'the intense emotions of these earnest souls, their longing for God's presence, their joyful faith, flaming hatred, agonizing doubts, black hours of despair all find expression in the Psalter' (i.e. Book of Psalms). Illustrate each of these five emotions by quoting verses in which they are expressed in the Psalms.

7

The Latter Prophets: Major

We now look at the books which come at the end of the English Old Testament: from Isaiah to Malachi. There are fifteen of them, known as the *Latter Prophets* to distinguish them from those known as the Former Prophets, which we studied in chapter 4. Mixed among the Latter Prophets are two books: Lamentations and Daniel, which belong to the third section of the Hebrew Scriptures. We shall study these books in turn with the Latter Prophets.

Three of the books of the Latter Prophets are long enough to have needed the space of a whole scroll in the Hebrew manuscript: Isaiah (66 chapters), Jeremiah (52 chapters), and Ezekiel (48 chapters). These are called the *Major Prophets*, and we study them in this chapter and the next.

The remaining twelve books are quite short. The two longest of them have only 14 chapters each: Hosea and Zechariah. The shortest has only one chapter: Obadiah. These twelve books are called the *Minor Prophets*. They were at one time contained in a single scroll called 'The Book of the Twelve', even though they record the work of prophets from widely different times in the history of Israel. We shall study the Minor Prophets in chapter 9.

THE USE OF WRITING

The earliest of the prophets made no use of writing themselves, and nobody attempted to keep a complete record of their work. If they were remembered at all, it was for the part which they had played in the history of Israel and Judah. The historians of ancient times thought it necessary to write about such men as Samuel and Nathan because of their importance in Israel's history. The books of Samuel and Kings, and from a later time Chronicles, contain the records of these and other early prophets.

Scholars believe that written records were made of events involving Elijah and Elisha, before the book of Kings was compiled, and that the editor of the book of Kings was then able to use these earlier records in preparing his book. But if there were such earlier records, they are lost, and we depend on the book of Kings for information about these prophets.

Amos was probably the first of the prophets for whom a special book was prepared, in order to record his work for its own sake. Careful study of the book shows that much of it was written after Amos had completed his service as a prophet. Perhaps it was written by one of his disciples. The writer's purpose was to record some of Amos's messages. But he also included an account of one of the major events of Amos's ministry; his visit to Bethel (Amos 7.10–17). Some parts of the book are written as if Amos himself is telling of what happened to him (Amos 7.1–9, etc.). But these sections were probably written down by his disciples to record how he explained his experiences to them. It is unlikely that Amos himself thought that his story should be recorded for later generations to read. The same may also be true of Hosea, the prophet who followed Amos in the history of Israel.

Isaiah of Jerusalem twice instructed his disciples to make a written record of the messages he had delivered, in order to preserve what he had said for the sake of later generations. The people of his own day refused to listen to him, but later generations would know he had spoken the truth. They would see that his warnings had been fulfilled (Isa. 8.16; 30.8). These records which Isaiah's disciples made were used later on when the book of Isaiah was prepared. It seems possible that Isaiah himself recorded the story of his call (Isa. 6). But it may be that his disciples recorded what he had told them, in the words he had used. They also wrote accounts in their own words of what he did (Isa. 7, etc.).

Jeremiah made use of writing for the sake of the people of his own day. At one time in his life he was forbidden to preach, and so he employed Baruch to write down his messages. He then sent Baruch to read them in public, so that people could hear again what Jeremiah felt God wanted him to say to them (Jer. 36.4–8).

Later prophets used writing as the normal way of preparing and delivering their messages. We can see this especially in Ezekiel, where the carefully recorded dates suggest that the prophet made his own record of his various prophecies (e.g. Ezek. 1.1; 8.1). Ezekiel explained to his readers how he received messages from God, and how he delivered them (e.g. Ezek. 11.1–12).

It is probable that chapters 40—55 in the book of Isaiah were written by an unknown prophet in Babylon. If he had preached openly about the defeat of Babylon and freedom for the Jews, he would have been imprisoned. Instead, he wrote down his message, and it was passed round secretly among the Jews. Nobody knew who had written it. The people looked simply for a message from God. These anonymous chapters were later added to the scroll of Isaiah, and are included in the Bible as part of one book under the same title.

The first part of Zechariah also was probably written by the prophet himself, as he tells his own story. In contrast, the book of Haggai may have been written by somebody else after Haggai preached.

So we see that the prophets made more and more use of written records. And more and more, as the years went by, prophets' disciples took care to preserve full information about them.

Sometimes extra verses of prophecy were added to the older records, when writers believed that these came from the same time and belonged together. So some of the older books were enlarged with fresh material. This tended to disturb any sort of order that these earlier books may originally have had.

The later prophetic books were prepared in as orderly a way as possible. The writers did this to show how the changing events of history were related to what the prophets had said about them.

MAKING SENSE OF THE PROPHETIC WRITINGS

Only a few of the prophetic books contain the messages of the prophets set down in the order in which they were actually spoken. In most cases many different items on prophecy have been placed one after another, together with stories about the prophets. Usually there is no clear reason for the order in which the various items have been included. We find an example of this in Isaiah. Isaiah of Jerusalem preached over a long period of time, and it is possible to distinguish some of his earlier prophecies from those which he preached at a later time in his ministry. But in his book the prophecies are *not* set down in order of time. They are mixed up, and out of order. Even the story of Isaiah's call to be a prophet (Isa. 6), comes *after* several chapters of his prophecies (Isa. 1—5).

In Jeremiah the prophecies are often grouped according to their subject, rather than their date. For example, there is a group of prophecies against false prophets (Jer. 23.9–40), and another about the kings of David's family (Jer. 21.11—23.8). It is unlikely that these prophecies all belong to the one day's preaching. Jeremiah must have returned to the same important themes many times in his ministry. Somebody then gathered several separate prophecies about the same subject and wrote them down side by side, so that we can read what Jeremiah had to say about the matter without having to search for verses on the subject in various parts of the book.

Because the prophetic books contain many separate prophecies from different occasions, which are not always set out in any clear sequence, we need to examine each prophecy as an individual item. We have to discover for ourselves, and with the help of commentaries, the place which each prophecy had in the work of the prophet. We need to know as far as possible the exact events which led the prophet to give the particular message that we happen to be studying.

The chapter divisions in the prophetic books do not always help us to distinguish each separate prophecy in order to study it on its own. In the RSV Common Bible the passages in the prophets are printed with wider spaces between the lines where scholars believe that one prophecy seems to end, and another to begin.

To discover how to divide each section from the next, scholars have used clues from the prophetic books themselves. They draw our attention to the three main sorts of writing found in these books.

1. Some passages are *autobiography*. They tell us in the prophet's own words what happened to him, and the things which he felt led to say in God's name.
2. Some passages are *biography*. They tell us what the prophet said and did, as seen by other people.
3. Many passages are *verses of prophecy* without any explanation attached to them. Many of these verses of prophecy are poetry, but not all.

One way to discover the original divisions in the prophetic books is to look for these three different sorts of writing, and to notice where one ends and another begins.

Another way to discover how these books should be divided into sections for study depends on the fact that the words '*says the Lord*' are often used as a way of introducing a new prophecy (e.g. Jer. 23.1, 5, 7, 15, 16). The same words are sometimes used to end a prophecy (e.g. Jer. 23.4, 11, 12). When these words occur, they often show the dividing point between one prophecy and the next. This phrase should also serve to remind us that all the prophets felt they had something to say on behalf of God. Out of their experience of God, and out of their understanding of His purposes for His chosen people, they rebuked or encouraged the Israelites as the situation seemed to demand.

ISAIAH: ONE PROPHET OR TWO?

There is a very clear division in the book of Isaiah between chapters 1—39, and chapters 40—66. Three differences in particular suggest that the two parts of the book were written at different times and by different people:

1. The first 39 chapters refer to the time when Judah was being troubled by Assyria (from about 742 to 688 BC). Assyria and the Assyrians are mentioned many times (e.g. Isa. 7.18; 10.5; 14.25). Sennacherib, king of Assyria, is mentioned in Isaiah 36.1, and three times in Isaiah 37.

In the final 27 chapters of the book of Isaiah, on the other hand, Assyria is only mentioned once, and then only as part of the past

7.1 'We know that Isaiah did instruct his disciples to prepare a written record of his sayings' (p. 128). This manuscript of Isaiah, dating from the time of Christ, was among the Dead Sea Scrolls found at Qumran in 1947.

7.2 A cuneiform tablet of the 6th century BC is inscribed with a list of events in the Assyrian Empire under Nabopolassar and Nebuchadnezzar II, including the conquest of Jerusalem, 'the City of Judah'.

history of Judah (Isa. 52.4). Instead, these chapters are about Cyrus, king of the Persians (550–530 BC) (Isa. 44.28 and 45.1). In this part of the book the prophecies give hope to Israel that Babylon will be destroyed, and that the Israelites will be free to return to their own land in the near future (e.g. Isa. 48.14, 20).

2. In the first part of the book Jerusalem stands condemned by God (e.g. Isa. 3.8; 10.11). The city can only hope to be saved from destruction if the people accept God's judgement (e.g. Isa. 1.24–26; 4.3–6). In the second part of the book, on the other hand, Jerusalem is the centre of hope and joy, even though it stands in ruins (Isa. 52.9–12).

3. The division between the two parts of the book is made especially clear by the four chapters of historical writing (Isa. 36—39) which have been placed at the end of the first part of the book as an appendix. These four chapters contain almost exactly the same words as are found in 2 Kings 18.13—20.19. They tell the story of Sennacherib's attack on Jerusalem, and Isaiah's part in guiding the decisions of king Hezekiah. The title given to the book of Isaiah in Isa. 1.1 makes it clear that the prophet completed his ministry in the time of Hezekiah. The historical section was probably added to the earlier part of the book in order to complete the account of all that the prophet Isaiah had done in Jerusalem. Isaiah is not mentioned at all in the later chapters of the book. There is no record that he was deported to Babylon, and none to show that he continued his work there. In fact he would have needed to live for more than two hundred years in order to be both in Jerusalem at the time when the Assyrians were a powerful enemy, and *also* in Babylon at the time when Cyrus set the Israelites free to return home.

Nobody suggests that Isaiah did live for over two hundred years, and work in both periods of the history of Israel. So we are left with a major problem. How should we explain the fact that the book which records the prophecies of Isaiah of Jerusalem also contains words of comfort and encouragement for the Jews in Babylon at the end of their Exile in that country? Two suggestions have been discussed between scholars over many years, and a third possibility has been presented by those who use Canonical Criticism in their work.

THE FIRST ANSWER: ONE PROPHET

According to this answer, Isaiah of Jerusalem foresaw what would happen to the people of Judah in exile, and prepared a written prophecy which could be published when it was needed in Babylon at the time when Cyrus was gaining power. We know that Isaiah did instruct his disciples to prepare a written record of his sayings (Isa. 8.16; 30.8).

We can see from the description of the two parts of the book that in some ways the second part of Isaiah follows on and completes the ideas of the first part. In both parts the prophet recognizes the need for judgement, (Isa. 3.14–15; 58.1–2), cleansing (Isa. 1.18; 44.22) and justice (Isa. 1.17; 42.1–4). In the first part judgement is regarded as a future event, in the second part it is something already completed. Both parts show that God uses foreign nations to fulfil His plans, and that what happens to Judah is always according to God's purposes. All through the book a special title is used for God which is seldom found in other parts of the Bible: 'The Holy One of Israel' (e.g. Isa. 1.4; 5.19, and Isa. 41.14; 48.17).

But many scholars do not accept that Isaiah 40—66 was written by Isaiah of Jerusalem such a long time before these prophecies were needed or could be used. It is true that most of the prophets had something to say about the future. But usually it was a message of warning or of hope, based on the behaviour of the Israelites at the time when the prophet was at work. The message of most prophecy was either: 'Because you have rebelled, God will punish you by sending this trouble . . .', or 'If you repent and turn back to God He will save you from this trouble . . .'. The warning or encouragement was uppermost in the thoughts of the prophets. They only mentioned future events because they would result from people's present attitudes and behaviour, which either deserved punishment or could lead to blessing. Isaiah of Jerusalem could not know what words of rebuke or encouragement would be needed by the people of Israel living in Babylon at the time of Cyrus.

Some scholars argue in response to this that though Isaiah as a man could not have known these things, God did know, and could inspire him to write about them. But this could only be true if the pattern of people's behaviour was already fixed long before they were born. To accept this argument we would have to believe that there is no such thing as free will. It would mean that even repentance is prearranged for people, without their own will and intention being involved. If this were true it would mean that the prophets were warning and encouraging people who could not decide for themselves how they would respond. The righteous would not be free to sin, and the sinners would not be free to repent. It would all be fixed beforehand and settled for ever. Extreme Calvinists will rejoice in such an idea, believing that it gives glory to God. They will find no difficulty in believing that Isaiah of Jerusalem prepared Isaiah 40—66 for people who would live in Babylon at the time of Cyrus. But most people find it impossible to take this view, and we have to look for some other explanation.

THE SECOND ANSWER: TWO PROPHETS

The second explanation is that there was another prophet at work in Babylon in the time of Cyrus. We do not know his name, but he was fully aware of the needs of the people of his time, and was responsive to God and His purposes for that time. This prophet probably wrote his message in secret, and passed it round anonymously as an encouragement to those who were willing to do the will of God.

The links that we have seen between his messages and the words of Isaiah of Jerusalem can be easily explained. This later prophet must have been a man who had studied the records of the work of Isaiah, and as a result had come to understand God's purposes. He did not simply repeat the ideas of Isaiah of Jerusalem, because his own experiences of God, while in exile, had deepened and enriched his understanding. But he was not afraid to use the ideas which had helped him as he had studied Isaiah 1—39. His writings were probably added to those of Isaiah of Jerusalem because people saw that they carried on, developed, and enriched those earlier writings.

There was also a practical reason for joining the two sets of writing together. Isaiah 1—39 was not long enough to fill a whole scroll, and there was room to add these latter writings. This would prevent the wasting of valuable writing materials.

Afterwards, because the prophet in Babylon was not known by name, there was no new title to place over his work, and the whole scroll became known as the Book of Isaiah. The division between the two separate writings was only marked by the differences we have already noticed, and not by special headings giving new titles as in the 'Book of the Twelve'. Modern scholars have given this unknown prophet the name 'Deutero-Isaiah', which means in Greek 'the Second Isaiah'.

A DEVELOPING LITERATURE

Most scholars have accepted that the book of Isaiah as we know it shows many signs of editing, and they have produced a wide range of theories to explain the form in which the text has reached us. The prophecies of Isaiah of Jerusalem are not presented in the order in which they were proclaimed. Some of the literature contained in Isaiah 1—39 was probably written down later than the time of the prophet. For example, chapters 24 to 27 may come from a much later time, even after the writing of chapters 40 to 66. The writings contained in chapters 40 to 66 are not all from the same time. In fact it is generally agreed that chapters 40 to 55 are the ones that were prepared in Babylon, and that chapters 56 to 66 belong to an even later time, when a Jewish community had been re-established in

Palestine. Some scholars believe a different prophet prepared chapters 56—66. They call him Trito-Isaiah, meaning 'Third Isaiah'. Books which are hand-written can very easily be adapted and extended as fresh copies are prepared, and there are many signs of development in the book of Isaiah.

Perhaps at some stage in the development of the book, Deutero-Isaiah intentionally produced a fresh edition of the prophecies of Isaiah of Jerusalem. If so, he adapted what was originally written and added his own writings to provide a unified book. He set out the material available to him to give an account of God's judgement on Israel, which led to the Exile. He added to it the second half of the story, saying that after the judgement a time of new hope was promised for the Jews.

This process may seem strange to us, because the books we use are printed and produced in large quantities all with the same contents. But we know that constant editing was an accepted activity in the production of the books of the Old Testament, for example the Pentateuch or the Torah. The time of the Exile was essentially a time when all the traditions, including earlier writings, were being studied and prepared in a written form to preserve the knowledge of what God had done among His people. It was normal practice to publish books under the name of a great poet or wise man of earlier times: for example early editions of the Psalms of David, and the Proverbs of Solomon. So this book would be accepted in Israel as based on the work of the prophet Isaiah. The editor's name would not be remembered even if it had been publicly known at the time.

The book of Sirach in the Apocrypha, or Ecclesiasticus as the book is also called, mentions the book of Isaiah (see Sir. 48.20–25). Sirach comes from early in the second century BC. These verses indicate that by that time the work of Deutero-Isaiah was already included. A copy of Isaiah much in the form we know was among the Dead Sea Scrolls, and comes from about that time, showing that by then the book of Isaiah was known and valued as Scripture.

In the remainder of this section on the book of Isaiah we shall study the work of Isaiah and the writings of Deutero-Isaiah in more detail, so as to see how the two men's activities were related. We cannot do this with complete accuracy because the work of Isaiah of Jerusalem has reached us in an edited form for which Deutero-Isaiah may have been partly responsible. And later editing may have been carried out on the complete book after the time of Deutero-Isaiah.

STUDY SUGGESTIONS

WORD STUDY

1. What is the difference between 'biography' and 'autobiography'?

REVIEW OF CONTENT

2. We have noticed three chief sorts of writing in the books of the prophets: autobiography, biography, and prophecy.
   To which of these three sorts does each of the following passages belong?
   (a) Isa. 6 (b) Isa. 7.1–7 (c) Isa. 8.1–8 (d) Jer. 25.15–16 (e) Jer. 36.1–8 (f) Ezek. 18.1–9
3. For what reasons did some prophets write down their message in their own lifetime, rather than preaching directly to the people?
4. (a) Describe two different ways in which writers and editors have grouped the items of prophecy in the major prophetic books.
   (b) Describe one of the clues which help scholars to discover how to distinguish where one prophecy ends and another begins, in those books where many items of prophecy have been set down one after another.

BIBLE STUDY

5. Look up the word 'Prophet' in a Concordance. Then make a list of the names of all the prophets whom you can find mentioned in the books of Samuel, Kings, and Chronicles.
   For how many of these men does the Bible contain separate books recording their work?

FURTHER STUDY AND DISCUSSION

6. What sort of people today, if any, do the work which the prophets did in Israel in Old Testament times?
   By what methods do they spread their message, and in what ways, if any, are their words recorded?
   Do people listen to them, and if so, what makes them listen?
7. Read Mark 6.1–6. What is your opinion of Jesus's words in verse 4? Is it possible to evaluate the 'success' or 'failure' of a prophet, either in his own lifetime or later? If so, how can it be measured?
8. Which of the following professions is nearest in method to the work done by the prophets of Israel:
   a fortune-teller a news announcer a water-diviner a weather-forecaster a witch.
   Explain your answer.

ISAIAH OF JERUSALEM (Isa. 1—39)

THE PROPHET HIMSELF

Isaiah was a married man with two children (Isa. 7.3; 8.3). He lived in Jerusalem, and had friends among the influential people of the city

(Isa. 8.2). He was able to talk freely to the kings who ruled over Judah (see especially Isa. 7). Jewish traditions suggest that he was a relative of king Uzziah, but there is no clear evidence to support this. He began his work in the year that king Uzziah died (Isa. 6.1), when Assyria first became a threat to Judah. He continued his work all through the period of Assyrian power, and many of his prophecies refer directly to the changing events of that time. His final words relate to the siege of Jerusalem, and probably to the second siege in 688 BC (e.g. Isa. 14.24–27; 17.12–14). If this is the date of his last prophecy, then his work as prophet continued for 54 years, and ended when he was about eighty years old. Jewish traditions from the second century AD say that Isaiah was martyred in the reign of Manasseh. One ancient writer says that Isaiah was 'sawn asunder', which perhaps explains the reference to this sort of martyrdom in Hebrews 11.37. Isaiah is said to have written an account of the reign of Uzziah (2 Chron. 26.22), and another of Hezekiah, which was included in the book of Kings (2 Chron. 32.32; see p. 83).

OUTLINE

Isaiah 1—12: Prophecies concerning Judah and Israel.
Isaiah 13—23: Prophecies against foreign nations.
Isaiah 24—27: A Vision of the final judgement, and God's kingdom on earth.
Isaiah 28—33: Prophecies concerning Judah, after the fall of Israel.
Isaiah 34—35: A vision of Liberation.
Isaiah 36—39: Historical appendix.

We have already noticed that scholars differ about the amount of this material that can be accepted as coming from Isaiah of Jerusalem, and the amount which must be regarded as belonging to a later time. Commentaries on Isaiah provide details of the varied ideas of scholars, but we can see the difficulty if we look at Isaiah 2.2–4. The footnotes in the RSV Common Bible draw attention to Micah 4.1–3 where the same prophecy is repeated. We do not know for certain which of the two prophets first produced this message. Perhaps one copied the other, or perhaps both borrowed these words from another, unknown, prophet. Clearly some editor valued these words and felt that they should be included with the record of the work of Isaiah. And we can share that editor's interest in these words, and value their insight into the purposes of God, even though we do not know for certain who first wrote them. Some scholars think that some of the best known passages from Isaiah 1—39 come from different sources; e.g. Isaiah 9.2–7; 11.1–9. Most scholars agree that Isaiah 24—27 comes from a long time after Isaiah of Jerusalem lived.

MESSAGE

We have already studied the message preached by the prophets who lived in the time of the Assyrian empire (see Vol. 1, pp. 125–129—in Revised Edition pp. 135–140). Isaiah was the most important among them, and as we studied his messages in detail there, we shall only summarize his words here.

Isaiah's chief duty was to guide the kings of Judah in all their dealings with Assyria: both in the early days when Ahaz wanted help from Assyria, and in the later days when the kings planned to throw off Assyria's control over Judah. In both situations the kings looked for help from other countries. But Isaiah repeatedly urged them to put their trust in God, who was well able to carry out His own purposes in Israel (Isa. 7.7–9; 14.24–27; 31.1–3). Assyria was a tool in God's hands sent to punish the Israelites, but was also liable to be punished in its turn (Isa. 10.5–19). If the leaders of Judah failed to trust God they would be replaced. God would choose and appoint a new leader who would rule in righteousness and justice (Isa. 7.14; compare Isa. 9.6–7; 11.1–5).

Isaiah believed that Jerusalem would play an important part in God's plans in the days that were to come, and so he taught that the city would not be destroyed (Isa. 29.5–8). Even so the people of Judah would be severely punished for their sins (Isa. 5.1–7, 13–17). Only a few survivors would remain to share in God's plans for the future, a mere remnant (Isa. 1.9; 11.11). Enemy nations would be destroyed and have no remnant left at all (Isa. 14.22, 30; 15.9).

DEUTERO-ISAIAH (Isa. 40–66)

THE PROPHET HIMSELF

We have no direct information about the prophet whose words are recorded in these chapters. We do not know his name, or anything about his experiences as a prophet. The prophecies fall into two groups, with a division at the end of chapter 55. Those in Isaiah 40—55 are concerned with the life of the Jews in Babylon, and those in Isaiah 56—66 with their experiences after the return to Jerusalem.

It is possible that there were two prophets, or even that these chapters contain the collected prophecies of a large number of people who worked during the time of Cyrus's rise to power, and the Jews' return from exile. (See Vol. 1, chapter 8).

There are similarities in the messages included in both halves of this part of Isaiah. But the chapters Isaiah 40—55 express greater confidence in God, and more hope for the future, than can be found in Isaiah 56—66. If the same prophet produced both parts, then his

7.3a and b 'The message of most prophecy was "You have rebelled ... God will punish you" or "repent and He will save you"' (p. 129). Isaiah warns Judah of punishment to come from the Assyrians, and encourages hope of eventual release from captivity in Babylon. Assyrian and Babylonian clay tablets from the 7th century BC recount the stories of the Flood, and of Creation and God's purpose and care for His people, underlining the teaching of the Torah which lay behind the prophets' message.

experience of the return to Jerusalem did not reach up to his high hopes, and the messages he declared in Jerusalem express something of his dissatisfaction and disillusionment.

OUTLINE

Isaiah 40—55: Prophecies of encouragement directed to the Jews living in Babylon, and preparing the way for their return to Jerusalem.
Isaiah 56—66: Prophecies of warning and encouragement directed to the Jews living in Jerusalem, urging them to be faithful to the way of life which God had given to them.

These prophecies are not accompanied by any details of the events which lay behind them. So their content is the only guide we have to the purpose for which they were written, or the time to which they belong. Some of them quite clearly belong to different times from the others. For example Isaiah 66.1–4 condemns the building of a place of worship, and some scholars think it is a message to the foreigners who lived in Jerusalem in the time of the Exile. If it belongs to the period after the Exile it does not agree with other prophecies which speak of the joy the people will experience in worshipping God in the Temple (Isa. 56.6–8).

THE SERVANT SONGS

Perhaps the most important sections of Deutero-Isaiah are those known as the Servant Songs: i.e. Isaiah 42.1–4; 49.1–6; 50.4–9; and 52.13–53.12.

Some scholars say that these passages can be taken out of their present place in the book of Isaiah without affecting the sense of the remainder of Deutero-Isaiah. They think this means that these Songs come from a different source from the other prophecies. But the whole book consists of a series of prophecies with very few links between them, and it would be equally possible to take out other passages without affecting what remained.

However, the main reason for treating these passages separately is that the ideas contained in the Servant Songs are in some ways different from those found in other parts of Deutero-Isaiah. The Songs are concerned with God's 'Servant', and in them the word 'servant' seems to be used differently from the way in which it is used in the rest of Deutero-Isaiah. In Isaiah 41.8–10 and 42.19, for example, 'the Servant' clearly stands for 'the whole People of Israel'. But in the Servant Songs the servant seems to be an individual person, with a work to do *for* the People of Israel (see especially Isa. 49.5–6). He is described as one who is righteous, who brings peace, and who suffers for others.

Various leaders and prophets of Israel have been suggested as the original Servant whose work is described in the Songs, e.g. Zerubbabel, Jehoiachin, Moses, or even Deutero-Isaiah himself. Among other suggestions have been Uzziah, Jeremiah, and Cyrus.

The idea of a Servant chosen for suffering probably developed when the prophet tried to face the fact that some of those who went into Exile did not deserve the condemnation which was due to the people of Israel as a whole, and that such people suffered with and for their fellow Jews. By their faithfulness in the face of suffering they prepared for the day of release from Exile, setting an example of humility and patience as an inspiration to others.

If this was the origin of the idea, then the Servant stands for any among the Jews who were faithful to God. And it stands for any people who share the sufferings of this world in obedience to God, and who share His concern for the salvation of His people. The One above all others who can claim to have fulfilled this role is our Lord Jesus Christ. Christians see this collection of prophecies as preparing the way for men to understand the work of Christ. But the original writer found his inspiration in the lives of faithful Jews.

The idea of the Servant in the other parts of Deutero-Isaiah is that of the people of Israel working with God for the fulfilment of His purposes. And the prophecies express the anguish of God, caused by the fact that as a nation they failed to fulfil this role (e.g. Isa. 42.18–25). In the Songs the writer tells of the problems created for those who were willing to fulfil God's purposes for them in the world. Thus we see that it is not really necessary to suppose that these Songs are quite separate in origin from the rest of Deutero-Isaiah.

MESSAGE: ISAIAH 40—55

Deutero-Isaiah working in Babylon presents a message of comfort to Zion (Isa. 52.1–2, 7–8). 'Zion' is another name for Jerusalem, and stands here for the people of God whose destiny is closely related to life in God's city.

The experience of exile has caused despair (Isa. 49.14), but God is preparing a 'new thing' for His people (Isa. 42.9). There is to be a new Exodus, and God will lead His people through the wilderness (Isa. 48.20–21; 49.9–11). Foreign nations will share in this pilgrimage with Israel as their leader (Isa. 45.14; 55.3–5). God will rebuild Jerusalem, and the whole world will find salvation through Him (Isa. 54.11–12; 45.22).

All this is different from what the exiles expect. There are many stronger nations than the Israelites, but they should remember that it was God who sent His people into Exile, and that He did so to punish them for their sins (Isa. 50.1–3). He now plans to redeem them, even though they are still unworthy (Isa. 48.9–11). The foreign gods have had no influence over the history of Israel, despite the boasting of their worshippers (Isa. 41.21–24). Even Cyrus is sent by God, although he does not know it (Isa. 44.24–45.7). God is the Creator of all things, and is in control of all things (Isa. 40.12–26, 28). He is the first and the last, and there is no other (Isa. 44.6; 46.9). His will for Israel will be fulfilled.

MESSAGE: ISAIAH 56—66

There are some prophecies in this part of Isaiah which are similar to those found in Isaiah 40—55.

The people of Zion are again to take comfort because God is about to renew His care for them (Isa. 61.3). The ruined condition of the city of Jerusalem has caused them despair, but now there is reason for joy (Isa. 64.8–12; 65.18–19). New people will come to Jerusalem as a result of the continuing new Exodus (i.e. the return from captivity in Babylon), and will make the city even more glorious (Isa. 60.4–7). Foreign nations have already provided some servants for God, but many more will follow (Isa. 56.3; 60.10–14). The only hindrance to the fulfilment of God's plans for Israel is the continuing disobedience of His people (Isa. 59.1–4). Their acts of worship are selfish and corrupt (Isa. 66.3–4). Their fasts are a mockery, for they do not express penitence (Isa. 58.3–5). God's judgement will come upon all who behave wickedly (Isa. 59.15–19). God's purposes cannot be hindered for ever, He will reign victoriously (Isa. 60.1–3; 66.22).

The differences between the prophecies of Isaiah 56—66 and Isaiah 40—55 reflect the differences between the experience of captivity in Babylon, and the experience of all that was involved in the return to Jerusalem.

STUDY SUGGESTIONS

WORD STUDY

1. What does the Greek word *deutero* mean?

REVIEW OF CONTENT

2. (a) Give at least two reasons why most scholars today believe that the prophecies in Isaiah 40—66 are the work of a different prophet from those in Isaiah 1–39.
   (b) What evidence can you find in Isaiah 1—39 that Isaiah of Jerusalem believed that after judgement would come new hope.
3. (a) What special title for God is used in the book of Isaiah which rarely occurs in other parts of the Bible?
   (b) What do we learn from this title about the relationship between God and the Jews?

4. What is the chief difference between the message of Isaiah 40—55, and the message of Isaiah 56—66?
5. Some passages in Deutero-Isaiah are known as the 'Servant Songs'.
   (i) Why is this name given to them?
   (ii) What difference is there between the way in which the word 'Servant' is used in these passages, and the way in which it is used in other parts of Deutero-Isaiah?
   (iii) On the basis of your answer to (i) and (ii) above, show which of the following passages belong to the Servant Songs.
   (a) Isa. 43.10–12 (b) Isa. 42.1 (c) Isa. 52.13 (d) Isa. 44.1–4 (e) Isa. 65.8

BIBLE STUDY

6. The book of Isaiah contains prophecies relating to two different periods in the history of Israel. Write a short paragraph about each of the following pairs of verses, and explain how they help scholars to distinguish the two parts of the book.
   (a) Isaiah 7.20 and Isaiah 43.14; (b) Isaiah 37.17 and Isaiah 45.1; (c) Isaiah 39.5–6 and Isaiah 48.20; (d) Isaiah 10.11 and Isaiah 40.2; (e) Isaiah 10.12 and Isaiah 52.4.
7. Isaiah of Jerusalem was a prophet in the reign of several kings (Isa. 1.1). Two of these were Ahaz and Hezekiah. Read about them in a Bible dictionary and then read the following passages. Then say which of the two kings you think was reigning at the time of each of these prophecies.
   (a) Isa. 7.4–6 (b) Isa. 9.8–12 (c) Isa. 17.1–3
   (d) Isa. 22.8–11 (e) Isa. 37.23–29

FURTHER STUDY AND DISCUSSION

8. Use a Concordance to discover how often each of the following words is used in each of the two parts of Isaiah (i.e. chapters 1—39 and 40—66):
   deliver destroy holy judgement justice mercy peace righteousness save transgression
   Do both parts of Isaiah contain all these terms? Do both parts contain them with the same frequency? Can you discover any kind of comparison between the two parts of Isaiah from the results you have obtained? What is the significance of what you have discovered?
9. 'Both parts of Isaiah show that ... what happens to Judah is always according to God's purposes' (p. 129).
   Did foreign nations serve God's purposes more readily than Judah did? How does God achieve His purposes in the history of the world?

8

The Latter Prophets: Major (continued)

JEREMIAH

THE PROPHET HIMSELF

Jeremiah was a young man when in 626 BC he received his call to be a prophet (Jer. 1.2, 6). He came from Anathoth, and his father was a priest (Jer. 1.1). He may have been a descendant of Eli, and distantly related to Abiathar (1 Kings 2.26). He believed that God had forbidden him to marry or to have children (Jer. 16.1–2). His ministry began at the time when the Assyrian empire was breaking up, and he continued work as a prophet at the time when Babylonia was becoming powerful (Jer. 1.2–3). The people of Judah imprisoned him for preaching that they should submit to Babylonian rule (Jer. 38.2–3, 6). The Babylonians allowed Jeremiah to stay in Jerusalem in 587 BC, when they took many of the leaders of Judah into exile (Jer. 40.4–6). After the assassination of the Babylonian governor, Gedeliah, some Jews forced Jeremiah to escape with them into Egypt (Jer. 42.19; 43.2, 5–7).

HISTORICAL BACKGROUND

A full account of the events of this period of the history of Israel was given in Vol. 1, chapter 7. Here we need only look at a brief summary of the main events, in order to understand the part played by Jeremiah:

621 BC King Josiah carried out a reform of religion in Judah.

612 BC Nineveh, the capital city of Assyria, was captured by the armies of Media and Babylonia.

609 BC King Josiah was put to death by command of Pharaoh Neco of Egypt. The Pharaoh appointed Jehoiakim in his place.

605 BC The Babylonians defeated the Egyptians at the battle of Carchemish.

597 BC The Babylonians captured Jerusalem, and took Jehoiachin and his court into exile. They appointed Zedekiah as king.

587 BC Zedekiah led a revolt against the Babylonians, who again attacked and this time destroyed Jerusalem and punished Zedekiah. They took more of the leaders of Judah into exile, and appointed Gedeliah as governor.

582 BC Further Jews were taken into exile, probably as the result of the assassination of Gedeliah.

OUTLINE

Jeremiah 1—25: Mainly prophecies against Jeremiah's own people:
Jeremiah 1. Call of Jeremiah.

Jeremiah 2—6. Early messages, mainly from the time of Josiah.
Jeremiah 7—25. Further messages, mainly from the time of Jehoiakim.
Jeremiah 26—45: Mainly stories concerning Jeremiah:
Jeremiah 26—29. Jeremiah preaches submission.
Jeremiah 30—33. Jeremiah preaches hope.
Jeremiah 34—38. Events before the fall of Jerusalem.
Jeremiah 39—45. Events after the fall of Jerusalem.
Jeremiah 46—51: Prophecies against foreign nations (including Egypt, the Philistines, Moab, the Ammonites, Edom, Damascus, Kedar and Hazor, Elam, and Babylon).
Jeremiah 52: Historical appendix (including a duplicate of 2 Kings 24.18—25.30).

TYPE OF WRITING

The book of Jeremiah contains the three types of writing found in many of the prophetic books: (1) autobiography, (2) biography, and (3) prophecy. Scholars have examined these separately and they have discovered evidence for the way in which the book of Jeremiah was prepared.

SOURCES

1. *Autobiography:* Jeremiah 36 describes how, in 605 BC, Jeremiah employed a scribe called Baruch to write out 'all the words that (God had spoken to him) against Israel and Judah, and all the nations, from the days of Josiah until today' (Jer. 36.1, 2). These 'words' declared that Judah would be destroyed by the Babylonians (Jer. 36.29). That first scroll was burnt by king Jehoiakim (Jer. 36.23), but Jeremiah had the words all written out again (Jer. 36.32).

Jeremiah's own record of the messages which he preached in God's name must have been used as a basis for the book for Jeremiah. We cannot be certain which parts of the biblical book came from that second scroll, but many of the passages of Jeremiah which are written as autobiography probably came from that source.

The Original Scroll: Jeremiah 25 is headed by the same date as Jeremiah 36. It contains a record written in the first person ('I', 'me', etc.), which mentions the earlier preaching of Jeremiah, and it tells of trouble to come from Babylonia. Probably this chapter is part of the original scroll. Other chapters written in the same style are likely to have come from the same source, provided that they refer to the period of Jeremiah's ministry up to 605 BC. These include Jeremiah 1.4–19; 3.6–13; 11.6–14; 13.1–14; 16.1–13; 17.19–27; 18.1–12; 22.1–5; and also part of Jeremiah 19, which now contains material from another source as well.

The Revised Scroll: When the second scroll was prepared it

8.1 'Baruch . . . wrote Jeremiah's scroll at his dictation' (p. 143). Baruch's work was like that of this scribe of an earlier period in Egypt.

contained the same original scroll, but 'many similar words were added' (Jer. 36.32). These may have been prophecies from a later time in the ministry of Jeremiah. If so, autobiographical passages from the later period which are now included in the book of Jeremiah may have come from the revised scroll, e.g. Jeremiah 24; 27; 32; and 35.

2. *Biography:* There are several sections of the book of Jeremiah which describe his experiences in the third person: i.e. 'he', 'him', etc. The man who knew most about Jeremiah's experiences was Baruch, the scribe, who shared many of Jeremiah's troubles. He wrote Jeremiah's scroll at his dictation in the time of king Jehoiakim (Jer. 36.4), and read the scroll publicly in the Temple (Jer. 36.10). He had to hide with Jeremiah to escape the king's anger (Jer. 36.19). Jeremiah gave a personal prophecy to Baruch, warning him to be patient in this time of trouble (Jer. 45.1–5).

When Zedekiah rebelled against Babylonian rule, and Jeremiah opposed the king, Baruch was still with the prophet. He took care of the deed of possession for the land which Jeremiah bought as an expression of his confidence in the future of Judah after Zedekiah had been punished (Jer. 32.3–5, 9–15). After the assassination of Gedeliah, Baruch was blamed for Jeremiah's condemnation of the people's plan to escape into Egypt (Jer 43.3). Jeremiah and Baruch were forced to go with the people of Judah when they left for Egypt (Jer. 43.6).

It seems probable that Baruch wrote the biographical sections of the book of Jeremiah. These include Jeremiah 20.1–6; 26; 36; 45; 28; 29; 51.59–64; 34.8–22; 37—44. Chapters 36, 45 and 51 are included in this list in the order in which they were probably written by Baruch. In the book of Jeremiah they have been rearranged by the editor, and are no longer in the right sequence. Many scholars believe that the biographical parts of the book of Jeremiah show evidence that their writer was influenced by the ideas of Deuteronomy. This is not surprising, because an early edition of this book was found in the Temple in the time of king Josiah, who based his religious reformation on it. Jeremiah himself probably approved of Josiah's activities, and certainly praised his qualities as a king. Baruch probably took a similar position, and so was influenced by the book.

3. *Prophecy:* Those of Jeremiah's prophecies which are not included within the autobiographical or biographical sections of the book are grouped according to their subject. It is highly unlikely that each group is the record of a single prophecy made all at one time. Jeremiah would have returned many times to the same themes in his preaching, and an editor has probably gathered together what he had to say on each subject. In this way readers could see Jeremiah's main themes set out clearly in the book.

Notice the following groups:

(a) Concerning the drought: Jeremiah 14.1—15.4,
(b) Concerning the kings of Judah: Jeremiah 21.11—23.8,
(c) Concerning the prophets: Jeremiah 23.9–40,
(d) Concerning future hope: Jeremiah 30—31,
(e) Concerning the nations: Jeremiah 46—51.

Most scholars believe that there are at least a few prophecies included in these sections which were not delivered by Jeremiah, but which have been added to the book by an editor who wished to preserve a prophecy though he did not know whose it was. Some scholars believe that there are a large number of these additions, especially among the prophecies concerning the nations.

The Confessions of Jeremiah: Scattered through the book are a number of prophetic passages which express the inward struggle which Jeremiah faced in trying to present God's message faithfully, when God's people were completely opposed to him, and were unwilling to hear what he had to say in God's name. The people supposed that Jeremiah was glad to preach their destruction, but his only motive was to proclaim what he had heard from God. Some of these passages show that Jeremiah felt anger and hatred towards those who persecuted him, but he expressed these feelings only to God, not outwardly to the people. These passages are known as the Confessions of Jeremiah, and are found in Jeremiah 10.23–24; 11.18—12.6; 15.10–21; 17.12–18; 18.18–23; 20.7–18. It is highly unlikely that Jeremiah used these passages as part of his preaching ministry. They were probably recorded privately, rather like a personal diary, and only published later. Baruch may have kept this record.

4. *Appendix:* Jeremiah 52 is taken from 2 Kings 24.18—25.30. It is a historical passage, recording the background history of the time of Jeremiah, but making no mention of the prophet himself. Verses 22–26 from 2 Kings are omitted because they are in fact a summary of the information about the assassination of Gedeliah which had already been given in Jeremiah 39—41. Jeremiah 52.28–30 is not found in the parallel passage in 2 Kings. It gives details of the three deportations of the people of Judah to Babylon.

MESSAGE

We can best understand Jeremiah's message if we consider what he said at different periods in his ministry.

1. *The fall of Assyria.* Jeremiah became a prophet at a time when Assyria was losing its control over world affairs. At that time he discouraged the people of Judah from trying to gain their independence by making treaties with other nations (Jer. 2.18). He believed that Judah would suffer further attacks 'out of the north' (Jer. 1.13–15). He may have been thinking of the Scythians as the new enemy. These

were nomadic people who usually lived north of Assyria. They took advantage of the decrease of Assyrian power by raiding many parts of the Assyrian empire. Some scholars believe that Jeremiah was already thinking of Babylon as the new enemy of Judah.

Jeremiah used many of the same words and ideas as Hosea, e.g. he described Judah as an unfaithful wife (Jer. 3.1, 6–10). His chief accusation was that the people of Judah had turned aside from serving God, and were worshipping the Baalim, the fertility gods of Canaan (Jer. 2.23). God had given them good crops, and they had praised the Baalim for it (Jer. 5.23–24). Jeremiah calls Judah a harlot, and says that the people committed adultery by turning away from the true God (Jer. 2.20 and 5.7). God would punish them for their unfaithfulness, but He would welcome them if they returned to Him (Jer. 6.6–8 and 3.12–14, 22). Jeremiah was doubtful whether they had the wisdom to return (Jer. 4.19–26).

2. *Josiah's reform.* Jeremiah had a high regard for king Josiah, and described him as a man who was both just and righteous (Jer. 22.15–16). Although there is no record of any prophecies on the subject, Jeremiah probably supported Josiah's reforms of the religious life of Judah, based on the law of Deuteronomy. This reform made it illegal to worship the Baalim, and prevented false forms of ritual being used at the shrines of Judah.

But later Jeremiah recognized that a book of law could not reform the people. They needed a change of heart. Without that, the people of Judah would probably distort the interpretation of the Law, and make it 'into a lie' (Jer. 8.8). Two false interpretations are especially mentioned in the book of Jeremiah:

(a) Because the book of Deuteronomy refers to one central place of worship chosen by God, the people felt confirmed in their belief that Jerusalem was especially sacred and would never be recaptured by an enemy. Jeremiah told them that this depended upon their obedience to God (Jer. 7.2–7).

(b) Secondly, because the book of Deuteronomy describes the forms of sacrifice which should be made to God in Jerusalem, the people were encouraged to think that sacrifice is especially important in the service of God. Jeremiah told them that God always wants obedience, and sacrifice could not be used instead of service (Jer. 7.21–26).

3. *The reign of Jehoiakim.* The greater part of Jeremiah's prophecies come from the reign of Jehoiakim, before the Babylonians had conquered Judah. Jeremiah preached judgement from God, and offered no hope to the people of Judah except through submitting to conquest (Jer. 15.1–3). The armies of Judah would be destroyed, and many of the young men would die (Jer. 15.8). The people of Judah would go into Exile by God's will (Jer. 17.4). Even in Exile

they would suffer severely (Jer. 8.3). Probably the Confessions of Jeremiah belong to this period of his ministry.

Jeremiah used picture-language, comparing God to a potter, to remind the people that God's judgement was the result of their disobedience. If they had responded to His will by obedience, judgement would not have been necessary (Jer. 18.1–12). On another occasion he suggested that God's rejection of Judah was as complete and final as when a potter has completed a pot, baked it, and then broken it because its shape was not perfect (Jer. 19.10–11).

Jeremiah's prophecies against foreign nations may perhaps belong to this part of his ministry. In the Septuagint, Jeremiah 46—51 comes immediately after Jeremiah 25, which suggests that there was a link between the two sets of prophecies. Jeremiah believed that God could judge other nations, as well as Judah.

Jeremiah was deeply troubled by the fact that false prophets were preaching that God would save His people from the Babylonians (Jer. 23.14, 21–22).

4. *After the first deportation*. Jeremiah did not entirely lose hope that God would be able to include the people of Judah in His plans for the future. But he believed that the people in Exile were the ones who would be able to serve God in the future. He wrote to the exiles in Babylon telling them to settle peacefully there, and to work for the prosperity of that country (Jer. 29.4–7). They must wait patiently for God to fulfil His plans by bringing them back to Judah (Jer. 24.5–7). Then they would be able to rebuild Jerusalem, and in those days the people would be faithful (Jer. 33.2–9 and 24.7). There would be a new covenant to replace the one which they had broken (Jer. 50.4). The old covenant was broken because it was based on laws written in books, which the people did not fulfil. In future God would write His laws in people's hearts, so that they would gladly serve Him (Jer. 31.31–34). There would be a new king in Judah, chosen by God from the family of David, who would rule wisely and well (Jer. 23.5–6).

THE LAMENTATIONS OF JEREMIAH

TITLE

Originally this book had no title. The Jews used the first word of the book as a title: 'How!' In Hebrew this is a special word used to express grief in funeral songs. The word is found again in the first verse of Lamentations 2 and 4, showing that the book is a collection of funeral songs mourning the 'death' of the city of Jerusalem. In the ancient Greek translation, the Septuagint, the Greek word for a funeral song is used as the title. In Jerome's Latin translation, the

Vulgate, the Latin word for a funeral song is used. The English title has a similar meaning.

The Hebrew version of the book does not mention Jeremiah. Some copies of the Septuagint add as an introduction the following words:

> 'And it came to pass, after Israel had been carried into captivity and Jerusalem had been laid to waste, that Jeremiah sat weeping and lamented with this lamentation over Jerusalem, and said . . .'

There was a tradition that Jeremiah had written a lament about the death of Josiah (2 Chron. 35.25), and those who translated this book into Greek seem to have supposed that it contained Jeremiah's laments.

They placed the book of Lamentations after the prophecies of Jeremiah, although in the Hebrew Scriptures the book was included among the Writings, and not among the prophetic books. As we shall see, there are good reasons for believing that those who prepared the Septuagint were mistaken in supposing that Jeremiah wrote Lamentations. But their tradition has survived in the English title of the book.

HISTORICAL BACKGROUND

There is no doubt at all that the book contains funeral songs composed shortly after the Babylonians destroyed Jerusalem in 587 BC. The hopes of the Jews had been centred upon the Temple, and upon the rule of David's family in Jerusalem. The Babylonian conquest of Judah, and the destruction of Jerusalem put an end to these hopes. The book makes no mention of any new circumstances that could bring hope to the Jews, so it must have been written before Cyrus rose to power and set the exiles free to return to Jerusalem, i.e. it must have been written before 538 BC. Zech 7.3 confirms the fact that during the time of the Exile mourning and fasting played an important part in the life of the Jewish community. We can compare with this the evidence of Psalm 137.

OUTLINE

The book is composed of five separate poems, each contained in a separate chapter. In the Hebrew the first four poems have the form of acrostics, each verse or group of verses beginning with a different letter in alphabetical order. The poems in Lamentations 2, 3, and 4 make one alteration in the order of the letter, which suggests that the final order of the Hebrew alphabet had not been fixed when the poems were written. Lamentations 5 is not in the form of an acrostic, but it does have the same number of verses as the number of letters in the Hebrew alphabet, i.e. twenty-two.

Lamentations 1: Jerusalem mourns her destruction.
Lamentations 2: National lament over the fall of Jerusalem.

Lamentations 3: A personal lament.
Lamentations 4: National lament over the fall of Jerusalem.
Lamentations 5: A prayer for deliverance.

SOURCES

All five poems are clearly to be dated between 587 and 538 BC. Probably Lamentations 2 and 4 were earliest, as they give the most detailed description of life in Jerusalem after the Babylonian attack. Lamentations 5, 1 and 3 were composed later in the period, possibly in that order. It is not certain whether one writer composed all five poems, or whether several writers contributed to the book. Lam. 2.9b, 'her prophets obtain no vision from the Lord', suggests that the Lamentations contained in this book were prepared by the community that remained in Jerusalem, rather than by the exiles. This is because the people in Babylon were well aware of the significant prophecies of Ezekiel.

A close examination shows that the writer or writers of these poems had known the prophecies of Jeremiah. At first they had rejected his message, but then they had seen his words fulfilled. The poems express their horror and sorrow that these things could be true. Notice especially:

(a) Jeremiah had warned the people not to trust the leadership of Zedekiah as a defence against the Babylonians, and they had seen him taken captive (Jer. 21.1–7; Lam. 4.20).

(b) Jeremiah warned them not to suppose that they were safe because God's Temple was in their city, and they had seen the Temple destroyed (Jer. 7.4–7; Lam. 2.6–7).

(c) Jeremiah had warned them that false prophets were misleading them, and they had discovered that this was true (Jer. 14.13–16; 23.16–17; Lam. 2.14).

(d) The people had rejected Jeremiah's warning that God would withdraw His inspiration from their leaders, and they had lived to see his words fulfilled (Jer. 18.18; Lam. 2.9–10).

But these writers did not simply take up and use Jeremiah's words. They still refused to believe some of the things that he had proclaimed:

(e) They believed that they were suffering as a result of the sins of their fathers, even though Jeremiah rejected this idea (Lam. 5.7; Jer. 31.29–30).

(f) They believed that God would give them an early deliverance from the rule of Babylon, even though Jeremiah had warned that the rule of Babylon would continue for a long time (Lam. 3.64–66; Jer. 29.10).

MESSAGE

The poems are an attempt to answer the urgent questions of the people of Judah: How could God allow His city to be destroyed, His royal line of kings to be defeated, and His Temple to be destroyed? It was because of the sins of His people (Lam. 1.8–9, 18). God's anger had led Him to hand them over to their enemies (Lam. 2.2–8). But God is merciful, and so there was hope for the future (Lam. 3.31–33). What He required of His people was repentance (Lam. 3.40–42, 55–58). He would then overthrow their enemies (Lam. 3.64–66). The book ends with less confidence, for the writer of the final poem feared that the people's sin might have led God to reject them finally and completely (Lam. 5.19–22).

The book of Lamentations is read at a Jewish festival which commemorates the fall of Jerusalem, and serves as a perpetual reminder that God requires righteousness from His Chosen People, and will punish their wrong-doing.

STUDY SUGGESTIONS

WORD STUDY

1. 'Jeremiah used many of the same words and ideas as Hosea' (p. 145). Give at least two examples of such words and ideas by setting side by side words from Jeremiah and the related words from Hosea. Give the Bible references in each example.

REVIEW OF CONTENT

2. Write short notes on the following verses, showing how each helps us to understand the life and work of Jeremiah.
   (a) Jer. 1.1–2 (b) Jer. 3.6–9 (c) Jer. 11.18–20
   (d) Jer. 36.1–3 (e) Jer. 43.2–3
3. (a) What reasons can you give to support the view that Lamentations was not written by Jeremiah?
   (b) What connection is there between the prophet Jeremiah and this book?

BIBLE STUDY

4. Jeremiah used the example of a potter to describe God's attitude towards His people. Other writers in the Bible also used the same comparison, but it led them to say different things about the relationship between God and His people. Use a Concordance to discover which prophets, and which New Testament writers, use the idea. Then write a paragraph on each showing how they used the idea.

5. Using a Concordance, read the verses in Jeremiah which are about God's covenant with the Israelites. Then summarize in your own words Jeremiah's preaching on the subject.

FURTHER STUDY AND DISCUSSION

6. 'These passages show that Jeremiah felt anger and hatred towards those who persecuted him, but expressed these feelings only to God' (p. 144). A student reading these words said, 'Surely a true servant of God would hide his feelings of anger and hatred. I cannot believe that the expression of such feelings would be acceptable to God.' What is your opinion?
7. 'Or hast thou utterly rejected us?' (Lam. 5.22). Do you think that God does reject nations, groups of people, or individuals? Use a Concordance to discover what other Old Testament books have to say on the subject.

EZEKIEL

THE PROPHET HIMSELF

From Ezekiel 1.1–3 we learn several things about Ezekiel. He was a priest, living in exile in Babylon beside the river Chebar, which was a canal off the Euphrates at Telabib (see Ezek. 3.15). Ezekiel received his call to be a prophet five years after 'the exile of Jehoiachin'. Jehoiachin was exiled at the time of the first deportation in 597 BC, so we know that Ezekiel became a prophet in 593 BC. The 'thirtieth year' (Ezek. 1.1) may perhaps refer to the age of Ezekiel at his call.

We also learn from the book that Ezekiel was influential among the exiles. He owned a house, and the elders of the people came to consult him there (Ezek. 8.1). Ezekiel was married, but his wife died at about the time of the siege of Jerusalem in 587 BC (Ezek. 24.15–24).

The ministry of Ezekiel had its own distinctive style. He was inspired by the Spirit of God (Ezek. 2.2; 11.5). The Spirit addressed him as 'Son of Man', emphasizing the contrast between his humanity and the glory of God (Ezek. 2.3; 3.17). The Spirit brought experiences of ecstasy, both controlling the prophet and setting him free from the normal limitations of human awareness and activity (Ezek. 3.12–15; 8.3–4). Ezekiel saw visions (Ezek. 1.1; 40.1–2). He recognized that the motive of all God's activities is that people will '*know that I am the Lord*'. This phrase occurs more than fifty times in the book.

Throughout his ministry Ezekiel kept a close watch on events in Judah, and adapted his message to the needs of the changing situations. He was an educated man, and used his knowledge effectively to present his message. His prophecies show his knowledge of history (Ezek. 16.3), of mythology (Ezek. 28.11–19; 31.1–9), and of ship-building (Ezek. 27.1–9).

Many of his prophecies are dated, and the latest of them gives a date in the twenty-seventh year of the Exile, i.e. 571 BC (Ezek. 29.17). Jeremiah was still working in Jerusalem when Ezekiel began his ministry in Babylon, but Ezekiel carried on for more than fifteen years after Jeremiah ceased to prophesy.

HISTORICAL BACKGROUND

The dates given under this heading on p. 140 provide the background to the work of Ezekiel, as well as to that of Jeremiah.

We can see how fully Ezekiel was aware of what was happening in South Western Asia in those years. He spoke of the defeat and destruction of the Assyrian empire (Ezek. 32.22–23). He knew that the Babylonians had captured Jerusalem, and had set Zedekiah as king over Judah, and that Zedekiah had rebelled against the Babylonians (Ezek. 17.11–15). He warned that the Babylonians would regain control of Jerusalem (Ezek. 17.16–21). He described the armies of Babylonia preparing to attack Judah (Ezek. 21.18–23), and declared that they would attack Tyre first, and destroy that city before they came to Jerusalem (Ezek. 26—27).

Later on Ezekiel remembered the long and difficult siege which resulted from that attack on Tyre (Ezek. 29.18). He knew when Jerusalem itself came under siege (Ezek. 24.2). He knew that the people of Jerusalem relied on Egypt for help, since he wrote about the failure of their ally to help at that time (Ezek. 30.20–26). He believed that Egypt would be conquered by the Babylonians (Ezek. 29.6–9). He waited for news of the fall of Jerusalem, and felt inspired to fresh work when the news came (Ezek. 33.21–22). In his latest dated prophecy Ezekiel spoke of the attack led by Nebuchadnezzar against Egypt after Amasis became Pharoah in 570 BC (Ezek. 29.17, 19–20; see Vol. 1, p. 133; rev. ed. p. 144).

Ezekiel's prophecies do not include any mention of Cyrus's rise to power in Persia. Ezekiel regarded the Persians as of little importance: some of them served as mercenaries in the army of Tyre (Ezek. 27.10). Nor did he record anything about the fall of Babylon, even though he looked forward to a time when the Jews would be free to serve God in Jerusalem. His prophecies were concerned with the events that took place during his ministry, and only looked to the future of Judah.

OUTLINE

Ezekiel 1—24: Prophecies against Jerusalem before the destruction of the city.
Ezekiel 25—32: Prophecies against foreign nations, especially against Tyre and Egypt.
Ezekiel 33—39: Prophecies concerning the restoration of Judah.
Ezekiel 40—48: Prophecies concerning the new Temple.

SOURCES

The prophecies of Ezekiel are carefully dated, counting from the exile of Jehoiachin. The prophet is described as sharing the Exile in Babylon, yet almost all his prophecies were addressed to the people still living in Jerusalem, and he was instructed to 'speak' to the people of Judah (Ezek. 2.7; 3.4). He strengthened the effect of his preaching by using many dramatic parables (e.g. Ezek. 4.1–3, 4–8), which needed to be seen in order to achieve their purpose.

These facts have caused many scholars to question whether the record of Ezekiel's work is historically accurate. They doubt whether Ezekiel could have worked in Babylon if his messages were intended for the people living in Jerusalem. Many different explanations are given by scholars for the fact that Ezekiel seems to be in Babylon too soon. They are of two chief sorts.

1. Some scholars reject the dates given in the book itself, for the various prophecies. Instead, they suggest that Ezekiel was living in Jerusalem until the city fell to the Babylonians in 587 BC, and only after that went into Exile.

However, the dates given are exact, and the prophecies seem so well suited to the changing circumstances of the period of the Exile, that it is highly doubtful whether we should reject their dates. The writer's knowledge of the Exile is too accurate for us to believe that he did not share its experiences, as he describes them.

There is also strong evidence in the book of Ezekiel that the prophet was not in Jerusalem. We know that Jeremiah faced severe opposition, imprisonment, and kidnapping as a result of his ministry in Jerusalem. But there is no record at all in the book of Ezekiel that the people of Jerusalem tried to silence him. Ezekiel was free to prophesy without interference, and this would have been very unlikely if he had been in Jerusalem. The authorities in Babylon would *welcome* what he had to say.

2. So we are left with the idea that Ezekiel was working in Babylon. His prophecies may have been recorded in writing and sent to Jerusalem, but second-hand accounts of his dramatic parables would not have been so effective as the dramas themselves in getting his

message across. So perhaps after all he was preaching to the Jews in Exile, and showing them what God was planning for Jerusalem.

It was a regular part of the work of the prophets to preach against foreign nations. Amos, Isaiah, and Jeremiah had all done so. Such prophecies were addressed to the foreign nations, but their message was for the people of Israel. The prophets were showing the Israelites what God would do with the foreign nations who were Israel's enemies. It is doubtful if much of what they said ever reached the nations they addressed. But the prophets had done their work if they had helped the Israelites to see God's hand in the events of their time.

Ezekiel was using the same kind of prophecy. He addressed it to the people of Jerusalem, but he really meant it for the people in Exile in Babylon. They needed to know whether God had forsaken the exiles, and forgiven the people in Jerusalem. Ezekiel assured the exiles that God would deal with the sins of those in Jerusalem as severely and as justly as He had dealt with the sins of those in Exile.

MESSAGE

Ezekiel received many of his inspirations to speak, as a result of visions. In particular he had visions of God, accompanied by cherubim (Ezek. 11.22). He saw God seated on a throne, which was mounted on wheels (Ezek. 1.26; 10.9–11). He most often described God Himself by the word 'glory' (e.g. Ezek. 3.23; 10.4).

These visions taught Ezekiel what he must say in God's name (Ezek. 11.1–4). He learnt from them that God is active in His world, and available to those who respond to His lordship. Ezekiel was in Babylon, but God appeared to him there and called him to service there. The people remaining in Judah and Jerusalem had rebelled against God's rule, and His message to them was 'words of lamentation and mourning and woe' (e.g. Ezek. 2.3; 2.10; 2.7–9). God would leave Jerusalem because His people would not serve Him there (Ezek. 11.22–23). But there would come a time when God would return with the faithful exiles, and His glory would be known in the Temple once more (Ezek. 34.11–16; 43.6–9).

Ezekiel believed that the Babylonians were God's tools for punishing the people of Judah (Ezek. 21.18–23; 24.1–14). He was quite certain that the Jews deserved this suffering. Throughout their history they had shown their unfaithfulness, even when they were in Egypt (Ezek. 20.5–9). All that had followed was equally evil, the people had become completely corrupt and indifferent to God's mercy (Ezek. 16).

God had laid down His Law for His people, but they refused to obey. They knew what was right, but they did not do it (Ezek. 5.6–8;

18.5–9; 33.25–26). These passages show that Ezekiel knew the early collections of laws which were gradually gathered together during and after the Exile to form the Torah which was published by Ezra.

Ezekiel came from a family of priests, and this may be why he spoke a great deal about the ritual impurity among the people in Jerusalem. The Temple itself had been defiled by pagan worship, and the people were not fit to worship God (Ezek. 5.11; 20.43). The priests had failed to teach people how to worship God in purity (Ezek. 22.26). Pagan cults had been taken up (Ezek. 8.7–13), and there was much idolatry (Ezek. 23.7, 30). Even infant sacrifice was practised among the people in Judah (Ezek. 16.20–21).

Ezekiel called himself a 'watchman' (Ezek. 33.7–9). It was his work to warn the people of Judah when God's punishment was likely to come on them because of their sin. They would then have the opportunity to 'turn from their wickedness' (Ezek. 3.19). Ezekiel believed that the future of each individual person depended upon his or her own personal attitude to God: either rebellion or repentance (Ezek. 33.11). Nobody could rightly claim that they faced disaster because their parents had sinned (Ezek. 18). Nobody could pass on to their children the blessings they had received from God as a reward for obedience (Ezek. 14.20). Ezekiel himself could only act as watchman, he could not compel the people to repent (Ezek. 3.19, 21).

God had repeatedly offered to save His people; not because they deserved His help, but in order to show His unbroken power among the nations (Ezek. 20.9, 14, 22). Judah's hope for the future was in the cleansing that could come from God, who would give His people a new heart and a new spirit (Ezek. 11.19–20; 36.25–27). Then they would look back on their evil past and loathe themselves for it (Ezek. 36.31). The nation which appeared to be dead because of its failure to serve God would be recreated by the Spirit of God. Ezekiel learnt this from his vision of the valley of dry bones (Ezek. 37). A new leader would come to God's people, and then they would keep His commandments (Ezek. 34.23–24; 37.24–25).

The last section of the book of Ezekiel describes in detail the new community which would be centred round the new Temple in Jerusalem, where God would dwell in His glory (Ezek. 40.1–16; 43.1–5).

DANIEL

APOCALYPTIC LITERATURE

The book of Daniel is placed among the Prophets in the Christian Canon, but belongs among the Writings in the Jewish Canon. It is not strictly a prophetic book, but tells in the first six chapters the traditional stories of Daniel and his companions in the time of the Exile, and then presents some important 'Apocalyptic' chapters. Daniel is the most characteristic example of apocalyptic writing in the Old Testament, just as the Revelation (which uses much of the same symbolic language that we find in Daniel) is for the New Testament. Scholars differ in describing the essential features of such writings. But we can notice some of the things they point to as significant. The writers are often anonymous, using the names of greater spiritual leaders of earlier times. They present history as a series of distinct ages under the control of God. These involve a conflict between good and evil, and lead to the completion of God's purposes for the world and humanity. The faithful must wait patiently and faithfully for His victory. The details of the apocalyptic record are given as having been received in visions or dreams. Angels and symbolic animals play an important part, but the timing of their activities is not spelled out. Mysterious numbers are used which need interpretation. The original purpose of most of these writings was to meet the needs of the faithful in a particular time of great persecution, but the books have been re-interpreted many times in the history of Judaism and the Christian Church to give encouragement and hope to the readers when facing such suffering.

TITLE

The book is named after the chief character of the stories in chapters 1—6, who is said to have received the visions recorded in chapters 7—12. Daniel is described as a Jew living in Babylon, who became influential in the court there, and continued to have authority when Darius the Mede conquered Babylonia. The stories tell how Daniel remained faithful to God in the time of the Exile, and how God protected him from his enemies. The visions describe the events of world history which followed the breakdown of Babylonian power, and the writer used these visions to show how God was directing events towards the establishment of His kingdom on earth.

Although Daniel is shown as playing an important part in the Exile and afterwards, there is very little information about him in other parts of the Old Testament. Ezekiel spoke of a Daniel who was one of the righteous men of much earlier times, and who could be counted alongside Noah and Job (Ezek. 14.14, 20; 28.3). One of the leaders who returned from the Exile with Ezra was called Daniel (Ezra 8.2). And the name appears again among those who made a new Covenant with God in the time of Nehemiah (Neh. 10.6). But it is unlikely that any of these were the same as the Daniel of Daniel 1—6. They belonged to different times.

HISTORICAL BACKGROUND

The stories describe events at the time of the Exile, and of the fall of Babylon to the Persians. The visions point forward from that time, and seem to reach their climax and conclusion at the time of Antiochus IV, one of the Greek rulers of the second century BC. The events of this whole period are described in Volume 1, chapters 7–9.

Scholars differ about the historical background to the writing of the book of Daniel. Some take it literally, and believe that Daniel both experienced the events described in Daniel 1—6, and also wrote the account of the visions in Daniel 7—12. Others are convinced that the stories are legends, which were not recorded until long after the fall of Babylon. They think that the visions were composed in the time of Antiochus IV, to encourage the Jews of that time, who were facing persecution and death.

Some people suggest that the interpretation which a scholar gives to the book depends upon his own basic ideas about the nature of prophecy. Some scholars emphasize that the powers of a prophet included the ability to foretell the future. They say that Daniel was quite capable of writing a detailed account of future events, and that the book did come from the time of the Exile. Other scholars deny that prophets were capable of knowing future events. They then say that because the book of Daniel shows such a detailed knowledge of the events up to the time of Antiochus IV, it must have been written at a later time.

The only satisfactory way to decide between the two views is to examine the evidence by ordinary historical standards, and to interpret the book in the light of what we discover. If the writer of Daniel lived in the time of the Exile and the Persians' rise to power, then we could expect him to have possessed detailed knowledge of those times. If he lived in the time of Antiochus IV, he might well have been ignorant of the earlier times, and have made statements which conflict with what we know of those times from other sources.

There is strong evidence that the writer of Daniel was ignorant of certain basic facts about the time of the Exile, and thus could not have lived at that time, i.e.:

(a) He thought that Jerusalem fell to Nebuchadnezzar in the third year of Jehoiakim (605 BC), and that the first deportation took place then (Dan. 1.1–4). But in fact Jerusalem fell in 598 BC, after the death of Jehoiakim.

(b) He thought that Belshazzar was the son of Nebuchadnezzar, and that he became king of Babylon (Dan. 5.1–2, 13; 7.1). But in fact Belshazzar was son of Nabonidus, and the greatest authority he possessed was as his father's regent.

(c) He thought that Darius the Mede conquered Babylon, and became the first king of the new empire (Dan. 5.30; 6.28). But in fact the first king of the new empire was Cyrus. His son Cambyses was next, followed by Darius who was a Persian.

The visions of Daniel provide accurate information about the Greek Empire, which might be the result of clear revelation. But when the visions refer to the time of the Persian Empire they are less accurate. Notice especially the prophecy about the coming of four Persian rulers (Dan. 11.2–3). In fact there were eleven Persian rulers before the Greek victories over Persia, led by Alexander the Great. It is difficult to see how Daniel could have foreseen accurately the more distant events, and yet make mistakes about things that were to happen nearer to his own time. But this difficulty disappears if we accept that the writer of the book of Daniel was at work in the time of the Greek Empire. His purpose in describing the visions was to convey an important message to the people of his own time. Probably he could only remember the four most famous of the Persian rulers, who were part of history by the time that he wrote. But this mistake was of little importance, and did not affect the message he was presenting.

OUTLINE

Daniel 1—6: The stories of Daniel and his companions:
Daniel 1: Daniel and his companions at the Babylonian court.
Daniel 2: Daniel interprets Nebuchadnezzar's dream.
Daniel 3: The three friends in the fiery furnace.
Daniel 4: Daniel interprets another dream, and it is fulfilled when Nebuchadnezzar goes mad.
Daniel 5: The writing on the wall at Belshazzar's feast.
Daniel 6: Darius sends Daniel to the lions' den.
Daniel 7—12: The visions of Daniel:
Daniel 7: Four beasts, and one like a son of man.
Daniel 8: The ram and the he-goat, and the little horn.
Daniel 9: Jeremiah's prophecy of 70 weeks explained.
Daniel 10—12: A vision of the Last Days.

In the Septuagint version of this book there are a number of additions to the contents of the Hebrew Scriptures, as given above. The three major ones are included as separate books in the Apocrypha, i.e. 'The Prayer of Azariah and the Song of Three Young Men', which was inserted after Daniel 3.23; and 'Susanna', and 'Bel and the Dragon', which were a postscript forming Daniel 13—14.

SOURCES

The language in which the book was written supports the idea that it was composed in the time of Antiochus IV. Daniel 2.4b—7.28 was in

Aramaic, the language widely used by the Jews after the Exile. The rest of the book was in a style of Hebrew known to belong to a much later time, and may have been a translation from an Aramaic original. Many Persian words were used, which would be more natural after a longer period of contact with the Persians than at the very beginning of their Empire. Some Greek words are used also.

The name of the real writer of this book is unknown. No new prophets would have been accepted in this period, after the people's bitter experience of false prophets before the fall of Jerusalem. A custom gradually grew up by which new writers used the names of people remembered from the past, in order to give their books authority. The stories of Daniel were probably told among the Jews before the book was written, and they provided an acceptable introduction to the visions which were newly composed. The writer used oral traditions which were incomplete, and this led him to make mistakes about the history of the earlier times, when he tried to give a complete background to the stories in their written form.

MESSAGE

The stories in the first half of the book show the victories over suffering which are possible as a result of faith. Daniel and his companions trusted God, and escaped the disasters which their enemies had planned for them. Clearly the writer intended these stories to encourage faith among those who face persecution, by assuring them that God is in control, and that He will care for His people.

The second half of the book is Apocalyptic (see Vol. 1, p. 181; rev. ed. p. 194). It refers in a hidden way to the things that were happening when it was written. In the same way, it describes how God's presence and power bring victory over evil, and lead to the establishment of His Kingdom. Such writing needs careful interpretation, with detailed explanation of the various signs and symbols used. When this is done, the book shows that the writer must have had a detailed knowledge of events in the Greek Empire up to the time of Antiochus IV. For example it mentions that:

(a) The Greek Empire was the fourth, counting Babylon, Media, and Persia as the previous ones (Dan. 7.17). It was also the greatest of them (Dan. 7.7, 23).

(b) The first ruler of the Greek Empire was the most powerful: Alexander the Great (Dan. 8.5, 21; 11.3).

(c) When Alexander died, the kingdom was divided into several parts under different rulers (Dan. 8.8, 22; 11.4).

(d) The two greatest of these kingdoms were one in the north (the Seleucid kingdom based in Syria), and one in the south (the Ptolemaic kingdom based in Egypt) (Dan. 11.5–6).

(e) Counting from Alexander the Great there were ten kings who ruled over Syria before Antiochus IV (Dan. 7.7).

(f) Antiochus IV did not inherit the right to become king (Dan. 11.21).

(g) He banned the morning and evening sacrifices which the Jews had been used to offering in the Temple (Dan. 8.11), and persecuted the Jews in other ways also (Dan. 7.25).

(h) He set up an altar in the Temple for the worship of Zeus, and sacrificed pigs' flesh on it, thus causing the 'abomination that makes desolate' (Dan. 9.27; 11.31; 12.11).

(i) The period of this desecration of the Temple was about three and a half years. In Daniel 9.27 the 'half of the week' in which sacrifices cease refers to the three and a half years, counting each day as a year. In Daniel 7.25 and 12.7 the 'time, two times, and half a time' also stands for this period of three and a half years. In Daniel 8.13–14 the 'two thousand and three hundred evenings and mornings' again stand for the three and a half years in which morning and evening sacrifices were forbidden, i.e. 1,150 days. This last prophecy is corrected twice in Daniel 12.11–12, probably because the time of this trouble was longer than the writer had at first expected.

Notice that nothing precise is foretold for the period following the end of the desecration of the Temple. The writer naturally looks forward to the death of Antiochus IV. But he does not say how it will happen, and only describes Antiochus as continuing his violent ways until the end (Dan. 11.40–45). This helps to confirm that the writer based his vision on events which had already occurred, and that he was writing at a time when Antiochus was still ruling over the Jews.

The book sets all these events into the background of God's purposes for the world. God's rule is more certain and more significant than all human empires. These will come and go, but God's purposes go from strength to strength, and His rule will crown all things. The rule of the righteous will come, and 'one like a son of man' shall lead them (Dan. 7.13–14, 27). In the meantime there is comfort concerning those who have died for their faith, for there will be a day of resurrection leading to eternal life. Some who have sinned greatly will rise to be punished (Dan. 12.2–3). Thus we see that the writer of Daniel grasped the truth which escaped the writer of Ecclesiastes.

THE FIVE SCROLLS

By examining the Lamentations of Jeremiah in this chapter (pp. 146–149) we have now completed our studies of the five books—Song of Solomon, Ruth, Lamentations, Ecclesiastes and

8.2 'The Five Scrolls . . . each of them is used in the Synagogues in connection with one of the main festivals of the Jewish year' (p. 161). Scrolls in richly decorated silver cases are held up high during a festival in North Africa today.

8.3 A modern scroll of the Torah belonging to a Synagogue in London.

Esther—which are placed together in the Jewish Canon as a sub-group of the Writings.

For the Jews they belong together as a group because each of them is used in the Synagogues in connection with one of the main festivals of the Jewish year. The Song of Solomon is read at Passover, Ruth at Pentecost, Lamentations at fasts held to remember the fall of Jerusalem, Ecclesiastes at the Feast of Booths, and Esther at Purim. We have noticed these connections as we have studied each of the books.

In the Christian Canon they are placed separately where they seem to fit in the sequence of books for historical reasons. Ruth comes first as belonging to the early history of Israel, and Esther next as from the later history. Ecclesiastes and Song of Solomon are placed among the books of Poetry and Wisdom. And now we have studied Lamentations in its place among the 'Latter Prophets'.

STUDY SUGGESTIONS

WORD STUDY

1. Use a Concordance to discover all the verses in the book of Ezekiel where the words 'the glory of God' are used. Which of the following meanings does 'glory' have in this phrase?
   (a) The praises people give to God,
   (b) The wonderful character and caring presence of God Himself,
   (c) The achievements of God in creation.
2. Ezekiel 'was inspired by the Spirit of God'. Use a Concordance to discover which of the other three prophets whom we have studied spoke about the Spirit being an inspiration to somebody who was serving God.

REVIEW OF CONTENT

3. What evidence is there in the book of Ezekiel that he knew what was happening in Jerusalem while he was working in Babylon.
4. Which book in the Old Testament uses the phrase 'son of man' most often, and what does it stand for in that book?
5. Why do scholars believe that the book of Daniel comes from the time of Antiochus? Is it that they say prophecy does not include a knowledge of events far in the future? If not, what other reasons are there?

BIBLE STUDY

6. 'Most of the prophets had something to say about the future. But usually it was a message of warning or of hope based on the

behaviour of the Israelites at the time when the prophet was at work' (p. 129). Give an example to support this statement from each of the four prophets whom we have studied so far.

7. Compare what each of the four prophets we have studied had to say about a new God-given leader who would help to establish the kingdom of God in Jerusalem.
8. Read Daniel 11.2–4 and then answer the following questions.
(a) Who were the 'three more kings' of Persia, besides Darius?
(b) What is strange about the order in which the kings are mentioned in the book of Daniel?
(c) Why did the writer not mention the remaining seven kings of Persia?
(d) Who was the 'mighty king' mentioned in verse 3? Was he more powerful or less powerful than the kings of Persia?
(e) When was his kingdom 'broken' (verse 4)?
(f) Who succeeded him on the throne of his empire? Was his successor a member of his own family?
(g) Is Xerxes I mentioned in any special way in this passage? If so, in which verse and in what way?
(h) What was the purpose of the writer of Daniel in including this passage among the visions that he describes?

FURTHER STUDY AND DISCUSSION

9. 'Nobody could rightly claim that they faced disaster because their parents had sinned' (p. 154). Ezekiel proclaims the justice of God, based on the righteousness or sinfulness of individual people. But does Ezekiel overstate his case? Is the sentence quoted above *always* true?
10. (a) The books which make up the Five Scrolls seem to be less well known among Christians than most other parts of the Bible. Ask some lay Christians the following five questions and see whether they can answer without prompting.
(i) Which book in the Bible contains human love songs?
(ii) Did David have any foreign ancestors? If so, who were they?
(iii) Which book of the Bible contains funeral songs about the destruction of Jerusalem?
(iv) Who said, 'Vanity of vanities! All is vanity', and what did he mean by it?
(v) Which Jewish woman became queen of Persia, and how did she help her own people?
(b) Make a note of the responses you get to these questions, and compare your notes with those of other students. Why was there difficulty in answering these questions, or how did your lay

Christians get to know about these things? How important is it that lay-people should be taught about these books?

(c) Why would Jewish people be likely to give more prompt answers to these questions?

9

The Latter Prophets: Minor

THE BOOK OF THE TWELVE

THE MINOR PROPHETS

These are the twelve books which together make up the scroll called 'The Book of the Twelve' in the Jewish Canon. They record the work of the prophets who represent several centuries of God's messengers, living between about 750 BC and about 300 BC in the time of the Assyrian, Babylonian, and Persian empires. Some of the prophets worked before the Exile, others during its time and yet others after the return from Exile. The books are not set out in the Bible in historical sequence, although Hosea and Amos are rightly placed early in the list because these prophets were from the time before the Exile. Similarly the books of Haggai, Zechariah and Malachi are rightly placed late in the list because they record the work of prophets who lived after the Exile. We must remember that the books themselves had a long and varied history, and were not put into their present form until long after the death of the prophets whose work they record.

Because scholars in recent years have emphasized the importance of Canonical Criticism, which involves recognizing that those who prepared the Canon believed that the impact of the total revelation of God was best presented in this way, we shall study these books in the order in which they are presented in the Bible. But it will be important for us to try to relate the prophets to the periods of history in which they worked, and so to understand the significance of their message for the people of their time. There is no direct evidence from outside the Bible to help us decide where each belongs in history. But there is evidence in the books of the Minor Prophets themselves which helps us to decide to which period each belongs. Sometimes the evidence is in the information about the circumstances the prophet faced in doing his work. Sometimes the evidence is in the anticipated outcome of events to which the prophet pointed. Sometimes the evidence is more technical, in that it depends on the vocabulary used in the book being studied. For example, some of the words are ones known to be used at a particular time in the history of Israel, or words are borrowed from other languages which could only have been known at a particular time.

As a result of such studies, many scholars believe that historically the Minor Prophets should be grouped as follows:

1. In the time of the Assyrian Empire:
   Amos, Hosea and Micah;
2. In the time of the Babylonian Empire:
   Zephaniah, Habakkuk, Nahum and Obadiah;
3. In the time of the Persian Empire:
   Haggai, Zechariah, Malachi, Joel and Jonah.

We should note that Zechariah chapters 9 to 14 do not belong with the rest of that book. Some scholars believe that they come from the time of the Greek Empire.

However, scholars do not all agree with the information set out above. There is not always clear evidence on which to make decisions about the dates. So some scholars suggest different dates and circumstances for some of the prophets. We shall notice any major disagreements as we study each book.

HISTORICAL BACKGROUND

For convenience we repeat here the outline of each of the historical periods mentioned above as it is given in the introduction to *History of Israel* Vol 1, Revised Edition. This will help us to relate information contained in each book to the circumstances of the prophet concerned. For further details about each period see Vol. 1, chapters 6 (Assyrian Empire), 7 (Babylonian Empire), 8 (Persian Empire) and 9 (Greek Empire).

THE TIME OF THE ASSYRIAN EMPIRE

In the early part of this period there was no nation strong enough to conquer and control the Israelites. It was a time of peace and prosperity for Judah and Israel. But the prophets Amos and Hosea condemned the injustice and false worship which marked the life of Israel at this time. They warned of trouble to come. New and powerful kings came to rule in Assyria, who conquered Israel in 721 BC, and took its people into Exile. This was the end of the Northern Kingdom. Judah submitted to the Assyrians, but several times rebelled against their control, relying on Egypt for help. Each time, the Assyrians regained control, and punished the people of Judah. Egypt could give no help. Isaiah the prophet urged the kings and people to put their trust in God, not in foreign alliances.

THE TIME OF THE BABYLONIAN EMPIRE

After a time the Assyrians found that they were unable to control the vast empire which they had created for themselves. Three nations fought against Assyria: Egypt, Media, and Babylonia. Assyria was defeated, and its empire was divided between the victorious nations. The Egyptians tried to regain control of Palestine, but were defeated by the Babylonians at Carchemish in 605 BC. The people of Judah tried to claim their independence, but were defeated by the Babylonians in 597 BC. After a period of rebellion, the Babylonians attacked Judah again, in 586 BC, and destroyed Jerusalem and the Temple. After each victory the Babylonians took some of the leading people of Judah into Exile in Babylon.

The prophets were active towards the end of the Assyrian Empire, and in the years when the Babylonians were gaining mastery over the nations which became part of their own empire. Important dates in this period were:

663 BC	The Assyrians captured Thebes in Egypt, and extended their empire so far that they eventually lost control of the peoples whom they ruled.
625 BC	Nabopolassar seized control of Babylon from the Assyrians.
621 BC	King Josiah carried out a reform of religion in Judah, which involved the rejection of Assyrian authority.
612 BC	The armies of Media and Babylonia attacked and destroyed the Assyrian capital, Nineveh.
597 BC	The Babylonians attacked and captured Jerusalem.
586 BC	After Judah had rebelled, the Babylonians destroyed Jerusalem.

Jeremiah was the great prophet of this period. Only Zephaniah shared his vision that the Babylonians were coming in order to punish the people of Judah for their sins. The other Minor Prophets of this period were chiefly interested in the punishment which God was preparing for Judah's enemies.

THE TIME OF THE PERSIAN EMPIRE

Cyrus, king of Persia, conquered Babylon in 539 BC, and gave permission for the Jews to return to Judah, and to rebuild the Temple in Jerusalem. They met with such difficulties that the work was not completed until 516 BC. In 445 BC Nehemiah was permitted to return to Judah to repair the walls of Jerusalem, and to establish a Jewish sub-province there. Later, about 397 BC, Ezra came from Babylon bringing a written record of the Law of God, which was perhaps the first five books of our Old Testament. But there is some doubt among scholars about the actual date at which Ezra came to Jerusalem, and about the exact nature of the book which he brought with him. It was to be used as the guide for the life of the Jewish community in Jerusalem.

By his prophecies in Babylon between 593 BC and 571 BC Ezekiel had helped to prepare the way for the people's return to Jerusalem. His great vision of the new Temple, and of the worshipping community in Jerusalem, was a source of inspiration for these later

9.1 The Minor Prophets 'represent several centuries of God's messengers' (p. 164), although in this engraving from a French commentary of the 18th century AD they are pictured as being all alive at the same time. The Nativity scene in the background reminds us that according to tradition some passages in their books point directly forward to the coming of Christ.

prophets. In one way or another all of them were concerned about the situation among the Jews who had returned to Jerusalem.

THE TIME OF THE GREEK EMPIRE

For the sake of understanding Zechariah chapters 9 to 14 it is worthwhile to recall part of the history of that period.

Alexander the Great of Greece conquered a large area of the Mediterranean and South Western Asia, including the Persian Empire. After his death the Greeks continued to rule, though the area was divided into separate kingdoms. From 323 BC to 198 BC the Jews were ruled from Egypt by a Greek family, the Ptolemies. In 198 BC the family of Seleucus took control of Judah, and ruled the Jews from Antioch.

1. HOSEA

THE PROPHET HIMSELF

According to the first verse of each of the following books the four prophets belonged to roughly the same period of the history of Israel: Isaiah, Hosea, Amos and Micah. But Amos and Hosea worked in the Northern Kingdom of Israel, while Isaiah and Micah prophesied in Judah. Amos was a man of Judah who preached in the Northern Kingdom of Israel. Hosea belonged to Israel, and preached to his own people there. His first prophecy, which was against the dynasty of Jehu, was fulfilled in 745 BC, when Shallum assassinated Zechariah (Hos. 1.4; 2 Kings 15.8–10). After that, several men, one after another, became king in Israel by violent means, and Hosea condemned those responsible for these troubles (Hos. 7.7; 8.4). He also prophesied when Israel and Syria formed an alliance against Judah (Hos. 5.8–12). He warned the leaders of Israel about the danger involved in forming alliances with foreign nations, and in attempting to maintain independence by making friends with Egypt and Assyria in turn (Hos. 7.11–12; 12.1). Clearly Hosea was prophesying over a longer period of years than Amos, but not for as long a time as Isaiah of Jerusalem.

(a) *Hosea's Family* Hosea 1—3 seems to contain details of Hosea's personal life, and of his relationship with the woman Gomer. But scholars interpret these chapters in widely different ways.

Hosea 2 is a parable in which God speaks as the husband (Hos. 2.16) and Israel is the unfaithful wife (Hos. 2.11, 15, 16). Some scholars regard Hosea 1 and 3 in the same way, and say that these chapters have nothing to do with the life of Hosea. But this interpretation is unconvincing, because in these chapters we read of Hosea's own experiences, and of what he did at God's command (Hos. 1.2; 3.1).

Some scholars regard Hosea 1 and 3 as two different accounts of the same events. It is clear that these chapters do come from different sources, because Hosea 1 is a piece of biography, while Hosea 3 is a piece of autobiography, i.e. in the first chapter somebody else tells Hosea's story, and in the third chapter Hosea tells his own story. But the two chapters give different accounts of Hosea's relations with his wife. According to Hosea 1.3, Gomer bore the prophet a son in due time after their marriage, but Hosea 3 makes no mention of children, and mentions a time of stern discipline, which may have included sexual abstinence. Even stronger evidence is the fact that Hosea 3.1 refers to Hosea's wife as an 'adulteress'. This word can only be used of a woman who is already married, so Gomer must already have been Hosea's wife at the beginning of the events described in this chapter. Even though she had been unfaithful, Hosea was to love her *again* (Hos. 3.1).

So we see that the most convincing explanation is that Hosea 1 and 3 give details of two different events in the relationship between Hosea and Gomer. Hosea 1 tells how the prophet took her as his wife; Hosea 3 tells how he reclaimed her after she had deserted him for a lover and then been taken into slavery to pay off a debt.

(b) *Gomer's Unfaithfulness* It is not clear whether Gomer was a prostitute before she married Hosea, or whether she fell into sin afterwards. According to Hosea 1.2, God told Hosea to marry a prostitute. Some scholars accept this as accurate; they explain that Gomer was a cult prostitute involved in sexual relationships as part of pagan worship and honoured by those in Israel who worshipped the Baalim. Other scholars, however, point out that though the verse describes God's first call to Hosea, it must have been written at a later time in his life. They suggest that in fact Hosea married a woman who only turned to sin after their marriage, and that later Hosea reinterpreted God's call in the light of what had happened, saying 'God gave me Gomer as a wife. She has become a prostitute. Therefore God has given me a prostitute as my wife.'

There is also doubt whether the children of Gomer belonged to Hosea, or were born as a result of her adultery. The first child was clearly Hosea's own child (Hos. 1.3). Nothing is said about the father or fathers of the second and third child, but their names, Not-pitied and Not-my-people (Hos. 1.6, 9), suggest that Hosea disowned them. Another interpretation of these verses is that Hosea gave these names to his own children simply as a sign to the Israelites of God's attitude towards them, in much the same way as Isaiah named his children in a way that would be a sign to Judah (see Isa. 7.3; 8.3).

OUTLINE

Hosea 1—3: Hosea and Gomer: God and Israel.
Hosea 4—9.9: Hosea condemns Israel's unfaithfulness in worship and in politics.
Hosea 9.10—13.16: A review of God's merciful dealings in the past with rebellious Israel.
Hosea 14: A call to repent, with hope for the future.

MESSAGE

In whichever way we choose to interpret Hosea 1—3, it seems fairly certain that Hosea came to understand the ways of God with Israel as a result of his own sufferings with an unfaithful wife. The direct comparison is drawn in Hosea 2. The people of Israel had been unfaithful to God because they had worshipped the Baalim, the fertility gods of Caanan (Hos. 2.13; 11.2). And the priests had misled the people. So the golden calf used in worship at Samaria would be destroyed: 'It is not God' (Hos. 4.4–10; 6.9–10; 8.4–6). Probably it was a copy of the calves set up in Bethel and Dan before Samaria had been built (1 Kings 12.26–33). The people had lost their knowledge of God (Hos. 4.1; 5.4; 6.6).

The righteous God must therefore punish the sins of His people (Hos. 7.2–3; 13.9–11). This punishment would be conquest by their enemies (Hos. 10.14–15; 11.6). The Israelites would find themselves enslaved again, as in Egypt (Hos. 9.3, 6; 11.5). Assyria would be their new oppressor, but it was God Himself who would punish them (Hos. 5.12, 14; 8.13). But God is merciful, and repentance could lead to renewal (Hos. 14.1, 2, 7). This was God's deep desire (Hos. 11.8–9). Sadly the prophet's words were not given the attention they deserved in Israel.

B. S. Childs has provided evidence for saying that the original prophecies of Hosea were adapted a century later to serve the needs of Judah. He suggests that our difficulties in understanding the story of Hosea arise because the theme of adultery has been adapted to refer to the spiritual unfaithfulness of Judah. This would help to explain the words of hope for the future of a repentant 'Judah' found in Hosea 1.7, 11, and 3.5.

2. JOEL

THE PROPHET HIMSELF

Joel was the son of Pethuel (Joel 1.1), but we know nothing of who Pethuel was. The prophet was inspired to preach as a result of a severe plague of locusts (Joel 1.4). The writer gives no date for any of the prophecies, but there are clues which suggest that Joel was at work about 400 BC.

There are no references to Assyria or Babylon, nor is there any mention of Persia. The words about Greece do not suggest that Greece was ruling the world (Joel 3.6). Probably the prophet was at work before the reign of Alexander the Great, who became powerful in 336 BC.

The information which the book provides about life in Judah clearly shows that the prophecies were made after the Exile. The Jews are described as scattered 'among the nations' (Joel 3.2). The people who lived in Jerusalem are called 'Israel', and there is no mention of the separate Northern Kingdom (Joel 3.16–17). This would only be natural a long time after the fall of Samaria.

There is no mention of kings or a royal court in the book. Priests and elders are named as the leaders of the community (Joel 1.13–14; 2.16–17). The Temple was in daily use, and the worship included the drink offering, a custom from the time of the second Temple (Joel 1.9, 13; 2.14). The walls of Jerusalem had been rebuilt by the time of this prophet, so he must have worked after the time of Nehemiah (Joel 2.9).

OUTLINE

Joel 1.1–20: The plague of locusts, a call to national mourning, and
Joel 2.1–27: God will save His people.
Joel 2.28—3.21: The Day of the LORD is near; He will pour out His spirit on all Judah, and judge the nations.

MESSAGE

Some scholars believe that the prophecies of Joel were concerned entirely with the plague of locusts, and that some later writer has added to them a symbolic message about God's judgement and the establishment of His kingdom on earth. But the idea of the Day of the Lord is found in both parts, and it is probable that the two parts belong together (Joel 1.15; 2.1, 2, 11).

The terrible destruction caused by the locusts led Joel to think of the Day of God's Judgement. Just as penitence would lead to recovery after the attack of the locusts, so it would be the proper preparation for the Day of God's judgement (Joel 2.17–19, 32).

3. AMOS

THE PROPHET HIMSELF

Amos lived in the time of king Uzziah of Judah and king Jeroboam II of Israel, i.e about 750 BC (Amos 1.1). He was a shepherd from the town of Tekoa in the hill-country of Judah, and was skilled in the care of sycomores, a kind of fig tree. (The fruit had to be pierced to allow juices to escape before it ripened fully – see Amos 7.14.)

Amos denied that he had belonged to any band of prophets, but he was convinced that God had called him to prophesy (Amos 7.14–15, see also 3.7–8). Although he was a man of Judah, he fulfilled his ministry in Israel (Amos 7.10). Amaziah, the priest of Bethel, ordered him to return to his home country, but Amos's only response was a stern rebuke (Amos 7.10–17). We do not know whether Amos was banished from Israel, but his ministry there was brief and severe.

OUTLINE

Amos 1—2: Prophecy of judgement on the nations, leading to a judgement on Judah and Israel.
Amos 3—6: Judgement sayings against Israel.
Amos 7.1—9.10: A series of five visions which all concern God's punishment of Israel. The story of Amaziah's rebuke is included here, with other judgement sayings.
Amos 9.11–15: A message of hope, from a later time when Jerusalem and the Temple were in ruins.

MESSAGE

Amos preached that God was preparing to punish Israel. Twice, out of compassion, He had delayed, but there was no doubt that punishment was deserved (Amos 7.3–9). There would be a military disaster which would lead to exile for the Israelites (Amos 2.13–16; 3.11; 6.7; 7.17). Amos did not name Assyria as the enemy who would defeat Israel, but he did believe that the Israelites' exile would be in a land to the north (Amos 5.27). The greatest hope that he could offer was for a few survivors, but they would be in great trouble (Amos 5.15; 3.12).

The reason for God's judgement was the 'transgressions of Israel' (Amos 2.6). The people ought to have known well how to serve God; but the rich were oppressing the poor, traders were dishonest, and judges accepted bribes (Amos 3.2; 5.7, 11–15; 6.12; 8.4–6). The words 'in the gate' in these verses refer to the fact that court was usually held in public at the entrance to the towns. Wealthy people were living selfish, indulgent lives, unaware of the troubles that were coming on Israel (Amos 6.1–6). Amos rejected the people's claim that God was pleased with them because they visited places of worship and made sacrifices there (Amos 4.4, 5; 5.4, 5, 21–24).

4. OBADIAH

THE PROPHET HIMSELF

The name 'Obadiah' which is used as the title of this book, means simply 'Servant of the Lord'. It may have been the personal name of the prophet, but it could also be a title which was given to the book, perhaps because the true name of the prophet was no longer remembered. The prophecy comes from a time soon after the destruction of Jerusalem (Obad. 11–12), and expresses hatred towards the Edomites who had rejoiced at Judah's time of trouble. The following verses from other parts of the Old Testament describe the Edomites' triumph when Jerusalem fell: Lamentations 4.21; Psalms 137.7; and especially 2 Kings 24.2, where 'Syria' is an error for 'Edom', probably made by a copyist because the Hebrew name for Syria, Aram, is so similar. (See also Ezek. 25.12–14; 36.5–6 and Isa. 34.8–9.)

OUTLINE

Obadiah 1—9: The threat of Edom's downfall.
Obadiah 10—14: The reason for the threat: Edom's rejoicing over the fall of Jerusalem.
Obadiah 15—21: The Day of the Lord against the nations, with a promise of God's kingdom established in Judah.

Notice that this is the shortest of the books of the Minor Prophets, and has only one chapter. As with other books of the Bible consisting of one chapter only, it is customary to refer to verse numbers alone in the book of Obadiah, without a chapter reference.

MESSAGE

Verse 15: 'As you have done, it shall be done to you', summarizes the message of the whole book. Edom had rejoiced in the sufferings of Judah, and had taken advantage of her defenceless condition. But Edom's own turn for trouble would come.

Jeremiah 49.7–22 repeats many of the ideas of Obadiah 1–9. Probably these verses were added to the book of Jeremiah at a later time, when people had forgotten where they came from.

STUDY SUGGESTIONS

WORD STUDY

1. Explain each of the following titles used in the study of the prophetic books:
   (a) Former Prophets (b) Latter Prophets (c) Major Prophets
   (d) Minor Prophets

To which, if any, of these groups does the book of Daniel belong? What kind of book is it?

REVIEW OF CONTENT

2. Prepare a table to show in three columns the Minor Prophets who were preaching in the time of each of the following empires:
(a) Assyrian (b) Babylonian (c) Persian
3. Which of the Minor Prophets preached in the Northern Kingdom of Israel? Say in each case:
(a) what evidence, if any, their books show, of an interest in Judah (give appropriate references for your answers);
(b) whether scholars believe that such evidence shows the passage was written by the prophet, or added by an editor.
4. What evidence is there, that Joel was written after the Exile in Babylon?

BIBLE STUDY

5. Write short notes about each of the following passages, showing how they help us to understand the work of Amos and Hosea.
Amos 7.1–3 Amos 7.14–15 Hos. 3.1 Hos. 8.4.
6. Obadiah said, 'As you have done, it shall be done to you' (Obad. 15). This is an expression of *vengeance*. Look up this word in a Concordance and discover which books in the Old Testament contain it. For each of these books, say who will have vengeance, and who will suffer it? Is vengeance an attitude which Christians should take towards wrong-doers? Give your reasons.
7. Which of the Minor Prophets you have studied make use of the phrase 'the day of the LORD'? What does each of them say about that day: is it a time of joy or of sorrow for the Jews?

FURTHER STUDY AND DISCUSSION

8. How would you reply to somebody who said to you, 'The transgressions of Israel happened a long time ago, and the people of Israel rightly suffered for their sins, but we should not expect to find in the prophecies of judgement any message for our own day'. Give reasons to explain your own attitude, drawing evidence from the prophetic books.

5. JONAH

THE PROPHET HIMSELF

There was a prophet, Jonah son of Amittai, in Israel in the reign of Jeroboam II, at the time when the Assyrians were not yet powerful enough to create an empire for themselves (2 Kings 14.25). The book of Jonah tells the story of how the prophet went on a successful preaching campaign to Nineveh, the capital of Assyria. So at first sight the book seems to be a record of part of the ministry of an eighth century prophet.

Some scholars believe that the prophet Jonah really did preach in Nineveh. Other prophets, for example Amos, declared messages against foreign nations in the eighth century. But as we have seen already, such messages were seldom actually preached to the people of the nations named. More often such prophecies were meant to teach the people of Israel that God ruled over *all* the nations (see pp. 152–154).

There is no evidence outside the book of Jonah that the people of Nineveh experienced a mass conversion and began to worship the LORD. The history of Assyria's relations with Israel and Judah would have been very different if they had all been worshippers of the LORD.

This book shows many signs of having been written after the Exile. It contains many Aramaic words which were only in use in those later times, e.g. 'mariners', 'message', and 'decree' (Jonah 1.5; 3.2; and 3.7). The writer made statements about the city of Nineveh which were not true, and could not have been written by anybody with a knowledge of Assyria. The city is said to have been 'three day's journey in breadth' (Jonah 3.3), where actually it was only about 2½ miles in diameter. It is said to have housed a population of 120,000 (Jonah 4.11), which is far too many people for its size. Its ruler is said to have been known as 'the king of Nineveh' (Jonah 3.6), but this title is never used in any of the historical records preserved from the days of Assyrian power.

Probably the whole story of Jonah is a parable which was composed after the Exile in order to teach a lesson which the people of Israel needed to learn: a lesson about God's care for *all* His people, not only for the Jews. The fact that Jesus referred to this story does not compel us to accept it as a piece of history (Matt. 12.41; Luke 11.29). He knew how to use parables to drive home some significant message, and would have treasured this one. The Jews of His day still needed to learn about God's care for all people, and about the willingness of many Gentiles to respond to a call for repentance.

The twelve Minor Prophets are mentioned in Sirach 49.10, a book which was probably written about 180 BC, and which, as we saw, is now included in the Apocrypha. As the book of Jonah is one of the twelve, it must have been written well before 180 BC for the writer of Sirach to have accepted it. Perhaps it was written about 400 BC.

OUTLINE

Jonah 1: Jonah's flight from God.
Jonah 2: A Psalm of thanksgiving, probably added to the story at a later time.
Jonah 3: Jonah's successful mission to Nineveh.
Jonah 4: Jonah's disappointment, and God's rebuke.

MESSAGE

The theme of the book is the fact that God cares for more people than His servants do. Jonah tried to escape from preaching in Nineveh, and was very angry when the people repented, and so evaded judgement. This story was a direct attack upon the narrow self-righteous attitude of many of the Jews after the Exile.

The people had remembered the messages of the prophets about God's judgement on the nations, and His blessings on the Jews. But they had forgotten the messages about God's judgement on Israel, and His blessings on the nations. They expected the blessings for themselves, and gave no thought to the needs of other peoples.

The writer of the book of Jonah was confident that God would bless all peoples, because He had created them all. The writer tried to show the Jews that they were failing in their service to God if they failed to work for the good of other peoples. God's plans for the world could only be fulfilled by overruling the wishes of the Jews.

B. S. Childs has rightly made the point that the addition of the psalm in chapter 2 strengthens the message of the book. Jonah gives thanks for his salvation in chapter 2, and complains bitterly about the salvation of the Gentiles in chapter 4. His attitude is shown to be selfish and out of step with the will of God.

Some scholars like to treat the story of Jonah as an allegory, i.e. they find a hidden meaning for each separate part, e.g. the 'great fish' is said to stand for the Exile. According to this interpretation, the return from Exile had given God's people another opportunity to carry out their ministry to other nations. But the essential message of the story is the same whether or not we accept the idea that it is an allegory.

6. MICAH

THE PROPHET HIMSELF

Micah came from the village of Moresheth, close to the ancient Philistine town of Gath. He probably began his ministry before Samaria was attacked by the Assyrians in 722 BC, but there is no evidence that Micah preached in the Northern Kingdom (Mic. 1.5–7). He continued his work in the period when the Assyrians threatened

9.2a, b and c 'Jonah gives thanks for his salvation in chapter 2 and complains bitterly about the salvation of Gentiles in chapter 4' (p. 176). The pictures above are from carvings on a Christian sarcophagus of Roman times, which illustrate Jonah 1.15–17; 2.10.

to capture Jerusalem (Mic. 1.9, 12). He believed that Jerusalem would be destroyed (Mic. 3.12). This prophecy was remembered more than a century later in Jeremiah's time (Jer. 26.18). Jeremiah reminded his hearers that Hezekiah had accepted Micah's warning, and because of Hezekiah's penitence God had given the city a reprieve (Jer. 26.19). This prophecy of Micah was quite different from the message of Isaiah, who was a prophet around the same time (Isa. 17.12–14; 29.5–8; 31.4–5). Some scholars suggest that the difference between the interpretations of God's will for Jerusalem, as given by these two prophets, resulted from the fact that Isaiah was a townsman living in Jerusalem, while Micah was a villager who did not much like towns.

OUTLINE

Micah 1—3: Prophecies against Jerusalem and Samaria.
Micah 4—5: Prophecies of hope for Jerusalem.
Micah 6.1—7.7: God's charge against Israel.
Micah 7.8–20: God's triumph, and the renewal of Israel.

MESSAGE

There is a strong contrast between the prophecies of warning, and those of hope. Micah was remembered for his warnings, and he spoke about the way in which the people of Judah refused to listen to him (Jer. 26.18; Mic. 2.6, 11). Many scholars believe that the messages of hope in this book come from other sources, and were added later to Micah's words of Judgement. The words of Micah 4.1–5 are repeated in Isaiah 2.2–4, and could have come from some other source. Micah 4.10 refers to Exile in Babylon, but at the time when Micah lived Babylon was too weak to be a serious threat to Judah. According to Micah 5.5, 6, Assyria would be defeated (contrast Mic. 3.12), and princes of Judah would lead the people to victory (contrast Mic. 3.9–12).

In his prophecies, Micah condemned the leaders of Judah, and said that the princes, the priests, and the prophets did not serve the LORD (Mic. 3.5–12; 7.3). Rich people were oppressing the poor, and traders were dishonest (Mic. 2.1–2; 3.1–3; 6.10–11). Families were divided against one another (Mic. 7.6). Worship was corrupt: the people were willing to give expensive gifts to God, but He called instead for justice, steadfast love, and humble obedience (Mic. 6.6–8).

7. NAHUM

THE PROPHET HIMSELF

Nahum came from a village called Elkosh, but we do not know where it was situated: probably somewhere in Judah. He knew about the

Assyrian conquest of Thebes in 663 BC (Nahum 3.8–10), and he prophesied about the fall of Nineveh which happened in 612 BC. Probably he worked as a prophet close to the latter date.

OUTLINE

Nahum 1.1—2.2: An alphabetic poem. In the Hebrew each line begins with a new letter of the alphabet in turn: but after Nahum 1.9 the pattern is lost, possibly through faults made in copying the text in later times.
Nahum 2.3—3.19: Threats against Nineveh.

MESSAGE

Both sections of the book express the belief that God was about to punish the Assyrians. Scholars are uncertain whether both parts were by the same writer. The book contains no challenge to the people of Judah to live uprightly, nor any warning of what would happen after the fall of Nineveh, when other nations would try to gain control of Palestine. There is simply a promise of freedom from the Assyrians (Nahum 1.15). The whole book expresses belief in God's punishment of that nation.

8. HABAKKUK

THE PROPHET HIMSELF

Habakkuk probably worked at about the same time as Zephaniah. The 'oppressor' described in Habakkuk 2.6–20 was probably Assyria (see especially verses 8 and 10, where 'many nations' are troubled by 'him'). Habakkuk believed that the Assyrians themselves would be punished in their turn by the coming of the Babylonians (Hab. 1.6). The prophet probably worked in the period between 625 BC when the Babylonians gained independence, and 612 BC when they helped to destroy Nineveh. Perhaps his ministry was at the beginning of that period, as he refers to the Assyrians as still oppressing Judah.

OUTLINE

Habakkuk 1.1—2.5: A dialogue between the prophet and God. Habakkuk speaks twice (Hab. 1.2–4; 1.12–2.1), and God replies (Hab. 1.5–11; 2.2–5).
Habakkuk 2.6–20: Five woes, i.e. accusations, with warnings, against the oppressor.
Habakkuk 3.1–19: The Psalm of Habakkuk, which includes musical instructions (3.1, 3, 9, 13 and 19).

MESSAGE

Habakkuk twice challenged God, complaining that the wicked were triumphing over the righteous (Hab. 1.4, 13). The answer received through prophecy was that God was sending the Babylonians to punish the wicked (Hab. 1.6–7). They were to break the power of the oppressor.

Some scholars believe that the 'wicked' mentioned in Habakkuk's first challenge were the evil people in Judah, and that the 'wicked' in the second challenge were the Babylonians. According to this interpretation, the prophet was teaching that God could use the Babylonians to punish Judah, but that He could equally well punish the Babylonians themselves if they overreached themselves and crushed the righteous.

The prophet was confident that all evil-doers would be punished, and that 'the righteous shall live by his faith' (Hab. 2.4). The Hebrew word used in this verse regularly stands for 'faithfulness' and it is only here, in the whole of the RSV Common Bible, translated by the word 'faith'. The distinction between these words is important: the RSV translators have used the word 'faith', but give the alternative, '*faithfulness*', in a footnote.

9. ZEPHANIAH

THE PROPHET HIMSELF

Zephaniah was a descendant of Hezekiah: possibly King Hezekiah of Judah, and he worked during the reign of Josiah (Zeph. 1.1). His condemnation of those who worshipped false gods in Judah suggests that he worked before Josiah's reform of religion in 621 BC (Zeph. 1.4–6). Zephaniah prophesied that God would punish the Assyrians by destroying Nineveh, so these verses must come from a time before 612 BC (Zeph. 2.13–15).

OUTLINE

Zephaniah 1.1—2.3: A warning about God's Day of Punishment for Judah and Jerusalem, and a call to penitence.
Zephaniah 2.4–15: An announcement about God's punishment of other nations: Philistines, Moabites, Ammonites, Ethiopians, and Assyrians.
Zephaniah 3.1–20: Further warnings to Judah, and a promise of a righteous remnant to serve the LORD.

MESSAGE

God rules over all the earth, but He was especially present in Jerusalem (Zeph. 1.1–4; 3.5, 17). The people of Judah had not served their LORD (Zeph. 1.6; 3.2). The officials were rebellious and corrupt

(Zeph. 3.3–4). As a result the Day of God's Punishment was coming, when the sounds of battle would be heard in Judah (Zeph. 1.7, 12, 14–16), and other nations also would be punished for their evil ways (Zeph. 2.5, 9, 12; 3.8). There would be a remnant of humble and righteous people in Judah, who would live under God's rule (Zeph. 2.7; 3.12–13).

10. HAGGAI

THE PROPHET HIMSELF

Haggai prophesied 'in the second year of Darius' (Hag. 1.1). This was Darius I, who was king of the Persians from 522 BC to 486 BC. Thus the second year of his reign was 520 BC. At that time Darius faced widespread revolt among the nations under Persian rule. Haggai seems to have found hope for the Jews in this situation (Hag. 2.6–7, 21–23). His work is mentioned in Ezra 4.24—5.2; and 6.14).

OUTLINE

Haggai 1.1–15: Haggai urged the Jews to rebuild the Temple, and they began work.
Haggai 2.1–9: Haggai encouraged the workers by describing the splendour of the Temple when it was completed.
Haggai 2.10–19: Haggai described the material blessings which would follow the rebuilding.
Haggai 2.20–23: Haggai said Zerubbabel would be God's Messiah.

MESSAGE

Haggai urged the Jews in Jerusalem to rebuild the Temple, because the day would come when God would make Jerusalem the religious centre of the whole world (Hag. 1.9; 2.7–9). People of other nations would learn to serve God by giving Him honour there. The Jews had already suffered because they had failed to honour God themselves by rebuilding the Temple (Hag. 1.6; 2.16–17), but they would find blessing when they began the work (Hag. 1.6; 2.16, 17, 19). Zerubbabel was specially chosen by God, and would be His 'signet ring' (Hag. 2.23), i.e. Zerubbabel's power would be a symbol of God's authority and rule.

11. ZECHARIAH

There are important differences between Zechariah 1—8 and Zechariah 9–14 which lead scholars to think that this book is two separate collections of prophecy. A verse in Matthew's Gospel (Matt. 27.9, where the writer quotes Zechariah 11.12–13 as though it came from the prophet Jeremiah) first drew scholars' attention to these differences. Probably in New Testament days people were not sure about the origin of the second part of the book of Zechariah.

A. ZECHARIAH 1—8

THE PROPHET HIMSELF

Zechariah is described as the grandson of Iddo, who returned from the Exile with Zerubbabel (Zech. 1.1; Neh. 12.4). They belonged to a family of priests (Neh. 12.12a, 16). Zechariah began his work a few months after Haggai began his. Both are also mentioned in Ezra 4.24—5.2 and Ezra 6.14. The date of Zechariah's latest prophecy was 518 BC (Zech. 7.1), so perhaps he did not live to see the completion of the Temple in 516 BC.

OUTLINE

Zechariah 1.1–6: Introduction: A call to repent.
Zechariah 1.7—6.8: Eight visions in the night, about the approach of the Age of God's rule through His chosen leader in Jerusalem.
Zechariah 6.9–15: The crowning of God's chosen leader (i.e. the Messiah).
Zechariah 7.1—8.23: A question about fasting.

MESSAGE

Zechariah shared Haggai's belief that the disturbances in the Persian empire were a sign of the coming of God's kingdom (Zech. 1.18–21). Jerusalem would be at the centre of God's plans, the Temple would be rebuilt, and blessings would follow (Zech. 1.16–17; 2.1–5; 4.9; 8.9–13). Zechariah seems also to have shared Haggai's belief that Zerubbabel would reign in God's name, and that beside him Joshua, as the second 'branch of the olive tree', would exercise spiritual authority as priest over God's house (Zech. 3.6–10; 4.9–14).

In contrast to these earlier prophecies, Zechariah 6.9–14 describes Joshua as the one to be crowned. According to Zechariah 6.12 he would *be* the 'Branch' even though according to Zechariah 3.8 he was to prepare for the coming of the 'Branch'. He would rebuild the Temple, even though according to Zechariah 4.9 it was Zerubbabel who would do so. According to Zechariah 6.13 he would have a priest by his side even though he as a priest had a direct relationship with God (Zech. 3.7).

Most scholars believe that Zechariah 6.9–14 originally named Zerubbabel as the Branch, as was to be expected from the earlier prophecies. But Zerubbabel did not become king in Judah; he may have been seized by the Persians because he was a threat to their authority. Some later scribe who copied out the prophecies of Zechariah probably altered the name to Joshua to take account of the disappearance of Zerubbabel.

B. ZECHARIAH 9—14

These six chapters do not belong with the actual prophecies of Zechariah. The prophet is never mentioned in them, and no dates are given relating these prophecies to his time. The prophecies do not mention the Persians who were powerful in the time of Zechariah. They do not refer to the Jewish leaders Joshua and Zerubbabel as the genuine prophecies do.

The title 'An Oracle: the word of the LORD' appears twice in these chapters (Zech. 9.1; 12.1), which suggests that chapters 9—11 and 12—14 should be treated as independent of what has gone before. But scholars differ widely in their ideas about these six chapters. Some regard them as a single unit, some as two distinct units, and others as containing a larger number of separate prophecies from different sources. Some scholars believe that they all come from around the same time in the history of Israel, and others think that they come from widely different periods both before and after the exile.

There is evidence that these chapters come from a time after the return from Exile, especially in the following passages:

(a) **Zechariah 10.6–10:** God will bring back to Judah his people who have been scattered among the nations (compare Isa. 41.8–10; 60.4);

(b) **Zechariah 12.1–6:** The people of Jerusalem will be victorious over their enemies (compare Isa. 60.10–14);

(c) **Zechariah 9.13–15:** Here there is a direct reference to Judah being victorious over the Greeks. This suggests that the chapters belong to the time of the Greek Empire, perhaps after the death of Alexander at a time when there were great conflicts for power among the Greeks. Possibly Assyria and Egypt in Zechariah 10.11 stand for the families of Seleucus and Ptolemy who ruled in those parts of the Greek empire.

The prophet or prophets who proclaimed these oracles revived the ideas of earlier times that God would make Jerusalem and Judah the centre of His rule over all nations, and that the Messiah would ride triumphantly into God's city to take up His rule (Zech. 9.9–10; 14.16–19).

12. MALACHI

THE PROPHET HIMSELF

We have no information about the life of this prophet. His name may not have been 'Malachi', as this word simply means 'My Messenger', and seems to have been adopted as a title for the book because of what is said in Malachi 3.1.

The date at which the prophet worked can be fixed with confidence as shortly before Nehemiah arrived in Jerusalem, i.e. about 460 BC. The evidence for this date comes from the prophecies, and what they tell us about the situation in Jerusalem. The people were ruled by a Persian governor, and the Temple had been rebuilt and was in use (Mal. 1.8, 10; 3.1, 10).

The prophet knew of the laws for worship that were in the Law Code of Deuteronomy. No lame or blind animal was to be offered as sacrifice (Mal. 1.8; Deut. 15.21). Tithes were to provide food for the needy (Mal. 3.8–10; Deut. 14.28–29).

But Malachi did not know the changes in the Law which were introduced by the Priestly Code, brought by Ezra. He regarded Priests and Levites as holding the same office, as they do according to Deuteronomy (Mal. 2.4–9; 3.3; Deut. 21.5). But the Priestly Code introduced a distinction between them: after that only the sons of Aaron could act as priests (Exod. 28.1).

The prophet attacked the same evils which Nehemiah found among the people of Judah when he became governor in Jerusalem. Malachi opposed mixed marriages as Nehemiah did (Mal. 2.10–12; Neh. 13.23–27). And he opposed the careless way in which the Jews worshipped God as Nehemiah also opposed it (Mal. 1.6–8; 3.7–10; Neh. 10.28–31). Both men faced the same problems in Judah, and they must have been at work at about the same time. Neither one mentions the other, so probably they were separated by an interval of a few years: Malachi about 460 BC, and Nehemiah 444 BC and later.

OUTLINE

Malachi answers the complaints of the people:
Malachi 1.1–5: 'How has the LORD loved us?'
Malachi 1.6—2.9: 'How have we despised His name?'
Malachi 2.10–16: 'Why does not the LORD accept our offerings?'
Malachi 2.17—3.5: 'How have we wearied the LORD?'
Malachi 3.6–12: 'How shall we return to the LORD?'
Malachi 3.13–15: 'How have we spoken against the LORD?'
Malachi 3.16—4.5: A promise for those who fear the LORD.

MESSAGE

The whole of the book of Malachi is a long debate between the prophet and the people of Judah. He accused them of turning aside from the sincere worship of the LORD, and of giving only half-hearted attention to His service. They openly disputed what the prophet had to say. He remained faithful to the best traditions in the religious life of Judah, and pleaded with the Jews for sincerity.

We can understand the background to this book if we remember the promises which many of the prophets had made in God's name, that He would rule the world through His people in Jerusalem. These promises did not seem to have been fulfilled even after the return from exile and the rebuilding of the Temple. The people had grown careless in their service of the LORD because they no longer believed that the future was in God's hands.

The prophet assured the people that God would come to His Temple, but warned them that they were not ready for His coming (Mal. 3.1–2). God would prepare for His coming by sending Elijah, the prophet who had led the people to say, 'The LORD, He is God; the LORD, He is God (Mal. 4.5–6; 1 Kings 18.39).

STUDY SUGGESTIONS

WORD STUDY

1. 'Faithfulness . . . faith . . . The distinction between these words is important' (p. 180).
   Choose from the following definitions the right meaning for 'faith' and for 'faithfulness'. Also write a sentence using each of these words in its proper meaning.
   (a) Trustworthy, reliable, loyal.
   (b) Factual, accurate, right.
   (c) Trust, belief, confidence in a person.

REVIEW OF CONTENT

2. Which of the Minor Prophets were at work at about the same time as:
   (a) Isaiah of Jerusalem?
   (b) The writer of Isaiah 55–66?
3. In which of the prophetic books would you expect to find each of the following verses:
   (a) 'For three transgressions of Judah, and for four, I will not revoke the punishment.'
   (b) 'This people say the time has not yet come to rebuild the house of God.'
   (c) 'What does the LORD require of you, but to do justice, and to love kindness, and to walk humbly with your God.'
   (d) 'Go, take to yourself a wife of harlotry.'
   (e) 'Lo, your king comes to you; triumphant and victorious is he, humble and riding on an ass, on a colt the foal of an ass.'

4. Three of the prophets named in each of the following groups had something in common, e.g. the country they worked in, the time at which they prophesied, or the length of their written records, etc. The remaining prophet in the group did not share this thing with the others named. For each group, say which was the 'oddman out'.
   (a) Amos, Hosea, Joel, and Micah.
   (b) Ezekiel, Isaiah, Jeremiah, and Zechariah.
   (c) Ezekiel, Jeremiah, Micah, and Obadiah.
   (d) Haggai, Jonah, Malachi, and Zechariah.
   (e) Haggai, Hosea, Jeremiah, and Micah.
5. Amos and Micah both condemned the rich for oppressing the poor.
   (a) Describe in your own words what the rich were doing that deserved the condemnation of the prophets.
   (b) Were the people of Judah any better than the people of Israel? Give references to support your answers.
   (c) Do the rich in your own country oppress the poor? If so, must your message be one of condemnation only, or is there hope for the rich?
6. Ezekiel's 'great vision of the new Temple, and of the worshipping community in Jerusalem, was a source of inspiration for these later prophets.' Explain what part this idea had in forming the message of Haggai, Zechariah and Malachi.

BIBLE STUDY

7. Use a Concordance to discover which books of the Old Testament refer to the Exile. Notice that some translators have preferred to use the word 'Captivity'.
   (a) List the books in three groups according to the time that they record: before the Exile, during the Exile, after the Exile.
   (b) Why was the Exile so important to those who preached or wrote about God's dealings with Israel?
8. The Jews 'had forgotten the messages of God about God's judgement on Israel, and his blessings on the nations', in the time when the book of Jonah was written (see p. 176).
   (a) Use a Concordance to discover from the Major and the Minor Prophets the verses where the words *bless*, *blessed* or *blessing* are used to describe God's care for the nations.
   (b) From these verses illustrate the way in which Israel was expected to bring this blessing to the nations.
9. Read Micah ch. 5, Zechariah ch. 9 and Malachi ch. 3. Which verses in these chapters do you see as pointing directly forward to Christ?

FURTHER STUDY AND DISCUSSION

10. Haggai and Zechariah both proclaimed that Zerubbabel was God's Messiah. Yet he never became king in Jerusalem. How would you explain these facts? What have they to teach us about the nature of inspiration?
11. Malachi opposed mixed marriages as Nehemiah did' (p. 184). Read Mal. 2.10–12 and Neh. 13.23–27.
    (a) Can you suggest why these leaders believed that mixed marriages were a danger to God's people?
    (b) If there are Jews living in your country, say whether you find that they still believe that they should live in religious isolation. If so, ask a friendly Jew about the reasons.

Summary

How the Books of the Old Testament are related to the History of Israel

Study of the origins and content of the various books of the Old Testament can leave us confused. We do need to know how each book is related to the history of Israel, in order to be able to read the Bible with understanding. But there are so many items of information to be remembered about each book, that it is difficult to keep them clearly in mind as we read the Old Testament itself. We need some kind of summary that will remind us quickly of the things we have learnt, and enable us to return to the relevant part of this book for further information.

The books of the Old Testament are related to the history of Israel in two separate ways:

1. Each book may tell us something about what happened at a particular time in the history of Israel, and what the people of that time thought about their experiences. Later editors may have added their own interpretation of the experiences described in the book. We gain information about the period, and learn something about the way Israelite ideas about God developed as a result of the experiences.

2. Each book also has its own history and development, and only reached the form in which we know it after many years in which traditions were gathered and early editions revised and enlarged. But at some particular point in time the book as we know it became available to the people of Israel, and from that time influenced their ideas and understandings in ways we can appreciate by reading the book for ourselves.

The charts given on pp. 190 and 191 help us to understand (a) which period in the history of Israel each book of the Old Testament relates to, and (b) from which period in that history the book itself was available in the form in which we know it today. We must be careful how we use these charts, as otherwise we may fail to reach the right conclusions from the information that they contain. Two things in particular need to be remembered each time we use the chart.

1. The books of the Old Testament were not written at one particular time, and preserved in that form for ever. As we have seen, most books were prepared over a long period of time, and were revised and adapted by later editors. The information given in the chart concerns the period at which each book was *probably*

completed, i.e. the *approximate* time when the book reached the form we know today. We do not know the precise time, and for some books we can only give a very uncertain suggestion.

According to the chart no books were completed before the time of the Assyrian Empire. But this does not mean that there were no written records in Israel before that time. Earlier editions of some books, and collections of traditions later used to prepare books, were both available in the earlier period, e.g. the J and E documents and the Book of Jashar. The chart does not include any information about these writings. Such information is given earlier in this volume, in the relevant places.

2. Some books in the Old Testament appear at first sight to refer to a particular period of the history of Israel, but in actual fact belong to a much later time. The writers have used information about the earlier times in order to provide a background for what they wished to include in their own time, and a great deal of the material they use in these cases does not belong to the period the book seems to describe. Such books are printed in brackets in the column of the chart which gives details of the period to which each book refers.

Two examples will make this matter clear.

1. *Leviticus* was probably prepared in the time of the Exile, and although it contains laws preserved from earlier times, it includes others which belong to the period at which the book was prepared. The writer describes Moses giving these laws to the people of Israel at Sinai, but this is only his way of saying that these laws are a fresh interpretation of the will of God who called Israel out of Egypt, and made a Covenant with them at Sinai.

2. *Jonah* appears to describe the activities of a prophet in the Assyrian Empire, who led the people of Nineveh to repent and serve the LORD. As we have seen there is ample evidence that this is a parable rather than a piece of actual history. Its purpose was to challenge the people in Palestine after the Exile to recognize God's care for all nations.

Note that for ease of reference the ten historical periods listed in the charts have been numbered to correspond with the chapter numbers in Volume I, which gives fuller information about these periods.

Date (approx)	Historical period	Books referring to the period Historical:	Prophetic:	Other:	Books probably completed in the period
2000–1550 BC	**1. The Patriarchs** Nomadic peoples settle in Mesopotamia and Egypt. The Patriarchs travel from Mesopotamia to Egypt.	Genesis 1 Chronicles			
1550–1250 BC	**2. The Exodus** Egypt strong, ruling over Palestine. The Israelites leave Egypt and travel to Sinai to make Covenant.	Exodus Numbers 1 Chronicles		(Leviticus) (Deuteronomy)	
1250–1000 BC	**3. The Twelve Tribes** Egypt weak, conflicting tribes in Palestine. The Israelites settle in Palestine and battle with many enemies	Joshua Judges 1 Chronicles		(Ruth)	
1000–922 BC	**4. The First Kings** Philistine defeated. United kingdom of Israel with Jerusalem as capital. Israel controls Palestine and lands beyond Jordan.	1 & 2 Samuel 1 Kings 1 & 2 Chronicles		(Psalms) (Proverbs) (Song of Solomon) (Ecclesiastes)	
922–802 BC	**5. The Two Kingdoms** A time of small nations. Brief invasions of Palestine by Egypt and Assyria. Israel and Judah as rival kingdoms.	1 & 2 Kings 2 Chronicles			

Date (approx)	Historical period	Books referring to the period: Historical:	Prophetic:	Other:	Books probably completed in the period	
802– 610 BC	**6. The Assyrian Empire** Israel attacked, Samaria destroyed, her people exiled. Judah defeated but later rebels	2 Kings 2 Chronicles	Isaiah 1–39 Amos Hosea Micah (Jonah)		1 & 2 Samuel Deuteronomy	
610– 539 BC	**7. The Babylonian Empire** A time of great nations: Egypt, Media, and Babylonia. Judah attacked, Jerusalem destroyed, her people exiled in Babylon.	2 Kings 2 Chronicles	Jeremiah Ezekiel Zephaniah Habakkuk Nahum Obadiah	Lamentations (Daniel)	1 & 2 Kings Isaiah 1–39 Jeremiah Ezekiel Amos Hosea Micah	Zephaniah Habakkuk Nahum Obadiah Lamentations Job
539– 331 BC	**8. The Persian Empire** People of Judah freed. Some return to Jerusalem and rebuild city and Temple.	2 Chronicles Ezra Nehemiah Esther	Isaiah 40–66 Haggai Zechariah 1–8 Malachi Joel		Isaiah 40–66 Haggai Zechariah 1–8 Malachi Joel	Jonah Ruth The Torah Joshua Judges
331– 65 BC	**9. The Greek Empire** Judah ruled by Greeks. Maccabees lead revolt against enforcement of Greek culture.		Zechariah 9–14		Zechariah 9–14 Psalms Proverbs Song of Solomon Ecclesiastes	Esther Daniel 1 & 2 Chronicles Ezra Nehemiah
65 BC –AD 70	**10. The Roman Empire** Herod family share rule of Palestine with Procurators. The Jews rebel, Jerusalem destroyed.					

Postscript

This volume has been an *introduction* to the books of the Bible. It is not complete in itself. To gain the full benefit of the work that we have done, we must use this introduction as a means to get to know the many writings of the Old Testament really well.

Consider what happens in human society when an introduction takes place. Somebody says, 'David, I want you to meet John Muntu. He's our Circuit Superintendent. He's the man who is helping our village congregations to witness to their faith.' When my friend tells me these things I recall all that I have heard others say about this man, and I am glad of the opportunity to meet him. But if the introduction is going to be any real help it must be the first of many meetings. The next time I will not need to be told who John Muntu is. As the months and years go by we shall work and think and plan together on many occasions. Then we shall gain full benefit from that first introduction. So it must be for us, that having been introduced to the Bible we go on reading and thinking and praying about all that the writers have to say. Then we shall gain full benefit from our studies. See the section of this book headed 'Further Reading' (p. xiv). It will be a guide for your later studies.

Just as today there are many different people with different experiences, different ideas, and different characters, who all seek to serve God in the best way they can, so too in Old Testament times there were many different people with an equally wide range of qualities who were seeking to know God, and to make Him known to others. As we read what they wrote, we can benefit from their knowledge of, and love for the Lord. They have shared many of the same hopes and fears, joys and sorrows, successes and failures that we experience. Their continuing faith can inspire us to face the perplexities of life with courage and confidence. Because they have known that the Lord was with them through it all, they can promise that we shall find the same.

You may feel that you want to reduce all that they have written to a few words which will summarize the beliefs of those who lived in Old Testament times. But that would be quite as difficult as it would be to summarize the beliefs of all the many Christian writers and teachers of the present time. However in Volume 3 of this course we shall compare what the Old Testament writers had to say about the chief questions of belief that surround faith in the Lord. Thus we shall try to draw together the theology of the Old Testament, and so gain full benefit from all that the Lord revealed to His people Israel.

Key to Study Suggestions

Please Note: This key provides information about where the answers can be found: it does not usually provide the answers themselves. Students should not answer questions by copying out the paragraphs and lines indicated here, but discover the answers and explain them in their own words, using the key to check whether they have answered correctly. No answers are given for questions suggesting the use of a Bible Dictionary or Concordance, since the answers are to be found there. Nor are answers given for topical questions depending on discussion or a knowledge of students' own country, customs, etc.

CHAPTER 1: PAGES 1–7

1. (a) See p. 1, and p. 2, para. 2.
   (b) See p. 1, paras 1 and 3, and p. 2, para. 2.
   (c) See p. 1, para. 1, and p. 2, para. 1.
2. (a) and (b) See p. 1, para. 3, and p. 2, paras 1 and 2.
3. See p. 3, paras 3 and 4.
4. See p. 3, para. 4.
5. See p. 5, para 3.
6. See a Concordance.
7. (a) See Vol. 1, p. 119, para. 3, lines 1–2; rev. ed. p. 128, para. 4, lines 1–2, and Vol. 1, p. 155, para. 1, lines 2–10; rev. ed. p. 167, para. 2, lines 3–11.
   (b) See Isa. 7.1 and Vol. 1, p. 155, para. 1, line 4; rev. ed. p. 167, para. 2, line 5.
   (c) See Isa. 7.9b; 44.22.
   (d) See p. 126, last 7 lines, and p. 127, lines 1–11.

PAGES 8–14

1. (a) See p. 2, para. 3.
   (b) See p. 5, lines 1–3.
   (c) See p. 5, last para. and p. 6, lines 1–2.
2. (a) See p. 5, para. 2.
   (b) See p. 5, last 2 paras, and p. 6, paras 1–3.
   (c) See p. 5, para. 3, and p. 14, para. 2, lines 3–7.
3. (a) Verses 1–3 describe events at the beginning of the Exile and the people involved in those events (see p. 1, para. 2).
   (b) V. 1 refers to a 'letter' recording the prophet's message (see p. 9, para. 4, last sentence).
   (c) In verses 4–10 Jeremiah is recorded as calling the exiles to accept their condition as being in accordance with God's will and His promises for their future, and to ignore the words of false prophets promising a quick deliverance.
4. (a) See Vol. 1, p. 171, last 12 lines, and p. 172, paras 1 and 2; rev. ed. p. 184, last 4 lines, and p. 185, paras 1–4.
   (b) See 1 Macc. 1.10, and Vol. 1, p. 174, para. 2; rev. ed. p. 187, para. 3.
7. Based on p. 14, paras 2–4.

CHAPTER 2: PAGES 16–25

1. (a) 'good things' (b) 'good things', 'prosperity', perhaps 'choice gifts' (c), (d) and (e) None.

2. 'Belief in God, trust in God, confidence.
3. See p. 16, para. 3, lines 1–3, and p. 17, para. 2, lines 1–5.
4. See details given on pp 20–21 and 24–25.
7. Your answers might indicate: for accuracy and care (b), (c), (e) and (f), for practical value (d), (e), (g), (h) and (l).

PAGES 27–35

1. (b) In all the verses quoted the human 'love', etc. is of a temporary or even selfish sort.
2. (b) See e.g. p. 18, para. 4, line 1, and p. 19, para. (b), lines 1–2, and para. (c) lines 1–4.
3. (a) See p. 29, para. 1, last 2 lines; (b) See p. 29, para. 2, last 2 lines; (c) See p. 30, para. 1, last 2 lines; (d) See p. 30, para. 4; (e) See p. 30, para 6.
4. (a) See p. 31, last 2 paras, and p. 33, para. 1.
   (b) See p. 33, para. 2.
5. (a) Based on p. 28, last para.
   (b) Compare pp 27–28 numbered para. 2.
   (c) See p. 28 numbered para. 3. The context relates the sound of the name 'Esek' with the quarrelsome herdsmen of Isaac.
   (d) See p. 28 fifth (last) para. lines 1–8.
   (e) See p. 28, fourth para. (unnumbered), lines 6–9.
6. Based on pp 27–28, numbered para. 2 headed 'Cross references': See the Bible passages given.
7. (i) (a) – (j) See the Bible passages given.
   (iii) Compare the way a Psalm is printed with e.g. Deut. 1, and see p. 53, section 3 headed 'Poetry'.

CHAPTER 3: PAGES 37–43

1. See p. 37, last 3 lines, and p. 38, lines 1–10.
2. See p. 43, para. 1.
3. (a) See p. 39, para. 2.
   (b) Instruction and Revelation: See an English Dictionary for the various words.
4. See p. 37, para. 2, p. 38, last para. and p. 39, lines 1–9.
5. See p. 39, paras 2 and 3.
6. See p. 40, para. 2.

PAGES 44–61

1. (a) See p. 45, section headed (b), and p. 46, section headed (c).
   (b) See p. 46, section headed (c), and p. 47 section headed (e), lines 1 and 2.
   (c) See p. 46, section headed (c), and p. 47, section headed (d).
   (d) See p. 45, section headed (a), and p. 47, section headed (d).
2. J: See p. 51, last para. lines 2–4.
   E: See p. 52, para. 3 lines 1–3.
   D: See p. 39, para. 3, lines 10–12, and p. 53, lines 1 and 2.
   P: See p. 52, para. 2, lines 1 and 2.
3. (a) See p. 53, para. 2, lines 2–5.
   (b) See p. 51, para. 4, lines 5–9.
   (c) See p. 52, para. 3, lines 5–6.
   (d) See p. 53, para. 2, lines 2–5.
   (e) See p. 52, last para. lines 9–11 and p. 53, line 1.

4. (a) What was the reason for celebrating the Sabbath?
   (b) Who should use the produce of the fallow years?
   (c) Should a Hebrew woman slave be released after six years?
5. See a Commentary on Exodus.
7. See a Bible Dictionary.

PAGES 63–71

1. Based on p. 63, paras 1–4.
2. See p. 63, para. 3.
3. Joshua: See p. 66, last 6 lines, and p. 67, lines 1–5; Judges: See p. 69, para. headed 'Message'.
4. See Vol. 1, p. 70, para. 2; rev. ed. p. 79, lines 15–24.
5. (a) See p. 63, para. 3, lines 6–10.
   (b) See p. 63, para. 3, line 7, and p. 70, para. 3, lines 4–5.
6. (a) See Judges 4.4–6 and 5.1.
   (b) See Judges 5.14 and contrast 4.6.
   (c) See Judges 4.2, and notice no mention of Jabin in Judges 4.
   (d) See Judges 4.6–7 and 5.19–21.
   (e) See Judges 4.21 and contrast 5. 25–27.
   See p. 69, para. 1, lines 1–2.
7. (b) See p. 71, para. 2, lines 1–2 and 8–9.

PAGES 72–79

1. See p. 65, para. 2, lines 4–8; p. 72, last 2 lines, and p. 73, lines 1–6.
2. (a) and (b) See p. 73, para. 3, lines 1–3; p. 75, last 2 lines, and p. 76, line 1 and para. 4 line 1.
3. See p. 78, section headed 'Sources', para. 2.
4. Group (a) How was Saul chosen to be king?
   Group (b) Did Saul know that David had fled?
5. See the Bible passages given.
6. See a Bible Dictionary and Concordance.
7. See a Concordance and discuss the question.

CHAPTER 5: PAGES 80–86

1. See p. 81, last para.
2. See p. 85, para. 5. Death was to be delayed by living a good life.
3. (a) 2 Chron. 10.1–19. (b) 2 Chron. 13.8. (c) Not used.
4. (a) The Levites, see Chronicles. The Editor was deeply interested in the Temple cult. See p. 83, section headed Sources, para. 4, lines 6–10.
   (b) David, see Samuel; the Levites, see Chronicles.
   (c) The account in Samuel is probably correct, and the account in Chronicles has probably been adapted to fit in with laws concerning sacrifice in the Priestly Code.
   (d) David's wild dance seems to have exposed his body. The editor of Chronicles attempts to cover this up, by his reference to long heavy clothes.
   (e) Samuel.
   (f) See Samuel 6.15, and compare 1 Chronicles 15.28. The editor of Chronicles again adapts the story to make it as similar as possible to later customs known to him after the Exile.

(g) (i) Because this was the beginning of the history of Jerusalem as a centre for the religious activities of the Jews.

5. For discussion after re-reading p. 86, last para. of text.

PAGES 88–95

1. See p. 91, para. (f), p. 92, paras (c) and (e), also last 3 lines and p. 93, para. 1.
2. See p. 89, section headed 'Sources', para. (c).
3. See p. 92, paras (d) and (e).
4. See p. 94, lines 24–36.
5. *Ezra 7.27—8.34* Ezra's own account directly copied, including list of names from official records in 8.1–14.
   Ezra 9.1—10.44 Summary from Ezra's own account, with official list of names in 10.18–44.
   Nehemiah 1.1—7.73 Nehemiah's own account, with official list of names in 7.6–72.
   Nehemiah 9.38—10.39 Record of a covenant in response to Ezra's presentation of the Law.
   Nehemiah 11.1–2 Nehemiah's own account.
   Nehemiah 11.3—12.26 List of names from official records.
   Nehemiah 12.27—13.3 Summary from Nehemiah's own account.
   Nehemiah 13.4–31 Nehemiah's own account.
6. (a) See Vol. 1, p. 156, para. 2, lines 3–4; rev. ed. p. 168, para. 2, lines 3–4.
   (b) See Vol. 1, p. 156, para. 2, lines 8–11; rev. ed. p. 168, para. 2, lines 8–11.
   (c) See p. 182, para. 2. Notice the slight confusion over the relationship. Ezra 6.14 is probably correct.
   (d) See p. 89, Outline, lines 1–2.
   (e) See a Commentary on Ezra 6.14. There was a decree of Artaxerxes referred to in Ezra 4.18–22, but this seems historically to belong to the time of rebuilding the walls of Jerusalem rather than the Temple.
7. See p. 92, para. (e).

CHAPTER 6: PAGES 97–106

1. See p. 98, para. 2. (b) See p. 99, para. 2. (c) See p. 100, para. (a). (d) See p. 100, para. (b). (e) See p. 100, para. (c).
2. See p. 100, Section 'Hebrew Wisdom', para. 1, and p. 102, para. 3.
3. (a) See p. 98, para. 2, lines 1–2, and p. 100, para. 2.
   (b) Based on p. 100, paras (a)–(d).
4. See p. 102, para. headed 'Title', lines 8–10.
5. Use a Concordance to discover the exact verse quoted in each example, and check this against the outline of Job on p. 103. In this way check your answers, which should have been based on your knowledge of the book.

PAGES 107–121

1. See p. 111, last para.
2. (a) See p. 108, para. 4, lines 1–2. (b) See p. 108, para. 3, lines 1–4. (c) See p. 108, para. 4, lines 3–4.
3. (a) See p. 114, para. 3, lines 1–4.
4. Ps. 8: See p. 111, para. 4, lines 1–3.
   Ps. 42: See p. 111, para. 2, lines 3–4.
   Ps. 75: See p. 111, para. 4, lines 3–5.
   Ps. 113: See p. 109, lines 3–6.
   Ps. 125: See p. 108, last line but one.

5. See a Concordance.
6. Use a Concordance and discuss.
7. (a) Check your answer against the list provided by G. Fohrer, see pp 110–111.
   (b) The Psalms express real human feelings about situations and offer those feelings to God through prayer. We too should learn to open our hearts to God.

CHAPTER 7: PAGES 123–131

1. See an English Dictionary and p. 126, first numbered para. 1 and numbered para. 2.
2. Autobiography uses 'I' and 'me' to describe experiences of the prophet; Biography uses 'he' and 'him'; prophecy does not necessarily mention the prophet at all. Apply these rules to the verses given.
3. See p. 124, para. 2, lines 1–5; para. 3, lines 2–5; para. 5, lines 2–5.
4. (a) See p. 125, para. 3, and para. 5, lines 1–4.
   (b) See p. 126, para. 4, lines 1–6.
5. See a Concordance.

PAGES 132–138

1. See p. 130, para. 4, last 3 lines.
2. (a) See p. 126, last 11 lines, and p. 128, first 4 paras.
   (b) See p. 128, numbered para. 2.
3. (a) See p. 129, para. 1, lines 9–11.
   (b) See p. 129, para. 1, lines 1–8.
4. See p. 134, para. 4, lines 3–6, and para. 6, lines 2–4.
5. (i) See p. 136, para. 7, lines 3–6.
   (ii) See p. 136, para. 7, lines 6–11.
   (iii) (b) (c).
6. (a) Which nation is enemy to Judah?
   (b) To which nation do the people named here belong?
   (c) Are God's people going to Babylon, according to those prophecies?
   (d) Are these messages of judgement or promise?
   (e) Is trouble from Assyria in the past or the future?
7. See a Bible Dictionary, or Vol. 1, p. 119, para. 4, lines 1–5, and pp 121–123, numbered sections 4 and 5; rev. ed. p. 128, para. 4, lines 1–5, and pp 130–132, numbered sections 4 and 4.

CHAPTER 8: PAGES 140–149

1. See p. 145, para. 2, lines 1–8.
2. (a) See p. 140, para. 1, lines 1–3 and 5–6. (b) See p. 145, para. 2, lines 1–5. (c) See p. 144, para. 3, lines 1–9. (d) See p. 141, para. 3 'Sources', lines 1–4. (e) See p. 143, para. 3, lines 5–8.
3. (a) See p. 147, line 3, and p. 148, last 10 lines.
   (b) See p. 148, Section headed 'Sources', para. 2, lines 1–5, and sub-paras (a)–(d).
4. See the word 'potter' in a Concordance.
5. See p. 146, numbered para. 4, lines 9–13.

PAGES 150–163

1. See p. 153, para. 4 and para. 5, lines 7–11. As used by Ezekiel 'glory' meant the character and caring presence of God Himself.
2. A Concordance will show you Isa. 48.16; 61.1.

3. See p. 151, para. 4.
4. A Concordance will show that in the Old Testament the phrase 'Son of man' appears most often in Ezekiel, and is God's way of addressing the prophet himself.
5. Based on pp 156–157, section headed 'Historical Background', and pp 157–158, section headed 'Sources' lines 1–3.
6. See e.g. p. 128, numbered para. 2; p. 145, para. 2; p. 153, para. 5, p. 159, last para. relating to the Book of Daniel.
7. See e.g. p. 134, para. 2, lines 9–12; p. 136, para. 6, lines 8–11; p. 146, para. 5, last 2 lines; p. 154, para. 4, lines 9–11.
8. (a) Probably those mentioned in the Old Testament: Cyrus, Ahasuerus (i.e. Xerxes I), and Artaxerxes.
   (b) See p. 157, para. (c).
   (c) See p. 157, para. 2.
   (d) See p. 158, para. (b).
   (e) See p. 158, para. (c).
   (f) See p. 159, para. (f).
   (g) Probably as the king 'richer than them all' in v. 2.
   (h) See p. 158, para. 4, lines 3–5.

CHAPTER 9: PAGES 164–173

1. See p. 3, section headed 'The Prophets'; p. 125, paras 1–3; p. 154, last 2 lines, and p. 155, lines 1–6; p. 164, para. 1.
2. Based p. 164, last 2 lines, and p. 165, lines 1–14.
3. See p. 168, para. 4, p. 170, section headed 'Message', p. 172, para. 2, lines 2–7 and section headed 'Message'.
4. See p. 171, lines 1–9.
5. In all four passages the prophets show how God related the message to be preached to their own life experiences.
6. Use a Concordance and discuss.
7. Joel, Amos and Obadiah all describe it as a day of judgement, with sorrow for the disobedient, and eventual joy for the faithful.

PAGES 174–185

1. See Faith = (c). Faithfulness = (a).
2. (a) See p. 133, lines 4–7. (b) See p. 138, para. 3, lines 1–6 and para. 4; and p. 164, lines 1–2 and 5–6.
3. Use a Concordance to check your answer.
4. (a) Three belong to the time of the Assyrian Empire, one does not.
   (b) Three are among the Major Prophets, one is not.
   (c) Three belong to the time of the Babylonian Empire, one does not.
   (d) Three are concerned with the re-establishment of worship in Jerusalem, one is not.
   (e) Three are Minor Prophets, one is not.
5. (a) See p. 170, Outline, Hosea 4—9.9, and p. 172, last para, lines 2–4.
   (b) Use a Concordance to see references to Judah in Amos and Hosea.
6. Haggai: See p. 181, para. 4, lines 1–3.
   Zechariah: See p. 182, para. 4, lines 3–4.
   Malachi: See p. 185, para. 3, lines 1–3.
7. See Vol. 1, pp 143–145; rev. ed. pp 155–156.
8. See especially prophecies about Jerusalem or Zion by looking up these names in a Concordance. The Servant Songs have a reference to help for foreign nations.

Subject Index

Please Note: Only the major references to each subject are given in this Index. Countries and their people are given as a single entry, e.g. *Ammon, Ammonites*. Many of the subjects are also dealt with in Volume 1 of this course, and important information can be gained by making use of the Subject Index of that volume.

Bible Reference Index

Please Note: There are a large number of Bible References in this Guide, but most references to any book of the Bible are in a single chapter, or section of a chapter, where the book is introduced. This index gives (a) the chapter or section of the Guide that contains the majority of references, and (b) the page numbers for references which are scattered in other parts of the Guide.

Cross-Reference

Showing where information contained in the first edition appears in this present revised volume

Zechariah 1–8, Malachi, Joel, and Jonah (p.84)	9	166,170,174,181,183
The Remaining Fragment: Zechariah 9–14 (p.92)	9	183
6. The Writings: Poetic		
Hebrew Poetry (p.96)	6	98
Psalms (p.99)	6	107
Proverbs (p.104)	6	111
Job (p.106)	6	102
7. The Writings: The Five Scrolls		
Song of Solomon (p.113)	6	119
Ruth (p.116)	4	69
Lamentations (p.118)	8	146
Ecclesiastes (p.120)	6	116
Esther (p.123)	5	93
8. The Writings: Apocalyptic and Historical		
Daniel (p.127)	8	154
Another account of the History of Israel (p.131)	5	81
1 and 2 Chronicles (p.132)	5	81
Ezra and Nehemiah (p.134)	5	88
Summary		188
Time Chart		190
Postscript (p.142)		192

NOTE: NEW BOOKS

Christian and other bookshops can usually give information about new theological books published locally or in the West. But in some parts of the world currency restrictions and complicated import/export and customs regulations hinder trade in books between one country and another. Serious students, as well as tutors and librarians, may therefore find it useful to subscribe to the Theological Book Review published by Feed the Minds, 3 times a year, which regularly includes titles issued in a number of Third World Countries, as well as books by African and Asian authors published in Europe and America. It also lists the addresses of publishers whose books are reviewed. (Address: Robertson House, Leas Road, Guildford, GU1 4QW, UK. Subscription 1991 £UK15, US$30.)